Sunday's Coming!

G. Edward Reid

Omega Productions
P.O. Box 600
Fulton, MD 20759

Distributed by
Review and Herald®
Publishing Association
55 West Oak Ridge Drive
Hagerstown, MD 21740

This book was
Edited by Lincoln E. Steed
Designed by Byron Steele
Cover design by Helcio Deslandes
Cover photo: © 1996 Douglas Peebles/Panoramic Images
Typeset: Times 11.5/13.5

PRINTED IN U.S.A

00 99 98 97 96   10 9 8 7 6 5 4 3 2

ISBN 1-878951-32-7

Introduction

I will come again" is a red print standout in the Bible. Jesus said it, and it's a promise we can bank on.

Regarding his confidence in Jesus and the plan of salvation, the apostle Peter stated, "We did not follow cunningly devised fables when we made known to you the power and coming of our Lord Jesus Christ, but were eyewitnesses of His majesty. . . . We have the prophetic word confirmed, which you do well to heed as a light that shines in a dark place, until the day dawns and the morning star rises in your hearts" (2 Peter 1:16, 19).

God's Word outlines very clearly the course of earth's history from the time of Daniel right to the end of the world and the second coming of Christ. Our loving Saviour has revealed to us what will happen just before He comes to earth the second time. And I believe we are seeing these events taking place right now.

This book presents in the plainest way possible the outline of prophecy as revealed in Scripture. "All that prophecy has foretold as coming to pass, until the present time, has been traced on the pages of history, and we may be assured that all which is yet to come will be fulfilled in its order" *(Education,* p. 178). The final test for the inhabitants of this earth will be over the issue of the true Sabbath. Clearly the final countdown has begun. It is time to renew our covenant with God. Time to get a vision of our God—high and lifted up above this ever more sinful world. This book will strengthen your confidence in the prophetic record, make an understanding of prophecy real and permanent with you, and aid in the realization that current events in the United States reveal that *Sunday's Coming!*

Stephen Covey, in his best-selling book *"The 7 Habits of Highly Effective People,"* suggests when discussing habit number two that the reader "Begin with the end in mind." "If the ladder is not leaning against the right wall, every step we take just gets us to the wrong place faster. We may be very busy, we may be very efficient, but we

will also be truly effective only when we begin with the end in mind."
As you read this book through consider the evidence in these pages as
one measure that will help you to determine whether or not your ladder is leaning against the right wall. Will the road you are now traveling take you to where you want to spend eternity? The question
demands a serious answer.

Contents

CHAPTER 1

Planning Ahead

T he millennium looms as civilization's most spectacular birthday. . . . The millennium is freighted with immense historical
symbolism and psychological power. . . . The millennium has
a gravitational pull that draws in the largest meanings. . . . The millennial drama represents nothing less than the ritual death and re-
birth of history" ("The End," a *Washington Post Magazine* article by
Peter Carlson, January 1, 1995).

The millennium is everywhere: on Broadway, the book industry, in
a growing number of millennial organizations, in magazines, and in
tabloids. Even in Christian publications there are discussions of the
millennium and the year 2000. *Christianity Today*, March 6, 1995, had
a review of the book *The Star of 2000*, by Jay Gary. Gary says that
more than 2,000 organizations—from United Nations and government
agencies to business, educational, and religious concerns—have special plans for the year 2000. More than 40 Christian organizations, including the Roman Catholic Church's Evangelization 2000, plan to
take the gospel to the whole world by the year 2000.

The Christian Coalition and the Millennium

Regent University in Virginia Beach, Virginia, is the intellectual and
theological center of the Christian Coalition. The cover story of the
Atlantic Monthly magazine for November 1995 featured a report by liberal Protestant theologian and Harvard professor Harvey Cox of his visit
to Regent. Cox says that Regent has been called the Harvard of the
Religious Right. He observed that the stated goal of Regent University
to invade society with Christian professionals is similar to that of the

Jesuit Order of the sixteenth century. Cox states, "This is just what gives many people the jitters. Pat Robertson is both founder and chancellor of Regent, and both founder and president of the 1.7 million-member Christian Coalition; so it is understandable that the idea of a university designed to dispatch waves of ardent young graduates into all professional spheres might sound ominous to those who harbor reservations about the coalition's potent mixture of old-time religion and up-to-date conservative politics.

"The concept behind Regent is hardly a new one. The idea of preparing an elite of religiously trained professionals to exert a spiritual influence on the secular realm has a venerable lineage. Shortly after the founding of the Catholic Society of Jesus [Jesuit Order], in 1540, its members began to study theology in combination with law, literature, history, and the natural sciences. Jesuits quickly became advisers to kings and tutors to princes, and they founded universities all over the world" *(Atlantic Monthly,* "The Warring Visions of the Religious Right," by Harvey Cox, November 1995).

Pat Robertson's views on the millennium make the Regent goals more significant. Cox reports, "Pre-millennial and post-millennial eschatologies generate opposing visions of what believers should be doing in a fallen world. If conditions are inevitably to degenerate until the return of Christ (as in [Hal] Lindsey's view), there is little point to political activism. But if the persistent efforts of the faithful can help to hasten the coming of the reign of God, there is some reason to lobby Congress or run for office.

"Pat Robertson apparently started out in his earlier years with the pre-millennial view about the imminent approach of the last days that then held sway among most fundamentalists. It seems, however, that he has since altered his opinions. He now subscribes to a post-millennial eschatology in which Christians—at least the ones who share his views— are called upon to try to assume positions of power wherever they can in order to build a more religious and God-fearing society" *(ibid.).*

The Pope Looks to the Coming Millennium
Apparently the pope shares the same basic view. For some time now Pope John Paul II has been working toward uniting the world by the year 2000 and participating personally in the "Great

Jubilee." The Sunday, April 3, 1994, issue of the Washington *Post's Parade* magazine featured the pope on its cover. During the interview for *Parade* the pope stated, "We trust that with the approach of the year 2000, Jerusalem will become the city of peace for the entire world and that all people will be able to meet there, in particular, the believers in the religions that find their birthright in the faith of Abraham."

On November 10, 1994, Pope John Paul II issued an apostolic letter from the Vatican. It was addressed: "To the Bishops, Clergy, and Lay Faithful on Preparation for the Jubilee of the Year 2000." This 62-page document outlines his plan to prepare for the "third millennium." He calls it the third millennium since the birth of Christ. Let's look at just a few excerpts from this apostolic letter. "The year 2000 will be celebrated as the Great Jubilee . . . Among the most fervent petitions which the Church makes to the Lord during this important time, as the eve of the new millennium approaches, is that unity among all Christians of the various confessions will increase until they reach full communion. I pray that the Jubilee will be a promising opportunity for fruitful cooperation in the many areas which unite us; these are unquestionably more numerous than those which divide us. It would thus be quite helpful if, with due respect for the programs of the individual Churches and Communities, ecumenical agreements could be reached with regard to the preparation and celebration of the Jubilee" (p. 23).

The pope says that as Bishop of Rome he has special responsibilities to prepare for the Great Jubilee of the Year 2000. He goes on to say that the increase of papal journeys over the past several years have been designed to bring about unity. In addition, the Holy Years that have been set aside by the Roman Catholic Church have also helped to prepare for the Jubilee. For example, "The Marian Year [1986-87] was as it were an anticipation of the Jubilee, and contained much of what will find fuller expression in the Year 2000" (p. 33).

The pope has divided the time between now and the year 2000 into two periods: The first phase is the prepreparation period—through the year 1996—and the second is the strictly preparatory phase for the years 1997, 1998, 1999. He states, "Only a few years now separate us from the Year 2000. . . . In these last years of the millennium, the

Church should invoke the Holy Spirit with ever greater insistence, imploring from him the grace of Christian Unity" (pp. 35, 39).

The second phase is divided in thirds among the Trinity with Mary added to each one.

"The first year, 1997, will thus be devoted to reflection on Christ, the Word of God, made man by the power of the Holy Spirit. . . . From an *ecumenical point of view,* this will certainly be a very important year for Christians to look together to Christ the one Lord, deepening our commitments to become one in him, in accordance with his prayer to the Father." The pope also suggests that "A detailed study of the *Catechism of the Catholic Church* will prove of great benefit." He concludes his thoughts on the year 1997 by stating, "*The Blessed Virgin,* who will be as it were 'indirectly' present in the whole preparation phase, will be contemplated in this first year especially in the mystery of her Divine Motherhood" (pp. 47-49).

The second year, 1998, will be dedicated in a particular way to the *Holy Spirit*, "and to his sanctifying presence within the community of Christ's disciples." "In this *eschatological perspective*, believers should be called to a renewed appreciation of the theological virtue *of hope.* . . . Christians are called to prepare for the Great Jubilee of the beginning of the Third Millennium *by renewing their hope in the definitive coming of the Kingdom of God,* . . . in world history itself." He continues his discussion of the second year countdown by emphasizing unity in the Spirit and His gifts and then, again, mentions the role of Mary. "Mary, who conceived the Incarnate Word by the power of the Holy Spirit and then in the whole of her life allowed herself to be guided by his interior activity, will be contemplated and imitated during this year <u>above all</u> as the woman who was docile to the voice of the Spirit" (pp. 51-53).

According to the pope's countdown, 1999 will be the third and final year of preparation and will be dedicated to God the Father. "The whole of the Christian life is like a *pilgrimage to the house of the Father.*" The pope emphasizes the role of conversion, penance, and charity in preparing for the Jubilee. He then goes beyond unity among Christians to include other world religions. "As far as the field of religious awareness is concerned, the eve of the Year 2000 will provide a great opportunity, especially in view of the events of recent decades, for *inter-religious dialogue*, in accordance with the specific guidelines set down by the Second Vatican Council. . . . In this dialogue the Jews and the Muslims ought to have a pre-eminent place. . . . Attention is being given to finding ways of arranging historic meetings in places of exceptional symbolic importance like Bethlehem, Jerusalem and Mount Sinai.

"In this broad perspective of commitments, *Mary Most Holy*, the highly favored daughter of the Father, will appear before the eyes of believers as the perfect model of love towards both God and neighbor." He concludes by saying, "The ecumenical and universal character of the Sacred Jubilee can be fittingly reflected by a *meeting of all Christians*. This would be an event of great significance. . . . I trust this responsibility of the whole Church to the maternal intercession of Mary, Mother of the Redeemer. She, the Mother of Fairest Love, will be for Christians on the way to the Great Jubilee of the third Millennium, the Star which safely guides their steps to the Lord" (pp. 53-62).

It is with this great event in mind that the pope is preparing the world.

CHAPTER 2

God Is Right on Schedule

W e Adventists have had some big celebrations recently. Maybe "celebration" is an inappropriate term; so we have just called these events "Adventist Heritage" weekends.

First there was the 150th anniversary of the Great Disappointment, out of which sprang the Adventist movement. We memorialized it with a program at the William Miller Farm in October of 1994. Then in October of 1995 many of us gathered in Battle Creek to recognize 140 years of Adventist heritage there.

Of course it was appropriate to conduct these meetings. They allowed us the opportunity both to review the Lord's leading in the past and to renew our vision for a finished work.

But the question remains in the minds of many Adventist Christians—Is the Advent message still relevant? Can we preach with a straight face and a clear conscience that "Jesus is just about to come back"? Will we have to wait much longer? Will there be more celebrations to remind us of the apparent delay?

In fact, it is quite astonishing how right on schedule God is. The diligent student of history and Bible prophecy sees a clear track of fulfillment—sees that we are at the very end.

We gain this understanding from our study of Bible prophecies. Of particular significance are the books of Daniel, Matthew, and Revelation. And of course, as Adventists, we have the additional details that are supplied by the Spirit of Prophecy—most notably *The Great Controversy.*

A quick overview of prophecy reveals that there would be only four world empires: Babylon, Medo-Persia, Greece, and Rome. From the ashes of Rome would spring up a little horn power. A power very different from the others. It was to dominate the world for a period of 1260 years. Then the little horn power would receive a "deadly wound," and there would arise another power destined to be a world superpower. Abraham Lincoln described this power as a new nation conceived in liberty.

In that new land of freedom a renewed study of Bible prophecy led to an 1844 awareness formation of the Seventh-day Adventist Church.

Prophecy continued to unfold, and Ellen White declared early in this century that terrible wars were coming. She stated: "Only a moment of time, as it were, yet remains. But while already nation is rising against nation, and kingdom against kingdom, there is not now a general engagement" *(Testimonies,* vol. 6, p. 14). The great "world wars" were still in the future.

She went on to say, "The tempest is coming. . . . We shall see troubles on all sides. Thousands of ships will be hurled into the depths of the sea. Navies will go down, and human lives will be sacrificed by [the] millions" *(Last Day Events*, p. 24).

History records that in those two great world wars whole navies did indeed go down and that 69 million military and civilian personnel lost their lives. More were killed in those two wars than in all the world's previous wars combined.

Yet, terrible as those world wars were, we are told by Jesus in Matthew 24:6 to be aware that "The end is not yet." Still ahead is the scenario of Revelation 13. The deadly wound of the papal power would be healed, and it would command the attention and admiration of the world. The United States would speak as a dragon, becoming a superpower. But in spite of their obvious differences, instead of declaring war against each other, these last two great powers would cooperate to dominate the world, forming a formidable religio-political power.

WE ARE WITNESSING THESE EVENTS TAKING PLACE BEFORE OUR VERY EYES!

What has brought these two powers together is the "common enemy strategy."

In essence, Pope John Paul told former U.S. president Ronald Reagan: "Though we may not have a lot in common between us, we do have a common enemy in Communism. Let's work together for its downfall." And so what *Time* magazine called the "Holy Alliance" was born (see *Time*, February 24, 1992).

With the success of that endeavor the papacy then turned its attention to cooperative ventures with the Protestants of America in working to defeat the common enemy of moral corruption in the United States.

The conditions in society in these last days have provided the "common enemy."

Ellen White described the breakdown of society in *Selected Messages,* book 3, page 418, in the chapter titled "The Last Great Struggle." "Fewer and fewer will become the sympathetic cords which bind man in brotherhood to his fellow man. The natural egotism of the human heart will be worked upon by Satan. He will use the uncontrolled wills and violent passions which were never brought under the control of God's will. . . .

"Every man's hand will be against his fellow man. Brother will rise against brother, sister against sister, parents against children [The Susan Smith story was not an isolated event. Every year in the United States over 2,000 children under the age of 5 are killed by their parents or those who should be their protectors.], children against parents. All will be in confusion. Relatives will betray one another. There will be secret plotting to destroy life. [Bombings] Destruction, misery, and death will be seen on every hand."

It was in an atmosphere of common cause that leading American Catholics and Evangelicals prepared and signed on March 29, 1994, the historic document entitled "Evangelicals and Catholics Together." In essence these two groups agreed to work together to defeat a common enemy.

Evangelical author Dave Hunt in his recent book, "*A Woman Rides the Beast,*" states that the signing of this document "was the most significant event in nearly 500 years of church history. . . . The document in effect overturned the Reformation and will unquestionably have far-reaching repercussions throughout the Christian world for years to come" (p. 5).

Recently I went to a Catholic bookstore to purchase the encyclical, "That They May Be One," by John Paul II. In it he appeals to Christians worldwide to come together in full communion, with the pope as leader by the year 2000. While at that bookstore I asked if they carried any books on prophecy or the book of Revelation. I was shown the book *The Thunder of Justice*, by Ted and Maureen Flynn. This book contains reports of "Marian Apparitions." A number of Catholic clergy and laypeople claim to have had contact with the virgin Mary. Consistent with what the Bible says about the state of the dead, we believe that Mary is resting in her grave awaiting the resurrection. Those being "contacted," however, say that Mary is in heaven and has entrusted them with the message that Jesus is coming soon—before the year 2000!

We can see further evidence that the two powers of Revelation 13 are cooperating as predicted in the activity of the Christian Coalition, headed by Pat Robertson. In early October of 1995 on the occasion of the papal visit to the United States, Robertson and other Evangelical leaders had a private meeting with John Paul II at the residence of Cardinal John O'Connor in New York. At this meeting Robertson presented the pope with a three-page letter pledging his support for the unity of Christians. Robertson later joined the pope on the platform for the papal mass in New York's Central Park.

The Christian Coalition recently announced the formation of the Catholic Alliance, its Catholic branch, already with over 250,000 members. Prominent Catholic leaders have just concluded the first national conference of the Catholic Campaign for America. As stated in their printed materials, "The mission of the Catholic Campaign for America is to activate Catholic citizens, to increase the Catholic electorate's influence in formulating public policy, and to focus the public's attention on the beauty and richness of Catholic teaching."

We need to look closely at this new Catholic/Protestant political alliance. It seems consistent with biblical prophecy that this union will bring about the final struggle in the great controversy—the Sabbath/Sunday issue. As you will see, the stage has already been set. The script outlined in prophecy is being played out—now!

When the great explorers left Europe in search of new lands, many times they had inadequate maps for guidance. The early maps were complete only to a certain point. When the map makers did not know what was beyond a certain point, they would draw pictures of various hazards or simply write "dragons beyond here." In other words, "From here on you are on your own. We have no idea what is ahead."

But are we traveling in uncharted waters today, prophetically speaking? No, thank God, we have the sure word of prophecy to guide us. Ellen White stated in the *Review and Herald* of November 27, 1900, that <u>"Everything has been moving on just as the Lord revealed in prophecy that it would."</u>

At some point even the most adventurous, ambitious traveler gets homesick and decides to head for home. I know the feeling. On many occasions when a meeting or appointment has concluded earlier than anticipated I have gone to the airport to try to get an earlier flight home.

Ellen White had a very busy travel schedule. She did not have the convenience of air travel and regular meal service. She once wrote in her diary, "It is a beautiful day. We feared we should be obliged to ride in a storm, but we have a very good road and everything seems favorable. We are homeward bound today and expect before night to meet husband and children. At noon took a dry luncheon at an old hotel, while the horses were feeding. Joyfully, we again met our family . . . There is no place to be so dearly prized as home" *(Manuscript Releases*, vol. 3, p. 139).

But many times in her experience she looked beyond her earthly home and toward our real home: "The time of tarrying is almost ended. The pilgrims and strangers who have so long been seeking a better country are almost home. I feel as if I must cry aloud, Homeward Bound!" *(Our High Calling*, p. 367).

And indeed we are homeward bound! I'm excited, aren't you?

CHAPTER 3

The Way From Eden to Eden

The entire "plan of salvation," the story of salvation history, covers God's dealing with man from the Garden of Eden all the way to the New Earth. It is the grand theme of Scripture. John Bunyan, in his book *Pilgrim's Progress,* described the salvation process as a road that each of us must travel. Nearing our heavenly home we look ahead and see the last waymarks—the "signs" telling us that it is very close. This is exciting to those who have traveled a great distance, a long time, or through difficult times. However, we know that the last mile of this grand quest may be the most difficult. Our adversary, the devil, has come down with great wrath because he knows that he has only a short time (Revelation 12:12).

Like Christian in *Pilgrim's Progress*, we have a weapon to counteract the devil's wiles. "The Bible, and the Bible only, gives a correct view of these things. Here are revealed the great final scenes in the history of our world, events that already are casting their shadows before, the sound of their approach causing the earth to tremble and men's hearts to fail them for fear" *(Education,* p. 180).

The Bible warns, "There is a way that seems right to a man, but its end is the way of death" (Proverbs 14:12). If the way that seems right—isn't—what does one do? Again the Bible has the answer. "Trust in the Lord with all your heart, and lean not on your own understanding; in all your ways acknowledge Him, and He shall direct your paths" (Proverbs 3:5, 6).

One of the truly awesome things about the Incarnation, the life of Christ, is that He came to this earth to show us the way. He said, "I am the way, the truth, and the life, no one comes to the Father except through Me" (John 14:6). The Sermon on the Mount makes it plain that each of us has a decision to make—a gate to pass through—and a destination at the end of the road. "Enter by the narrow gate; for wide is the gate and broad is the way that leads to destruction, and there are many who go in by it. Because narrow is the gate and difficult is the way which leads to life, and there are few who find it" (Matthew 7:13, 14).

When Adam and Eve sinned, God responded with love. He let them know of His love by providing clothes for them and outlining the plan of salvation. There was a way out of the mess, but it would take a long time. And yes, there was an immediate price to pay. They had to leave their garden home. They could no longer eat of the tree of life and thereby perpetuate their life of evil. As it was, in the course of his 930 years Adam lived to see the almost total degradation of the race. Late in his life he was for a time contemporary with Enoch and Methuselah. Possibly he learned from them of God's plan to destroy the earth with a flood.

To Noah, faithful Noah, God revealed His plan to save the righteous in an ark. For 120 years Noah's life was one of excitement—anticipating the Flood and building the ark—and also frustration by the constant barrage of criticism, scorn, and ridicule. He saved himself and his family. But after the Flood wickedness increased and God again acted in righteousness, scattering the rebels at the tower of Babel. But He gathered the righteous into one family through the promise to Abraham.

The call of Abraham, the birth of Isaac, and the experiences of Jacob began the long history of "the people of God." All three of these men made serious mistakes in their lives, but God has identified Himself since then as the God of Abraham, Isaac, and Jacob.

Later God called Moses to deliver Israel from bondage in Egypt. Moses, who had been adopted into the family of the pharaoh, had to decide between the wealth and pleasures of Egypt or joining with the people of God. He chose the latter, and with God's power delivered Israel and led them to the borders of Canaan.

Inspired by God, Moses wrote the first five books of the Bible. He outlined salvation history from the Creation to the Exodus. He chronicled the giving of God's laws in written form. The Law combines poetry, salvation history, legislation, and exhortation. The three major divisions of the Law, as outlined in Deuteronomy 4:44, 45, are the testimonies (moral duties), the statutes (ceremonial duties), and the judgments or ordinances (civil and social duties). The moral portion of the Law is summarized in the Ten Commandments.

The reign of King David, about 1,000 years before Christ, was a high point in the experience of ancient Israel, a golden age, the "Camelot" kingdom of a man after God's own heart. But David compromised God's will for Israel, sowing in his own family the seeds of discord that would later divide the kingdom. Later kings led the people into apostasy. Because of increasing worldliness and disobedience, God allowed the Babylonian captivity. But it was during this period that God used faithful young men to represent Him in that foreign land. Daniel, the statesman/prophet, was used by God to outline the course of history from his day to the end of time. The time prophecies of Daniel and those of the apostle John in his Revelation of Jesus Christ give us a picture of where we are in this world's history and what can be expected in the time remaining.

Questioned privately by His disciples, Jesus revealed much about end-time events. He gave a number of "signs of the end" and described events in the world and the church that would indicate His coming was near—at the very doors.

Of course it was Christ Himself who laid out all of history and prophecy. "The history which the great I AM has marked out in His word, uniting link after link in the prophetic chain, from eternity in the past to eternity in the future, tells us where we are today in the procession of the ages, and what may be expected in the time to come. All that prophecy has foretold as coming to pass, until the present time, has been traced on the pages of history, and we may be assured that all which is yet to come will be fulfilled in its order. . . . The final overthrow of all earthly dominions is plainly foretold in the word of truth. . . . That time is at hand. Today the signs of the times declare that we are standing on the threshold of great and solemn events" *(Education,* pp. 178, 179).

We have briefly traced the lives of some of the major players in God's salvation history. They are part of history. Their part is written in the Scriptures and the history books. Now the last chapter is being written and we are the characters!

"The word came to Noah, 'Come thou and all thy house into the ark; for thee I have seen righteous before Me.' Noah obeyed and was saved. The message came to Lot, 'Up, get you out of this place; for the Lord will destroy this city' (Gen. 7:1; 19:14). Lot placed himself under the guardianship of the heavenly messengers, and was saved. So Christ's disciples were given warning of the destruction of Jerusalem. Those who watched for the sign of the coming ruin and fled from the city, escaped the destruction. <u>So now we are given warning of Christ's second coming and of the destruction to fall upon the world.</u> **Those who heed the warning will be saved** " *(The Desire of Ages*, p. 634).

The purpose of this book, from the author's perspective, is to give assurance and warning. I consider myself to be a kind of investigative reporter and this book to be somewhat of a documentary on our times. Things are happening in detail just like we have been told that they would. Truly we live in a grand and awful time. It is a time for confidence and trust in God and His many wonderful promises. My hope is that this book will serve as a call to Christians everywhere to awake and be vigilant.

It is my personal judgment based on my study of prophecy and an observation of current events that the stage is set for the final events. I believe that the organization and activities of the Christian Coalition, the Catholic Alliance, and the Catholic Campaign for America, though in each case the participants are apparently sincere and God-fearing, will lead to consequences that will fulfill the 13th chapter of Revelation.

A statement from the inspired pen of Ellen White seems to be especially timely right now. "Through the two great errors, the immortality of the soul and Sunday sacredness, Satan will bring the people under his deceptions. While the former lays the foundation of spiritualism, the later creates a bond of sympathy with Rome. The Protestants of the United States will be foremost in stretching their hands across the gulf to grasp the hand of spiritualism; they will reach over the abyss to clasp hands with the Roman power; and under the influence of this threefold union, this country will follow in the steps of Rome in trampling on the rights of conscience" *(The Great Controversy*, p. 588).

Spiritualism is indeed making major inroads into the Catholic Church with Marian apparitions, and a great emphasis on contact with the dead. And in addition, there is a growing emphasis on urging Sunday as a mandated day of rest.

We are at the point where "Angels are now restraining the winds of strife, that they may not blow until the world shall be warned of its coming doom; but a storm is gathering, ready to burst upon the earth; and when God shall bid His angels loose the winds, there will be such a scene of strife as no pen can picture" *(Education,* pp. 179, 180).

Many readers with a foundation of prophetic study will realize that the last two major players in earthly history are the papacy or the Roman Catholic Church and the United States of America, now the world's only remaining superpower. Other readers may find it necessary to review the major prophecies of the Bible and trace God's outline of prophecy down through time. If you desire to review the prophecies or to see them explained in a simple manner as a foundation for the material that will follow, I have included several extra chapters as an appendix at the back of the book. The appendix includes a review of the world empires as given in Scripture and history, the rise and fall of the little horn power, the predicted role of the United States in world affairs, an unmasking of the antichrist, and an explanation of the seal of God and the mark of the beast.

This material brings the student of prophecy down to our day, when the great powers of the United States and the Roman Catholic Church cooperate to bring about some of the last events on earth. These last two powers do not simply emerge out of thin air. God has plainly and simply outlined the course of history that brings us to our present-day scenario—the last act in the drama of the ages.

CHAPTER 4

Full Diplomatic Relations

The timing was calculated. The result is prophetic. The consequences are serious. On January 10, 1984, upon the orders of United States President Ronald Reagan and the "Holy See," the central government of the Roman Catholic Church, represented by "The Holy Father," Pope John Paul II, full diplomatic relations were established between these two entities.

"This cordial and cooperative framework did not always exist. In fact it took 208 years for the United States to enter into full diplomatic relations with the oldest international personality in the community of nations" (Thomas P. Melady, *The Ambassador's Story—The United States and the Vatican in World Affairs*, p. 41).

There were some early contacts between the new republic, the United States, and the Papal States. Papal authority then was essentially over the territory of central Italy. At that time the recognition of this fact by the United States did not include any perception of the "Holy See" and the unique international personality of the pope that transcended his role as the sovereign head of a state and the head of a church.

In 1797 the United States established consular relations with the Papal States, whose capital was in Rome. This action was reciprocated at the same consular level in 1826 when the Papal States established a consulate in New York City. In 1848 President James Polk proposed that the United States appoint a charge d'affaires—a diplomat below the ambassador level—to the Papal States. Following extensive debate in the Senate, Jacob I. Martin was appointed.

Thomas P. Melady, the official U.S. ambassador to the Vatican, i.e. the Holy See, from 1989 to 1993, gives a short history of the early recognitions between the United States and the Vatican.

"Mr. Jacob I. Martin presented his credentials to Pope Pius IX in Rome on August 19, 1848. Seven days later, on August 26, he died of malaria. Mr. Martin was in a certain sense the first representative of the United States Government accredited to the Pope. That accreditation, however, was along the traditional line of a diplomatic representative from one state to another. At that time the recognition did not include the fact that the Pope regarded himself as the head of the Catholic Church and of the Holy See. The letter of credentials of Mr. Martin referred to the Pope as Chief of State. There was no reference to him as head of the Catholic Community. But nevertheless, he was the first representative of the Government of the United States accredited to the Pope.

"Mr. Martin was followed in a period of nineteen years by five other diplomates. They were: Lewis Cass, Jr., 1849-1858; John P. Stockton, 1858-1861; Alexander W. Randell, 1861-1862; Richard M. Blatchford, 1862-1863; and Rufus King, 1863-1867.

"Rufus King was the last minister resident to the Papal States. He left his post in August 1867. Beginning in that year, it would not have been possible to fund such a diplomatic post, as Congress in that year prohibited the financing of any diplomatic post to the Papal States.

"Mr. King's departure from Rome in 1867 initiated a long interregnum of seventy-two years when the United States had no diplomatic representative to the Pope" (Melady, *The Ambassador's Story, the United States and the Vatican in World Affairs*, pp. 42, 43).

Then in 1936 the relationship between the U.S. and the Vatican began to warm again with the visit of Eugenio Cardinal Pacelli to the United States. At the time of his visit to the U.S., Pacelli was the Secretary of State of the Vatican. In March of 1939 he became Pope Pius XII. At the time of his "papal coronation," President Roosevelt sent Joseph Kennedy, then U.S. ambassador to England, as a special representative of the United States.

On Christmas Eve, 1939, President Roosevelt announced his intention to send a personal representative to the Vatican. Shortly after that he named Myron Taylor, an Episcopalian and retired chairman of the United States Steel Corporation, to this position. Former ambassador Melady fills in some interesting details.

"The appointment did not require the consent of the Senate.

Consequently there was no public forum to debate the merits of President Roosevelt's action.

"Once he arrived in Rome, Myron Taylor was always treated as an Ambassador representing the Government of the United States. Taylor's ten years as his country's diplomatic envoy covered the World War II years. He had easy access to the Pope and top Vatican officials. His office was a source of valuable information to the United States" (Melady, p. 45).

Myron Taylor retired in 1949. Two years later President Harry Truman nominated General Mark Clark as the first "ambassador" to the Vatican. It is important to note that this "ambassadorship" was to the Vatican City State, not to the "Holy See." However, opposition to the nomination mounted quickly. A few questioned General Clark's qualification for the job. Most, however, were strongly opposed to the "recognition" by the U.S. government of a "church."

President Truman decided not to press the nomination and the confirmation process. According to Melady, "Another eighteen years would expire before a U.S. President would attempt to name any kind of a senior diplomate to the Holy See. There was no diplomatic representative in the administrations of Presidents Eisenhower, Kennedy, and Johnson.

"President Nixon broke the long interregnum in 1969 and appointed Henry Cabot Lodge as his personal representative to the Pope. Mr. Lodge, a former U.S. Senator, had the courtesy title of 'Ambassador,' as he had served as U.S. Ambassador to the United Nations, Vietnam, and Germany" (Melady, p. 46).

President Carter had two personal representatives to the Vatican. They were David Walters, followed by former mayor of New York City, Robert F. Wagner.

In the first few weeks after his election in November of 1980, President Ronald Reagan appointed William Wilson, his friend from California, as his personal representative to the Vatican. Then something happened that changed the course of history in this regard. President Reagan had a private meeting with the pope in the Vatican on June 7, 1982. Many modern historians use this date as the beginning of the "Holy Alliance" between the U.S. and the Vatican. (See my book *Even at the Door*, p. 232 for more details of this meeting and its aftermath.)

Following this historic meeting with the pope, in the last year of his first term as president of the United States, Ronald Reagan initiated a process for doing what had never been done before—sending a full "ambassador," not just to the Vatican City State but to the "Holy See"—the central government of the Roman Catholic Church!

From Personal Representative to Ambassador—the Process

President Reagan's staff, aware of what had happened to potential "ambassadors" in the past, made an extensive study of the subject. This review included looking at Section 2, article 2 of the Constitution that defines the president's authority to nominate diplomatic officials and the responsibility of the Senate to give its consent. The staff felt convinced that they could defend the proposed ambassadorship with their interpretation of the Constitution. In addition, though the legal situation had not changed (remember Congress had passed a law in 1868 that had prohibited funding for an embassy to the Vatican), the domestic political climate had changed significantly! Popular Protestant evangelist Billy Graham had stated publicly that he saw a significant difference in the national Protestant attitude. There would still be some opposition, but not of the magnitude as 30 years before.

Ambassador Melady states, "Once he [Reagan] was convinced that the nomination of an Ambassador to the Holy See was constitutional and in the national interest of the country, President Reagan approved a move to void the 1868 law which prohibited the expenditure of public funds for an Embassy to the Vatican. This action was successful. The relative ease with which this action took place reassured the Reagan White House about proceeding with their project" (Melady, p. 52).

Melady adds these very significant statements: " On January 10, 1984, President Ronald Reagan announced the establishment of formal diplomatic relations with the Holy See . . . The announcement gave full recognition to the unique international sovereign role of the Pope and his government, not only in Vatican City State but throughout the world where the Pope and his government exercised their spiritual and political authority. There was no equivocation. **The United States was extending full recognition for the first time to the government of the Holy Catholic and Apostolic Church.**

"The announcement implied the acceptance of the international law principle that the Holy See is a bona fide international personality. Thus

the announcement by President Reagan acknowledged the papacy as a religious organ with international rights and duties. This was not a qualified
recognition of Vatican City State. In previous times it would have caused
a firestorm of protest. But it immediately became evident, both in tone
and substance, that there had been a major change in domestic U.S.
political opinion" (Melady, pp. 50, 53).

Understanding the Holy See

To the average Protestant layman the term "Holy See" has no
meaning whatsoever. It is probably not even in common usage among
Catholic laymen. The reason for this uncertainty is the unusual "nature
of the beast." It would be best, I believe, to get the definition of the
Holy See from someone who ought to know. Back again to Thomas
Patrick Melady, a Roman Catholic career diplomat and formerly the
official Ambassador of the United States of America to the Holy See.
His explanation is as follows: "The Government of the United States
has diplomatic relations with the government of the Roman Catholic
Church; that is, the Holy See.

"The Holy See is the composite of the authority, jurisdiction, and
sovereignty vested in and exercised by the Pope and his advisers in the
temporal and spiritual direction and guidance of **the Roman Catholic
Church throughout the world. The Holy See,** consequently, **is a
moral entity;** in modern terms, **it is the central government of the
Roman Catholic Church"** (Melady, p. 178).

The Holy See is not just the small city-state of 110 acres called the
Vatican within the City of Rome, Italy. It is the worldwide body of
over 900 million Roman Catholic members with the pope at its head.
The Holy See has formal diplomatic relations with over 145 nations including the United States.

"The Pope's Ambassador [the individual representatives of the
Holy See to the 145 nations] has two functions. One is diplomatic as
an ambassador of the Holy See to the government where he is accredited. The other is religious, as a representative to the local church of the
Pope to assure that canonical regulations are being followed. He also
recommends appointments of new bishops. When there are no diplomatic relations, the Pope's representative has solely a religious role.
. . . Vatican City State is the physical seat of the Holy See. The Holy

See is a sovereign entity that has this unique universal sovereignty because of the role of the Pope of the Catholic Church in the world" (Melady, p. 179).

The Holy See Not Democratic

In the summer of 1995 I visited the Vatican, the museum, the treasury, St. Peter's Basilica and related facilities. There in the Vatican treasury I saw the famous triple crown of the pope. It appears to be made of pure gold with large jewels attached to it.

In the treasury gift shop I purchased the official full-color directory and gift book of the treasury printed by the Vatican press. I noted that the triple crown photo has this caption: "The Triple Crown—papal tiara comprising the three crowns which symbolize the Pope's threefold power as Father of Kings, Rector of the World, and Vicar of Christ." Thomas Melady stated that upon arrival in Rome he presented his credentials to the pope as "Vicar of Christ, head of the Universal Catholic Church, and sovereign of Vatican City State."

In his explanation of how the government of the Holy See functions Ambassador Melady states, **"The Pope exercises supreme legislative, executive, and judicial power over the Holy See. He is the equivalent of an absolute monarch.** This authority is not restricted to the State of Vatican City. The sovereignty of the Holy See is a universal historical fact accepted by international society. The Holy See has sent and received diplomatic missions since the fourth century. The Pope rules the Holy See through the Roman Curia and the Papal Civil Service which staffs it" (Melady, p. 179).

The pope is elected for life, and there is no such thing as a deputy pope. Consequently, no one is "a heartbeat away from the papacy." In the only electoral process in the Roman Catholic Church the pope is "elected" by the cardinals who have been appointed by a pope. "Cardinals" are medieval creations with no scriptural foundation. The cardinals will choose the next pope, "the 265th successor of Saint Peter," from among their own number. By current canon law there can be only 120 eligible cardinals. Once they reach the age of 80 years they are no longer eligible to vote.

Noted Roman Catholic journalist Peter Hebblethwaite, who was widely respected as a commentator on events and trends in the Catholic

Church, gave some insight into the papacy's political process. In his book *The Next Pope,* printed in 1995, just a few months after his death, he states many interesting things about the papal electoral process. For example, "There is a great difficulty in speaking honestly and directly about popes, for as soon as a man becomes pope a process of mythologization sets in that transforms overnight the mediocre into a genius and the merely talented into a superluminary" *(The Next Pope*, p. 89).

All this about the politics of the papacy underlines the irony of the Holy See talking loudly about human rights and religious freedom in its affairs with nations. Ambassador Melady goes into considerable detail in his book about the Holy See's efforts to bring about democracy and religious freedom in Poland, the Baltic States, Czechoslovak Federal Republic, Hungary, Romania, Bulgaria, Albania, Cuba, Central and South America, and in Africa. Yet it is not democratic in its own process nor is it interested in religious freedom for anyone but Roman Catholics and the Holy See. For example, Ambassador Melady, when commenting on his work of getting the U.S. and Holy See officials together to discuss the situation in China, states, "Both the Holy See and the United States were confronted by the same human-rights and religious-freedom concerns in China . . . When I arranged for a meeting of Secretary [of State James] Baker with Cardinal Angelo Sodano [Secretary of State of the Holy See—newly appointed] on November 8, 1991, the promotion of human rights and religious freedom in China was on the agenda.

"This was the first meeting of Cardinal Sodano, first with Secretary Baker, then with President Bush . . . The exchange with Secretary Baker focused on how to accelerate the process of change in China that could reduce the current abuses. Cardinal Sodano brought up the matter of the right of the Catholic Church to carry out its mission in China" (Melady, p. 92).

The Senate Hearings

To reverse the current situation in which the United States has a full and formal diplomatic relationship with the Holy See would quite literally take the proverbial "act of Congress." The Congressional Records give a word-by-word transcript of the hearing before the Committee on Foreign Relations of the United States Senate regarding the nomination of William A. Wilson to be the U.S. ambassador to the Holy See on

February 2, 1984. The committee met, pursuant to notice, at 2:31 p.m., in room SD-419, Dirksen Senate Office Building, with the Hon. Richard Lugar presiding. The committee announced before the hearings that their deliberations would focus on the question Should the United States have diplomatic relations with the Holy See? However, as the record states, several speakers noted that the Senate had already settled that question and they were just now going to consider the qualifications of Mr. Wilson for the post. Since he had already served at the Vatican as President Reagan's personal representative for the past three years no one was more qualified than he to be named as ambassador. The vote of the committee was 15 in favor and 1 opposed.

The nominee, Mr. William Wilson, was introduced to the committee by the Hon. Pete Wilson, then U.S. Senator from California. His remarks were, in part, as follows:

"Thank you very much, Mr. Chairman, for giving me the privilege of introducing to you a fellow Californian, a very distinguished American . . . Mr. Chairman, in the interest of the committee's time and that of the nominee, I will try to come quickly to the point. There will, I assume, be witnesses who follow me and who follow the nominee wishing to address the committee with respect to what they term the propriety or lack of propriety of an action that I would point out is an accomplished fact. Diplomatic relations were established between the United States and the Vatican as of January 10 of this year.

"I mention that not to excite counter argument. That probably will not be necessary. But I would point out that the action has been taken. That debate has occurred in Congress and the decision has been taken. So what we are concerned with, quite properly, today, Mr. Chairman, is not the propriety of this relationship. The relationship exists."

Senator Richard Lugar, the presiding chairman of the Committee on Foreign Relations for this hearing, then gave an opening statement in which he said, in part, "I believe the President has made a wise decision in establishing diplomatic relations with the Holy See and in nominating William Wilson to conduct those relations at the ambassadorial level.

"The Holy See maintains a diplomatic presence and has wide influence and unique access in areas of great concern to the foreign policy of the United States. . . .

"Vatican officials and diplomats are not simply observers or moral guides but play an active role in international affairs. . . .

"Over the past two years, the President, the Vice President, the Secretary of State, and other Cabinet officers have had audiences with the Pope to discuss a wide range of political and moral problems which confront the world. Every President of the United States in recent memory has indicated his respect for the prominent international standing of the Papacy by meeting with the pope. . . . Pope John Paul II is a powerful force for the political and moral values which we in the United States cherish and which are so important to the dignity of men and women everywhere. . . .

"I will not argue the case further today. I will simply say I believe the burden of proof lies upon those who would argue that there is a special reason to abrogate the President's clearly stated constitutional authority to name Ambassadors. <u>The President established diplomatic relations with the Holy See on January 10, 1984.</u> Strictly speaking, Senators will be called upon not to judge this action but to judge the suitability of Mr. Wilson for the post for which he has been nominated."

The die was cast before the "hearing" was ever held. The action had already been taken! Another major step had been taken to form the image to the beast.

Where to From Here?

This is only half of the story, of course, because when we are dealing with the Holy See we must consider not just the political side but also the religious side. This we will do in the next chapter. But first, let's consider one more important factor. In his book *Keys of This Blood*, Malachi Martin noted that there would be a struggle for world dominion between the three great powers on earth—Communism, Capitalism, and Catholicism. Martin predicted, in essence, that by the year 2000 only one would remain—that being the Roman Catholic Church with the pope as its leader.

Ambassador Melady outlines how this struggle played out with a "common enemy" factor. "Both <u>the United States and the Holy See faced the same powerful opponent.</u> The years following World War II (when the then Soviet Union acquired superpower status) were especially difficult for the United States and the Holy See. Both the United

States and the Holy See were deeply involved—from 1945 to the late 1980s—in efforts to thwart the advance of atheistic communism. . . . Senior Vatican officials told me on several occasions that the world owed a great thanks to the United States for having orchestrated and played a leading role in this collapse [of the Soviet Union] and having done this in a non-violent way. . . ."

Melady goes on to say, "With the arrival of Gorbachev on the scene in 1985, the Holy See sensed that **the time was approaching when significant changes could take place"** (Melady, pp. 74, 75). This statement reminds one of Ellen White's statement in *The Great Controversy*, page 580: "Marvelous in her shrewdness and cunning is the Roman Church. She can read what is to be. She bides her time . . ."

So what will the future bring? Ambassador Melady concludes, **"I believe that the U.S., as the world's only superpower, and the Holy See, as the only world-wide moral-political sovereignty, have significant roles to play in the future. Their actions will impact the lives of people in all parts of the globe"** (Melady, p. 10). Surely, he doesn't realize how "prophetic" his words are.

CHAPTER 5

Ecumenism in High Gear

E cumenism is a fairly new term, used since 1948 to describe the tendency of modern Christian groups or bodies to cooperate and unify. It certainly brings to fulfillment the prophetic prediction that Protestants of the United States would eventually cooperate with the Roman Catholic Church. Early on, the ecumenical movement was primarily centered within Protestantism, for example, within various Lutheran denominations. But now we are seeing a major coming together of Protestants and Catholics.

Two recent documents on ecumenism and the unity of Christians have major significance. One was written in Rome—at the Vatican—and the other was written in the United States.

The first is *Evangelicals and Catholics Together: The Christian Mission in the Third Millennium.* This 25-page document was developed by Protestant Chuck Colson and former Protestant Richard John Neuhaus and signed by 40 well-known Evangelical and Catholic leaders. The document was signed on March 29, 1994. Among the Catholic signatories are John Cardinal O'Connor, Richard John Neuhaus, Keith Fournier, Nathan Hatch, and Matthew Lamb. The Protestant signatories included Pat Robertson, Bill Bright, Chuck Colson, Mark Noll, and Richard Mouw.

On March 30, 1994, *USA Today* reported the signing of the document this way: "In what is being called a historic declaration—though not an official stance of either denomination—evangelicals including Pat Robertson joined with conservative Roman Catholic leaders Tuesday in upholding the ties of faith that bind the nation's largest and most politically active groups. . . . The leaders, in a statement are urging the nation's 52 million Catholics and 13 million evangelicals to no longer hold each other at theological arm's length and stop aggressive proselytization of each other's flocks—in short, to turn their theological swords into a recognition of a common faith."

Christianity Today noted the signing of the document by pointing out "the way it was and the way it is." "In 1534, Abbot Paul Bachmann published a virulent anti-Protestant booklet entitled, 'A Punch in the Mouth for the Lutheran Lying Wide-Gaping Throats.' Not to be outdone, the Protestant court chaplain, Jerome Rauscher, responded with a treatise of his own, entitled, 'One Hundred Select, Great, Shameless, Fat, Well-Swilled, Stinking, Papistical Lies.'

"Such was the tenor of theological discourse among many of the formative shapers of classical Protestantism and resurgent Roman Catholicism in the sixteenth century. How surprised those feisty forbearers would be to learn that their 'conservative' heirs, removed by five centuries and an ocean, could find so much on which to agree in the historic document—'Evangelicals and Catholics Together'" *(Christianity Today,* May 16, 1994).

The Christian Coalition gave the document front page coverage in their *Christian American* publication. Their report states: "After nearly four centuries of division and hostility, <u>Protestants and Catholics have taken an important step toward unity.</u> Forty key Evangelical and Catholic leaders signed a statement at the Institute on Religion and Public Life in New York City, on March 29, 1994, urging their followers to accept each other as Christians, <u>put aside differences and contend for common civil causes.</u>

" 'This is the wave of the future. It is as significant a coalition to the future of American Politics as the unification of blacks and Jews during the civil rights struggle,' Dr. Ralph Reed, executive director of the Christian Coalition, told the *Wall Street Journal."*

The "common enemy" syndrome is at work here again as Pat Robertson explains. "The moral crisis facing society today and the obvious social breakdown mandates a closer cooperation between people of faith. <u>The time has come</u> where we must lay aside minor points of doctrinal differences and focus on the Lord Jesus Christ. . . . This statement lays the groundwork for moving forward in a spirit of cooperation," Robertson said. <u>"I am lending my support because I believe it's</u>

imperative that we work to bring the body of Christ together"
(Christian American, May/June, 1994).

Of course, not all Evangelicals believe ECT is a positive step.
"Bob Jones III regards it as evidence that the 'ecumenical church,
which will be the church of the Anti-Christ, is rapidly forming'"
(Christianity Today, May 16, 1994).

Author Dave Hunt is very troubled by this move toward unity.
"The most significant event in nearly 500 years of church history was
revealed as a *fait accompli* on March 29, 1994," he writes. "On that
day leading American evangelicals and Catholics signed a joint declaration titled 'Evangelicals and Catholics Together: The Christian
Mission in the 3rd Millennium.' The document, in effect, overturned
the Reformation and will unquestionably have far-reaching repercussions throughout the Christian world for years to come." Hunt added,
"The key element behind this historic declaration is the previously un-
thinkable admission of the part of leading evangelicals that active par-
ticipation in the Catholic Church makes one a Christian. If that is
indeed the case, then the Reformation was a tragic mistake. The millions who were martyred for rejecting Catholicism as a false gospel
have all died in vain. If, however, the Reformers were right, then this
new agreement between Catholics and evangelicals could well be the
cleverest and deadliest blow struck against the gospel in the entire history of the church. Either way, the consequences are staggering" (Dave
Hunt, *A Woman Rides the Beast*, pp. 5, 6).

In the same vein, Ellen White asked a similar question years ago:
"Shall this power, whose record for a thousand years is written in the
blood of the saints, be now acknowledged as a part of the church of
Christ?" *(The Great Controversy,* p. 571).

Another significant fact is that though Adventists have been cham-
pions in the past, with literally hundreds of articles in the *Review and
Herald* on this topic between 1863 and 1915, today the leading spokesmen for the Protestant cause seem to be outside our church. This, too,
is a fulfillment of prophecy. Under the heading **"Many Not in Our
Ranks to Come to the Front"** Ellen White predicted, "There are
many souls to come out of the ranks of the world, out of the
churches—even the Catholic Church—whose zeal will far exceed that
of those who have stood in rank and file to proclaim the truth hereto-

fore. For this reason the eleventh hour laborers will receive their penny. <u>These will see the battle coming and will give the trumpet a certain sound"</u> *(Selected Messages*, vol. 3, pp. 386, 387). For example, author Dave Hunt has written two major books recently that have exposed the errors and aims of the papacy. They are *Global Peace and the Rise of the Anti-Christ* and *A Woman Rides the Beast.* Hunt still holds to the secret rapture and other teachings that we believe are not supported in Scripture, but his studies on the role of the Roman Catholic Church in prophecy and world affairs are significant.

Why is the ECT document so controversial? Perhaps a quick look at it from the perspective of its authors will add some light. The principal developers of ECT were Chuck Colson and Richard John Neuhaus. In 1995 they edited a 236-page book by a similar name, *Evangelicals and Catholics Together: Toward a Common Mission.* This compares with the title of the ECT document—*Evangelicals and Catholics Together: The Christian Mission in the Third Millennium.* I will refer to the above references as ECT-book and ECT-doc. Colson and Neuhaus give as reasons for the development of the ECT-doc. as "Evangelicals and Catholics had been finding one another as Christian brothers and sisters in various activities, <u>notably in the pro-life movement and the charismatic renewal.</u> . . . There was another factor. Along with many other evangelicals and Catholics, we were anguished by the growing conflicts between our communities in various parts of the world, especially in Latin America. That was the original focus of the meeting that we convened in New York City in September, 1992. Our concern was (and is) that animosities between evangelicals and Catholics threatened to mar the image of Christ by turning Latin America into a Belfast of religious warfare" (ECT-book, p. xi).

What was causing the "animosity" between Evangelicals and Catholics in Latin America? Just in Brazil over 500,000 people a year have been leaving the Catholic Church and becoming Protestants! As a result, Catholics were becoming extremely irritated. The pope visited the area and stated how he deplored the fact that various Protestant sects were "proselytizing among our poor ignorant peasants." It is interesting to note here that four of the Catholic participants and/or endorsers of the ECT document were Jesuits. They are: Fr. Juan Diaz-Vilar, S.J. of Catholic Hispanic Ministries; Fr. Avery Dulles, S.J. of Fordham University; Fr.

Joseph P. Fitzpatrick, S.J. of Fordham University; and Bishop Carlos A. Sevilla, S.J. of the Archdiocese of San Francisco. The "S.J." after each of their names indicates that they are of the "Society of Jesus" or more commonly known as "the Jesuit order." Remember, the Jesuit order was established in the sixteenth century as part of the Counter-Reformation, the anti-Protestant campaign of the Catholic Church.

Apparently, in order to address the problem of Catholic defections to the ranks of Protestantism, and because of the Jesuit influence, the ECT document in the "witnessing" section condemns "sheep stealing" from each other's communions.

Written in support of the ECT-doc. is *House United*, by Roman Catholic attorney Keith Fournier, the executive director of the American Center for Law and Justice, the "religious liberty" arm of the Christian Coalition. The foreword to the book was written by Pat Robertson, founder of the Christian Coalition. Fournier states in his book, "My experience with the pro-life movement has inspired my conviction that alliance building between Christians on this issue is not only possible but essential. To me, pro-life efforts are the greatest example of how convergence and cooperation can effectively take place among Christians of very different theological perspectives" (pp. 273, 274).

Near the conclusion of the book Fournier reports, "Catholics, Protestants, and Orthodox can come together, must come together, and are coming together. <u>The wall of separation is cracking, portions of the wall are beginning to fall away.</u> Christians are waking up and starting to see each other as Family. We still have a long tough road ahead of us. But it is a road we need to travel together—with courage and confidence" *(ibid.,* p. 336).

The ECT-doc. begins by saying, "We are Evangelical Protestants and Roman Catholics who have been led through prayer, study, and discussion to common convictions about Christian faith and mission. . . . As the Second Millennium draws to a close, the Christian mission in world history faces a moment of daunting opportunity and responsibility. If in the merciful and mysterious ways of God the Second Coming is delayed, we enter upon a Third Millennium that could be, in the words of John Paul II, 'a springtime of world missions.' "

And then the document puts that mission emphasis in a monolithic context. "As Christ is one, so the Christian mission is one." Other statements in the document illustrate the nature of the agreement. "We affirm together that all who accept Christ as Lord and Savior are brothers and sisters in Christ. Evangelicals and Catholics are brothers and sisters in Christ."

"Christians individually and the church corporately also have a responsibility for the right ordering of civil society. . . . In the exercise of these public responsibilities there has been in recent years a growing convergence and cooperation between Evangelicals and Catholics. We thank God for the discovery of one another in contending for a common cause. Much more important, we thank God for the discovery of one another as brothers and sisters in Christ. Our cooperation as citizens is animated by our convergence as Christians. We promise one another that we will work to deepen, build upon, and expand this pattern of convergence and cooperation.

"Together we contend for the truth that politics, law, and culture must be secured by moral truth."

"The pattern of convergence and cooperation between Evangelicals and Catholics is, in large part, a result of common efforts to protect human life, especially the lives of the most vulnerable among us. . . . That the unborn child has a right to protection, including the protection of law, is a moral statement supported by moral reason and biblical truth.

"We contend together for a comprehensive policy of parental choice in education. This is a moral question of simple justice." There is strong support in the Catholic and Evangelical communities for the educational voucher system that would give families state support to enroll their children in the school of their choice—either state, private, or parochial.

The ECT document has an entire section dealing with evangelism and the Christian witness. Several paragraphs condemn the practice of proselytizing or "sheep stealing." The following is representative: "In view of the large number of non-Christians in the world and the enormous challenge of our common evangelistic task, it is neither theologically legitimate nor a prudent use of resources for one Christian community to proselytize among active adherents of another Christian community."

ECT Summary

The motivation for the development and signing of the ECT document came from Evangelicals and Catholics finding common ground in the charismatic renewal movement and a common enemy in the abortion/pro-choice movement. It is significant to note that once these areas of commonality developed then the condemnation of proselyting followed.

Actual practice since the signing of the document indicates that Catholics expect Protestants to live up the agreement regarding sheep stealing, but apparently they do not intend to keep their end of the bargain. For example, a best-selling book, *Rome, Sweet Home,* and a widely circulated audiocassette tape series, *Answering Common Objections,* and *Protestant Minister Becomes a Catholic,* is the dramatic telling of Scott and Kimberly Hahn's journey from the Presbyterian ministry to the Roman Catholic Church, where Scott is now a professor training priests at the Franciscan University of Steubenville, Ohio. Other converts to Catholicism such as Richard John Neuhaus, Deal Hudson, and Episcopal Bishop Clarence Pope are publicly lauded in Catholic circles.

The ECT book includes treatises on the ECT document by six of the signatories. They all agree on one point. Literal, organic unity of one superchurch is probably a long way off—unless "the Spirit of God intervenes." The unity sought at this moment is a cooperative unity on common beliefs and common enemies. In his treatise under the title "Reaching Across the Boundaries," Chuck Colson states, "The ecumenical movement among liberal Protestants sought to unite various denominations by eliminating doctrinal distinctions. For those who no longer believe in the Bible or any kind of supernatural revelation, such doctrinal compromises come easily. But the deepening alliance between groups of evangelicals and Catholics that is occurring today is wholly different, because it is a cooperation among Christians who take doctrines very seriously indeed" (ECT book, p. 34).

Colson concludes by saying, "Christians do not have the luxury of limiting their energies to theological debate. True believers must reach across theological divides and embrace one another as brothers and sisters in Christ. Our obligation is nothing less than to join together in a defense of the truth of our shared faith. All Christians who confess that

Jesus is Lord must unite for the sake of our Lord and for the sake of our culture" (ECT-book, p. 38).

Another prominent signatory of the ECT document is Dr. Mark Noll of Wheaton College. His chapter in the ECT book outlines how and why relations have changed between Evangelicals and Catholics. First he gives a brief history to set the stage for the dramatic shift seen today. "Although the number of Catholics in the thirteen colonies was small (only 25,000 by 1790), Protestant anti-Romanism was a staple of the American theological world. It was fueled especially by the background of Catholic-Protestant strife in the English Reformation. That antagonism was enshrined for English-speaking readers everywhere in the pages of John Foxe's *Book of Martyrs*, which added Catholic persecution of Protestants to the long line of sufferings endured by true servants of Christ. As merely one instance of the antagonism as it came to America, it is helpful to note the language used when the Massachusetts Judge Paul Dudley in 1750 left a legacy to Harvard College for the purpose of establishing a series of theological lectures. The third of the lectures in a rotating cycle was to be devoted to 'the detecting & convicting & exposing of the Idolatry of the Romish Church, Their Tyranny, Usurpations, damnable Heresies, fatal Errors, abominable Superstitions, and other crying Wickednesses in their high Places; and Finally that the Church of Rome is that mystical Babylon, That Man of Sin, That apostate Church spoken of, in the New Testament'" (ECT-book, p. 87).

Dramatic Changes in Attitude

That was then. Only short decades later, the situation has become very different. Dr. Noll lists a number of factors that help explain why the Catholic-Evangelical climate has changed and why that change has been so dramatic.

1. The most visible public signal of a shift in the United States was the election of a Catholic as president in 1960. John F. Kennedy's victory was itself a milestone for overcoming Protestant bias and fulfilling earlier Catholic efforts at public service.

2. The Second Vatican Council (1962-1965) was another turning point as a part of Pope John XXIII's ecumenical spirit. After "Vatican II" there was a more active role played by the Catholic

Church in encouraging the return of "separated brethren." Also during his pontificate the pope had sent Catholic observers to the 1960 assembly of the World Council of Churches in New Delhi and had established a Secretariat for Promoting Christian Unity.

3. In the international arena, even more damage was done to Protestant notions of Catholic tyranny by the contribution of the Catholic Church to the Solidarity movement in Poland, the public leadership of Pope John Paul II in combating Communism in Europe, and the pope's temperate statements on explosive political situations in Latin America, Africa, and Asia. [From my perspective, the Catholic Church gets involved in these political situations in order to further its own ends. For example in Poland, once the people were freed from Communism, the Catholic bishops there demanded a place at the table when the new constitution was drafted and later mandated the teaching of Catholicism in every public school in Poland.]

4. Following Vatican II—The Second Vatican Council—the Catholic Church began to "dialogue" with other churches. Of many examples that could be cited, the U.S. Lutheran-Roman Catholic dialogue on justification by faith, published in 1983, is one of the most remarkable. The document contended that much of the disagreement on this issue between Protestants (or, here, Lutherans) and Catholics was based on conditions that no longer prevailed.

5. The spread of the Charismatic movement (and then of songs, prayers, and worship styles going well beyond officially Charismatic circles) has done a great deal to reduce the barriers between Catholics and Evangelicals.

6. The influence of Billy Graham, the most visible Protestant in the world, has played a major part in warming relations with the Catholics. Early in his career he enjoyed less than cordial relations with the Catholics. Then following the election of John Kennedy, Graham began to work at improved relations with Catholics. His efforts were unusually successful. Catholics now make up a considerable portion of those who attend his meetings, record decisions for Christ, and watch the crusades on television. In 1977 Graham was granted permission to hold a crusade in one of American Catholicism's most hallowed locations, the football stadium at the

University of Notre Dame. In 1978 he became the first Protestant leader to be entertained by the abbot of the shrine of the Black Madonna in Czestochowa, Poland. In 1981 he sought and was granted an audience at the Vatican by Pope John Paul II, who short years before as Cardinal Karol Wojtyla had made it possible for Graham to preach in Catholic churches during his evangelistic tour of Poland. (Points above are summarized from ECT-book, pp. 93-99.)

Dr. Noll concludes his chapter by stating, "European Catholics and Protestants have concluded that the condemnations of the Reformation were based on misconceptions, were aimed at extreme positions on the other side, and no longer apply to today's situations" (ECT-book, p. 108).

Several contributors to the book, like Richard John Neuhaus, who joined the Catholic Church, state that either the Reformation was much ado about nothing or else the problems that the Reformers sought to address have been corrected.

In some ways the ECT document is only the latest in an ecumenical tide. Author Michael Semlyen, writing from England, points out that "September 1st 1990 was a date of great historical significance. On that day the British Council of Churches gave way to *Churches Together* in Britain, and the Inter-Church Process formally came into being. For the first time the Roman Catholic Church is participating. Indeed it is sure that she is destined to play a major role. *Churches Together in England* (CTE) was launched in St George's Cathedral, symbolizing, according to the journal *The Tablet*, the Roman Catholic Church's 'senior partnership' in the new venture. In a real sense, in the year of the anniversaries of J. H. Newman and Ignatius Loyola's Jesuit Order, the Counter-Reformation, the comeback of Roman Catholicism, was complete. The Protestant Reformation has now effectively been abandoned by the visible Church in Britain and is widely represented as a tragic mistake" (Michael Semlyen, *All Roads Lead to Rome*, p. 15).

The last three of the six chapters in the ECT book are the most interesting. Jesuit Avery Dulles states in a rather hard-line position, "It is hard to see how Catholics could consider themselves to be fully reconciled with churches that did not acknowledge the papacy as the bearer of a divinely instituted 'Petrine ministry' within the universal Church. . . . Some of these obstacles, but not all could be removed if

the parties were to agree that the condemnations of the sixteenth century no longer apply to the churches as they exist today." And then referring to the documents of Vatican II he continues, "The recent
council taught that all the essential features of the Church of Christ
'subsist' in the Catholic Church and that full communion requires acceptance of the 'whole structure' of the church, including 'all the
means of grace that have been established within it'" (ECT-book, pp.
122, 123).

Dulles then develops an interesting and subtle line of reasoning.
He states in essence that there are almost insurmountable hurdles to
full communion unless we go back to the early New Testament church
and follow a biblical model. "As already seen, evangelicals and
Catholics have a common ground insofar as both groups accept the reality of a spiritual unity based on faith, hope, and charity. They also
recognize the canonical Scriptures as a peremptory norm, one that may
under no circumstances be contradicted. Holy Scripture therefore provides a common resource for giving specific content to the prayer of
Christ for unity. It helps us to know what kind of unity prevailed
among the early Christians and to identify the signs by which that unity
was expressed and the means by which it was maintained.

"As any reader of the New Testament can easily verify,
Christianity in the lifetime of the apostles was in some sort a universal
religion, embracing in a single fellowship adherents of every race, nation, and linguistic group . . . Among the visible bonds uniting
Christians to one another, common practices of worship should not be
overlooked . . . [Notice now how he brings Sunday into the ecumenical mix.] In the New Testament we begin to find hints that Christians
regularly assembled for the Eucharist on the first day of the week (Acts
20:7, 8, observing it as the Lord's day (Rev. 1:10)" (ECT-book, pp.
125, 129).

Dulles, remember, was one of the four Jesuits who signed the ECT
document. He states in no uncertain terms what will be necessary for full
communion. For this reason there will probably not be full organic
union, but rather, as the pope states, "a unity in diversity."

Here is the bottom line from Dulles' perspective: "In Catholic
teaching the papacy is understood preeminently as a unitive agency. In
the words of the First Vatican Council, repeated almost verbatim by

the Second Vatican Council: 'In order that the episcopate itself might be one and undivided, and that the whole multitude of believers might be preserved in unity of faith and communion by means of a closely united priesthood, [Christ] placed blessed Peter at the head of the other apostles, and established in him a perpetual principle and visible foundation of this twofold unity.'

"According to the Catholic understanding, then, the visible unity of the church, as intended by Christ, includes three constitutive elements: the sacramental, the doctrinal, and the governmental. The members of the Church are in communion with one another to the extent that they enjoy the same sacramental life, profess the same faith, and acknowledge the same authoritative leadership" (ECT-book, p. 134).

Packer Tells, "Why I Signed."

One of the Protestant Evangelical signers of the ECT document is Dr. J. I. Packer, of Regent College in British Columbia. His chapter in the ECT-book attempts to explain why he signed the document. He says he has received a stream of letters suggesting that as a Protestant he should withdraw his name from the document. He states that he could not accept an invitation to have communion [participate in the mass or Eucharist] with Catholics and that he could never become a Catholic, but that there are many wonderful committed Christians within the Catholic communion (a position which Adventists have always held), that we have some teachings in common with Catholics, and that we share many common civil and/or moral goals.

Packer is a member of Christians United for Reformation (CURE). In August 1994 (the ECT document was signed in March of that year) CURE issued a statement over the signatures of 35 Evangelical leaders. It listed seven major areas of concern, doctrinally, for Evangelicals as regards Roman Catholic theology. The following gives a brief overview of their concerns.

"The council of Trent [called by the Roman Catholic Church in the sixteenth century to counteract the Reformation] anathematized those who embrace this doctrine [salvation by faith alone], and all subsequent magisterial declarations, including those of the Second Vatican Council, continue to bind Roman Catholics to the conviction that this Gospel of free justification by faith alone, apart from works, and the assurance of salvation that springs from it, is not consonant with Roman Catholic teaching . . . we radically disagree with the teaching of the Second Vatican Council that unbelievers may be saved by their good works, apart from faith in Christ.

"We further affirm that the unity we seek is shaped, bounded, and controlled by the teaching of canonical Scriptures, the written Word of God, comprising the Law and the Gospel in its message of reconciliation with God and new life in Christ. To this Word the Church must submit and by it must correct its understandings, so that its unity will be **unity in truth.** The Roman Catholic Church claims to be graced with an infallibility that attaches to conciliar declarations and Papal pronouncements ex cathedra, such that these are in principle irreformable, and must be treated as decisive guides to the theological interpretation of the Bible. **We deny that the defined doctrines of the Church's infallibility, Papal primacy, justification according to Trent, transubstantiation and eucharistic sacrifice, and the immaculate conception and assumption of Mary, can be proved from Scripture, and we cannot accept any form of joint action that appears to imply agreement with them."**

Then after pointing out that there are no doubt many individual Roman Catholics who do not assent to the errors stated above and have indeed experienced a new birth experience, they (CURE) go on to say, "We deny, however, that in its present confession it is an acceptable Christian communion, let alone being the mother of all the faithful to whom every believer needs to be related" (ECT-book, pp. 158, 159).

It should be noted here that many Protestants and even Evangelical Protestants were very upset that the ECT document had been signed as a joint statement of understanding between Evangelicals and Catholics. Many of them were not even happy with the CURE statement referred to above. Accordingly, Dr. D. James Kennedy hosted a meeting at his church in Fort Lauderdale, Florida. Joining Kennedy were Chuck Colson, J. I. Packer, Bill Bright, John Ankerberg, Michael Horton, John McArthur, R. C. Sproul, Joe Stowell, and John Woodbridge. Their meeting produced a five-point statement. Two items, however, were strongly emphasized. We affirm "the historic Protestant understanding of salvation by faith alone *(sola fide)*" and to counteract the antisheep-stealing part of ECT they stated, "We hold that evangelism and church planting are always legitimate, whatever forms of church life are present already" (ECT-book, p. 161).

After listing these problems with Roman Catholic theology, Packer makes a very definitive statement: "At this point I must state explicitly that I am not and could not become a Roman Catholic because of certain basic tenants to which the Roman system, as such, is committed." He then lists some of the most prominent erroneous teachings. "Bowing to Peter among the apostles as having definitive personal and pastoral authority over all the congregations, in the way that Roman Catholicism today makes acceptance of the papacy a defining mark of Catholic identity, is not however part of the New Testament. Nor does the fact that John Paul II is a wonderful man who has done a wonderful job as a world Christian ambassador make the papacy a credible institution or the Catholic claim to conciliar and *ex cathedra* infallibility at all plausible." Packer goes on to condemn "all modes of the Marian cult, the invoking of other saints, and the belief in purgatory, and all reliance on the disbursing of indulgences," which, he says, "still goes on, as in Luther's day, and is explained and justified in the new 1994 unabridged, updated, version of *The Catechism of the Catholic Church.*"

In concluding his second list of major theological problems in the Roman Catholic Church, Packer states, "I am not able to affirm of the Roman Catholic Church that 'in its present confession it is an acceptance Christian communion.' What I mean by that is that Rome's official doctrinal disorders, particularly on justification, merit, and the Mass-sacrifice, so obscure the gospel that were I, as a gesture of unity, invited to mass—which of course as a Protestant I am not, nor shall be—I would not feel free to accept the invitation. Why then should I, or any Protestant like me, want to develop mission activity in partnership with Roman Catholics?"

His answer is simple. "Despite the shortcomings of Rome's official teaching, there are many Roman Catholic Christians: believers in the Trinity, the Incarnation, the Atonement, and the historic Resurrection, present heavenly reign, and future personal return of Jesus Christ; disciples, worshipers, and lovers of Jesus; humble, self-despairing, joyful, Holy Spirit-oriented people with a story to tell of how God made himself known to them" (ECT-book, pp. 162, 163).

It is hard to understand Packer's reasoning here. In essence he says that the teachings of the church are erroneous, the system is unbiblical, and he could not if invited partake of Communion with them, but because there are sincere Christians among them—a fact that we all agree upon—he wants to cooperate with the system. The Adventist position is to call the sincere individuals out of the erroneous system.

The Richard John Neuhaus Perspective

As you may recall, Richard John Neuhaus, along with Chuck Colson, was a prime mover in the development of the ECT document. Neuhaus, a former Lutheran minister, has become a Roman Catholic priest. He believes that the document is the beginning of greater cooperation to come. He states, "The Greek *kairos* suggests an opportune and decisive moment, a 'fulness of time' when something can happen, when something must happen, that could not happen until then. . . . In his many comments on the coming of the third millennium [since the time of Christ], Pope John Paul II, while rejecting all forms of millennialistic enthusiasm, calls Christians to a heightened sense of expectation, to be on full alert to a new thing that God may be doing . . . a 'springtime of evangelism' and a 'springtime of Christian unity.' "

"There is a tremor of an intimation that something like a *kairos* may be at hand."

"One of America's most prominent evangelical scholars told me that, upon receiving the declaration [the ECT document], he stayed up all night reading and rereading it, and fell on his knees to thank God that something so long prayed for was at last happening."

"It is not too much to say that, as we enter the third millennium, the world-historical stage has been largely cleared to make room for the presentation of the Christian understanding of the human drama, the Divine-human drama that is the story of salvation. And it is not too much to believe that it is for this moment that God is bringing evangelicals and Catholics together to present to the world its promised future in Jesus Christ."

Ignoring what Packer and other Evangelicals have said about the erroneous Catholic teaching regarding salvation by faith alone and that true unity is based on truth, Neuhaus states, "The most important affirmation of ECT is this: 'And all who accept Christ as Lord and

Savior are brothers and sisters in Christ. Evangelicals and Catholics are brothers and sisters in Christ.'"

Then in a strange line of reasoning he asserts, "There are different ways of being Christian. . . . From a number of evangelical friends, I have received the objection that there is only one right way of being a Christian and that is the way revealed in the Bible. True enough, and it is precisely with Saint Paul that ECT wants to underscore the varieties of gifts, service and obedience that are all the gifts of the one Spirit. (I Cor. 12)." While we can understand the variety of gifts and service, it is difficult for a true Bible Christian to comprehend a variety of obedience.

In his attempt to explain what ECT means, Neuhaus states: "In thinking about the relationship between different Christian communities, one might have in mind a spectrum of five stages: from **hostility** to **coexistence** to **cooperation** to **sharing** to **full communion.** How does 'Evangelicals and Catholics Together' fit into that spectrum? Clearly, the declaration calls for an overcoming of **hostility** and moves beyond **coexistence** when it endorses **cooperation** in those things that Christians can and must do together in the world. With great care, it also invites us to **share** in some of those sacred activities that spring from the heart of being Christians together—evangelization, prayer, Scriptural study, and correction and edification in the gospel" (ECT-book, pp. 175-186). Apparently, from his perspective the only step left is **full communion.**

The Papal Encyclical *Ut Unum Sint*

Earlier in this chapter I spoke of two significant documents that had been released—one in the United States, the other from the Vatican. We have looked at the one from the United States, *Evangelicals and Catholics Together*, at some length. The one from the Vatican is the Papal Encyclical Letter issued over the signature of John Paul II on May 25, 1995—about 13 months after the ECT document. The Latin title of the encyclical, *Ut Unum Sint,* translates to *That They May Be One.* It is given as John Paul II's commitment to ecumenism in what is called a letter, but it is actually a 115-page book.

The secular press picked up the story shortly after the encyclical was issued. The Washington *Post* reported, "The encyclical, a pastoral letter addressed to the whole of Christendom, appears designed to reenergize three decades of discussions on Christian harmony that some theologians say have been overtaken by an 'ecumenical winter.'

"In particular, the pontiff apparently hopes to make <u>dramatic progress toward reconciliation</u> with both Eastern Orthodox and Protestant churches in time for the Christian millennial celebration of 2000, long-time Vatican observers say" (Washington *Post,* May 31, 1995).

U.S. News noted, "In a new encyclical 'That They May Be One,' he [Pope John Paul II] acknowledged that the papacy 'constitutes a difficulty for most other Christians,' and <u>he apologized for past sins and errors committed in the name of Roman Catholicism.</u> But he stopped short of renouncing his own supreme authority as the successor to St. Peter. Instead, he said he would seek to 'find a way of exercising the primacy' of his office that is 'open to a new situation.' He did not elaborate, but some Vatican observers suggested the 'new situation' could entail shifting some papal authority to local bishop's conferences.

"Besides the papacy, issues that he said must be resolved if Christians are to reunite include the relationship of scripture and tradition, the Eucharist, the ordination of priests, the church's authority and the role of Mary, mother of Jesus. <u>Reaction from Protestant and Orthodox leaders was generally positive</u>" *(U.S. News and World Report*, June 12, 1995).

Just three days before the official issuance of the encyclical, *USA Today* reported, "Pope John Paul II on Sunday asked the world's forgiveness for the historical sins and errors of the Catholic Church. 'Today I, the pope of the church of Rome, in the name of all Catholics, ask forgiveness for the wrongs inflicted on non-Catholics during the turbulent history of these peoples.'

"In a bid to forge Christian unity, the 75-year-old pope also pledged to forgive those who caused Catholics to suffer.

"'He is pushing hard on the accelerator toward unity,' said Vatican spokesman Joaquin Navarro-Valls. 'The main obstacle is not doctrine but history with all its prejudices'" *(USA Today*, May 22, 1995).

Before examining the encyclical itself and the Catholic reaction to it, let's review two statements made by Ellen White and compare them to the statement above. "Marvelous in her shrewdness and cunning is the Roman Catholic Church. She presents a fair front to the world, covering with apologies her record of horrible cruelties, and declaring that her spirit of persecution no longer exists [i.e., a kinder, gentler papacy]. But she is the same as in the days of the Reformation, when men of God stood up at the peril of their lives to expose her iniquity; the same when she assumed the power to control kings and princes, and claimed the prerogatives of God. She may clothe herself with Christlike garments, the better to carry forward her purposes; but she still retains the venom of the serpent, and her principles are exerting their influence in legislative halls, in churches, and in the hearts of men. Her spirit is no less cruel and despotic now than when it crushed out human liberty, and slew the saints of the Most High" *(The Signs of the Times*, Nov. 8, 1899). It is so uncanny that events that are happening today have been predicted in exact detail many years ago.

"The Roman church now presents a fair front to the world, covering with apologies her record of horrible cruelties. She has clothed herself with Christlike garments; but she is unchanged. Every principle of the papacy that existed in past ages exists today. The doctrines devised in the darkest ages are still held. Let none deceive themselves. The papacy that Protestants are now so ready to honor is the same that ruled the world in the days of the Reformation" *(The Great Controversy*, p. 571).

We must keep reminding ourselves that the erroneous doctrine of indulgences, the sale of which financed the building of St. Peters in Rome and that caused Luther to nail the 95 theses to the church door in Wittenberg, is still promoted today in the latest Catechism! And the false gospel that was promoted at the Council of Trent is still current Catholic teaching.

Richard John Neuhaus admits, "Trent's *Decree on Justification* does declare: 'If anyone shall say that by faith alone the sinner is justified, so as to understand that nothing else is required to cooperate in the attainment of the grace of justification, and that it is in no way necessary that he be prepared and disposed by the action of his own will: let him be anathema.'" Then he asks, "Why does the Catholic Church not recant what was said by Trent? . . . Because it is Catholic teaching that a council teaches authoritatively, and the Church is not authorized to repudiate retrospectively a conciliar decree" (ECT-book, pp. 208, 209).

Let us look at some brief statements from the encyclical itself. It begins, "Ut Unum Sint! The call for Christian unity made by the Second

Vatican Ecumenical Council with such impassioned commitment is finding an ever greater echo in the hearts of believers, <u>especially as the Year 2000 approaches,</u> a year which Christians will celebrate as a sacred Jubilee, the commemoration of the Incarnation of the Son of God, who became man in order to save humanity.

"I myself [the pope] intend *to promote every suitable initiative* aimed at making the witness of the entire Catholic community understood in its full purity and consistency, especially considering the engagement which awaits the Church at the threshold of the new Millennium. That will be an exceptional occasion, in view of which <u>she asks the Lord to increase the unity of all Christians until they reach **full communion**</u>. . . . In our ecumenical age, marked by the Second Vatican Council, the mission of the Bishop of Rome is particularly directed to recalling the need for full communion among Christ's disciples."

Quoting extensively from the documents of Vatican II, the pope says, "The Lord of the Ages wisely and patiently follows out the plan of his grace on behalf of us sinners. In recent times he has begun to bestow more generously upon divided Christians remorse over their divisions and a longing for unity. Everywhere, large numbers have felt the impulse of this grace, and among our separated brethren also *there increases from day to day a movement*, fostered by the grace of the Holy Spirit, *for the restoration of unity among all Christians* . . . almost everyone, though in different ways, *longs that there may be one visible Church of God,* a Church truly universal and sent forth to the whole world that the world may be converted to the Gospel and so be saved, to the glory of God." (Italics in original.)

"Ecumenism is directed precisely to making the partial communion existing between Christians grow towards full communion in truth and charity."

"It is true that we are not yet in full communion. And yet, despite our divisions, we are on the way towards full unity, that unity which marked the Apostolic Church at its birth and which we sincerely seek."

"As the Church turns her gaze to the new millennium, she asks the Spirit for the grace to strengthen her own unity and to make it grow towards full communion with other Christians . . . At the dawn of the new millennium, how can we not implore from the Lord, with renewed enthusiasm and a deeper awareness, the grace to prepare ourselves, together, to offer this *sacrifice of unity?*" (John Paul II, *That They May Be One*).

A *Wall Street Journal* article by Richard John Neuhaus entitled "The Religious Century Nears" gives some very interesting insights from a Catholic perspective. He asks, "What is it that, however tenuously, holds the world together at the end of the second Christian millennium? The alliances formed by the Cold War have fallen into disarray, and very few today view the United Nations as the precursor of some kind of world government. There are of course global markets and technologies, but, while very important, they cannot provide the moral adhesion necessary for human solidarity. Beyond markets, technology and politics is what, for lack of a better term, is called the spiritual. As Andre Malraux observed before his death in 1976, 'The next century will be religious or it will not be at all.'

"Enter the papal encyclical 'Ut Unum Sint' ('That They May Be One') issued on May 30.

"There are 1.8 billion Christians in the world, about one third of mankind. A little over one billion are Roman Catholic, more than 300 million are Eastern Orthodox, about 100 million belong to the 'classic' Reformation churches (Lutheran, Anglican, Presbyterian, etc.), and the rest <u>are part of the maddeningly diverse and rapidly growing world of evangelical Protestantism.</u> The other growing and culturally assertive religion on the world stage is Islam, with almost a billion adherents. Because it has been largely excluded from the centuries of modernity, much of Islam is in a reactive posture marked by resentment and suspicion."

Neuhaus then outlines the papal strategy for unity. "The Catholic Church under John Paul II has been working hard to develop a non-confrontational relationship with Islam as we together cross the threshold of the third millennium. <u>But the first order of business is Christian unity, or ecumenism.</u>

"As the second millennium has been one of Christian division, so John Paul says that the third millennium must be one of Christian unity. The division between the Christian West and the Orthodox Church of the East dates from 1054, while the division in the West issued from the

16th century Reformation. <u>During the pontificates of John Paul and his predecessor, Paul VI, dramatic steps have been taken toward healing the breach.</u> Just last month the pope met with Bartholomew of Constantinople, the ecumenical patriarch. The Catholic Church and the Orthodox Church are in essential agreement on doctrine, ministerial order and the sacraments.

"'Ut Unum Sint' makes clear that <u>the Catholic Church is irrevocably committed to the restoration of 'full communion' between East and West.</u> Historically the orthodox have objected to the jurisdictional claims of the papacy. This pope is saying that unity is more important than jurisdiction, and no pope has said that in a thousand years. If in the years ahead full communion is restored between Catholics and Orthodox, <u>it will be one of the largest and most momentous religious configurations in world history.</u>

"Turning to the Protestant communions in the West, 'Ut Unum Sint' acknowledges that there are substantial disagreements on doctrine, sacraments and ministerial order. John Paul further recognizes that the papacy itself has in the past been a cause of division. <u>In Catholic teaching, the pope, as bishop of Rome, is the successor of Peter, and this continuing 'Petrine ministry' belongs to all Christians, **whether they recognize it or not**</u>" (Richard John Neuhaus, *The Wall Street Journal*, July 6, 1995).

The June-July 1995 issue of the Catholic magazine *Inside the Vatican* devoted the cover and a five-page article to comments about the pope and his ecumenical goals. "One of the central messages of John Paul II's pontificate has been—and remains—the urgent need to reunify Christians for the coming Millennium. His latest encyclical Ut Unum Sint reiterates that message with force.

"The Pope hopes that all Christian Churches will celebrate the year 2000 together—perhaps praying together at the great holy sites of Rome, Jerusalem, and Mt. Sinai. The Pope's latest encyclical, the first devoted entirely to ecumenism, is one of his most impassioned and personal documents, the result of three years of intense work. His plea is that all those who believe in Christ should arrive at the year 2000, if not entirely united, at least much closer to overcoming the divisions of the Second Millennium.

"<u>Pope John Paul II's latest encyclical is</u> surely one of the broadest, most emphatic pleas for Christian unity ever issued by a Pope, perhaps even *the most* insistent and considered call for the reunion of divided Christians ever made by any Christian Church leader."

Have you taken note of the flavor of these comments—by the year 2000, irrevocable commitment to full communion, the first order of business, the Petrine ministry belongs to all Christians, etc.? Let there be no misunderstanding here, Roman Catholicism is "pushing hard on the accelerator for Christian unity." There is, however, this "maddeningly diverse and rapidly growing group of evangelicals," some of whom want to uphold the gospel purity of salvation by faith alone in Jesus Christ and to find their beliefs in the Word of God alone. What is to be done with them? The Roman Catholic weekly, *Our Sunday Visitor*, gives an insight in an article entitled "Why Ecumenism Is So Crucial for the Pope." Note the overall goal of full Christian unity and an intermediate goal of unity in diversity.

"The Week of Prayer for Christian Unity has been observed every January since 1908 with varying degrees of interest by the denominations that call themselves Christian.

"This year's observance (Jan. 18-25), however, is particularly significant because of a renewed thrust toward Christian unity signaled by the 1995 papal encyclical, Ut Unum Sint. In addition to putting the weight of an encyclical behind this movement, Pope John Paul II also has expressed an urgency to make greater progress toward Christian unity by the year 2000.

" 'The encyclical comes at an important time for a number of reasons,' explained Paulist Father Ronald Roberson, an expert on Eastern churches who formerly served on the staff of the Pontifical Council for Promoting Christian Unity.

" 'The Pope sees the year 2000 as a very important milestone in the history of the Church—as well as of humanity—and he wants, as much as possible, for that event to be able to symbolize the end of this millennium, which was marked by so many divisions,' Father Roberson said. Pope John Paul wants to enter the third millennium 'with very strong movement toward unity,' he added, a unity that would allow for diversity.

" 'The pope doesn't want everyone to become Latin Catholics,' he explained. 'To achieve unity, for example, does not mean that everyone has to celebrate the Eucharist the same way. With Eastern churches, especially, you're talking about a great diversity liturgically, and that's just fine.'

"The Pope does use the term 'hierarchy of doctrine,' Father Roberson said. 'Obviously, some teachings are more important than others, and there has to be agreement on those essential points, while leaving considerable latitude on other points that are less essential to the faith'" *(Our Sunday Visitor,* January 14, 1996).

The pope here concedes that though he would like to see full communion by the year 2000 we can still have "unity in diversity." We can work together with what we have in common—the essential points. This is the same conclusion drawn by the drafters of the ECT document—and expressed in the ECT book—no organic unity right now but we can work together on points we share in common. Another reference from *The Great Controversy* comes to mind, "When the leading churches of the United States, uniting upon such points of doctrine as are held by them in common, shall influence the state to enforce their decrees and to sustain their institutions, then Protestant America will have formed an image to the Roman hierarchy, and the infliction of civil penalties upon dissenters will inevitably result" (p. 445). That process is happening now!

Together Again

A recent editorial in the Catholic magazine *Crisis,* under the title *Together Again,* said, "Many people are surprised that Catholics and evangelicals are starting to get along so well—the media is surprised and disappointed, liberals are surprised and scared. I'm not surprised, I was a Baptist who became a Catholic at the age of 33.

"Some evangelicals have greeted this propitious moment in our cultural history by trying to reopen the wounds of the Reformation. It is a mistake to spend time fighting over who are the real Christians when we should rather confront this culture of death together, exactly as the signers of the *Evangelicals and Catholics Together* declaration of March 1994 urged.

"It is a pity that some powerful evangelical leaders are shunning cooperation with Catholics. Evidently they don't think it is a priority to take the culture back from the secularizers. They want to fight over church doctrine at a time when we have an unprecedented opportunity to win the political battles necessary, once again, to have influence in our social institutions.

"We can revisit the controversies of the Reformation in the classroom, around the dinner table, and over the phone, but in the public arena we should thank God that Catholics and evangelicals have found one another. If some people find that scary, it's because they realize that the tide is turning" (Deal Hudson, *Crisis*, November 1995). And indeed the tide is turning, as we shall see.

CHAPTER 6

The Man of the Year
Comes to America

People who see him—and countless millions have—do not forget him. His appearances generate an electricity unmatched by anyone else on earth. That explains, for instance, why in rural Kenyan villages thousands of children, plus many cats and roosters and even hotels, are named John Paul. Charisma is the only conceivable reason why a CD featuring him saying the rosary—in Latin—against a background of Bach and Handel is currently ascending the charts in Europe. It also accounts for the dazed reaction of a young woman who found herself, along with the thousands around her in a sports stadium in Denver [1993 visit], cheering and applauding him: 'I don't react that way to rock groups, What is it that he has?'

"Pope John Paul II has, among many other things, the world's bully-est pulpit. Few of his predecessors over the past 2000 years have spoken from it as often and as forcefully as he. When he talks, **it is not only to his flock of nearly a billion; he expects the world to listen.** And the flock and the world listen, not always liking what they hear. This year he cast the net of his message wider than ever. *Crossing the Threshold of Hope*, his meditations on topics ranging from the existence of God to the mistreatment of women, became an immediate best-seller in 12 countries. **It is an unprecedented case of mass proselytizing** by a Pontiff—arcane but personal, expansive but resolute about its moral message."

So begins the major article "Empire of the Spirit" in *Time* magazine, December 26, 1994/January 1995. Naming Pope John Paul II "Man of the Year" the issue featured him on the cover and through a total of 27 pages of pictures and text! The pope had been scheduled to visit the United States in 1994, but hip surgery kept him confined to the Vatican during that period and so of course the trip was canceled and rescheduled for 1995.

In preparing the "Man of the Year" issue five *Time* editors and correspondents traveled to Rome and had a private audience with the pope. In addition, in preparing the text for the articles *Time* also talked to dozens of religious leaders of all faiths, including the Dalai Lama and Billy Graham, asking them to assess the importance of John Paul. Billy Graham is quoted as saying, "He'll go down in history as the greatest of our modern Popes. He's been the strong conscience of the whole Christian world."

In listing some of the pope's accomplishments *Time* stated, "The *Catechism of the Catholic Church* appeared in English translation, the first such comprehensive document issued since the 16th century. It clearly summarizes all the essential beliefs and moral tenets of the church. Some Catholics believe it will be the most enduring landmark of John Paul's papacy. [This new Catechism sold over 10,000,000 worldwide in the first six months after printing.] In June [1994], John Paul oversaw the establishment of diplomatic relations between the Holy See [the central government of the Roman Catholic Church] and Israel, ending a tense standoff that had existed ever since 1948."

Though the pope is fluent in eight languages he rarely watches television or reads a newspaper. Instead he gets regular news briefings from his prime minister, Cardinal Sodano, and confers with cardinals and bishops around the world. According to *Time*, every Friday evening the pontiff meets with Joseph Cardinal Ratzinger, his friend for over 30 years. Ratzinger is the "perfect for the Congregation for the Doctrine of the Faith." This position was for many years called the "Office of the Inquisition." We'll look at this newly reopened office a little further on.

It seems that no one visits with the pope these days without learning of his plans for the year 2000. *Time* reports, "John Paul's ambitions for the millennial year are vast. He dreams of having a summit of all monotheistic religions at Mount Sinai and of concelebrating a Mass with Patriarch Aleksey II of Moscow to mark the reconciliation of Roman Catholicism with Russian Orthodoxy. Last month the Pope issued an apostolic Letter on preparing for the year 2000." We've looked at that apostolic letter in chapter 1.

Newspapers all across the country ran stories about the pope and his charismatic appeal. For example, the St. Louis *Post-Dispatch* featured a report by Archbishop Justin Rigali on his trip to Manila to be with the pope on "World Youth Day." Rigali stated, "About 5 million young people attended the four-day event's final papal Mass in a park. It was extraordinary, with just millions and millions of young people, as far as the eye could see . . . really farther," he said. "So much youthful energy in the name of God."

The paper pointed out, "Rigali is no newcomer to papal crowds. While posted in Rome for 20 years, he traveled with the pope. He helped the Vatican on a papal visit to Dublin where 1.3 million attended an outdoor mass, and at the crush at Chicago's Grant Park with over 1 million."

"'Those [events] were nothing like this—as far as eyes could see young people, it was spectacular,' he said, recalling how at the end of the pope's homily they chanted over and over his last words: 'Jesus Christ'" (St. Louis *Post-Dispatch,* January 28, 1995).

Coming to America

The October 4-8, 1995, visit by Pope John Paul II to the United States was an historic occasion. The media coverage, the government expense, the speeches, all played a part in what *USA Today* called "the Hottest ticket around." The pope made 11 public speeches, all of which are recorded verbatim in a book entitled *Make Room for the Mystery of God.*

Largest Security Operation in History

"Pope John Paul II's October 4-8 visit to the United States was one of the biggest security operations in history," reported the Catholic News Service on October 9, 1995. "New York police were out in massive force to give what Commissioner William J. Bratton called the 'presidential package.' But while U.S. presidents usually visit New York for a day or two, police maintained the security for five days.

"Gary Byrnes, New York spokesman for the U.S. Secret Service, said his organization mounted its largest security operation in history, to protect the pope.

"The pope confounded security officials Oct. 7 when, after reciting the rosary in St. Patrick's Cathedral, he walked down Fifth Avenue.

"'The pope's escaped on foot down Fifth Ave.!' said one. The pope walked to the corner of E. 50th St. and over to <u>Cardinal John J. O'Connor's residence on Madison Ave,</u> surrounded by a couple dozen Vatican officials and <u>hundreds of security officials.</u>

"Security in Manhattan, near the residence of Archbishop Renato Martino, the Vatican's representative to the United Nations, jammed traffic for days in what one cab driver described as 'popelock,' a papal version of gridlock.

"At many events, people without tickets were kept out of cordoned-off areas.

"Participants in the pope's Mass at Central Park Oct. 7 spent hours waiting in line to pass through metal detectors. Outside Newark, N.J. before the pope arrived on Oct. 4, police closed the New Jersey Turnpike in both directions for the pope and President Bill Clinton's motorcades—just in time for afternoon rush hour.

"Later that evening, at Newark's Sacred Heart Cathedral, cloistered nuns passed through metal detectors, while security officials used scanners to electronically frisk cardinals and archbishops.

On Oct. 8, when the pope flew out of Newark's airport to Baltimore, the Associated Press reported that "security at the Newark airport was so tight that the Secret Service agents inspected under the hoods of all vehicles—including New Jersey State Police cars."

The United Nations Visit

In his greeting to President Bill Clinton, church leaders, and the American people at the Newark International Airport on October 4, 1995, the pope said, "Mr. President, dear friends, dear people of America, it is a great joy for me to return to the United States, as I had hoped to do last year. Thank you all for receiving me so warmly. This is a land of much generosity, <u>and its people have always been quick to extend their hands in friendship and to offer hospitality. Thank you especially, President Clinton, for coming here today in that same spirit. For my part, I greet you and all representatives of the federal, state, and local governments.</u>

"I come as a pilgrim of peace and understanding among peoples.

Tomorrow, in observance of the United Nations' 50th anniversary, I shall return there to express my deep conviction that the ideals and intentions which gave origin to that worldwide organization half a century ago are more indispensable than ever in a world searching for purpose.

"The world, in fact, is undergoing a profound transformation. . . . Especially since the events of 1989 [the fall of Communism], the role of the United States in the world has taken on a new prominence. Your widespread influence is at once political, economic, military and, due to your communications, cultural" *(Make Room for the Mystery of God*, pp. 7-9).

The Catholic News Service reported, "Pope John Paul II's appearance at the United Nations on October 5 has produced a constant stream of favorable comment from U.N. diplomats since then, Archbishop Renato R. Martino reported.

"The Vatican nuncio to the United Nations said in an interview at his mission Oct. 11 that the diplomats appreciated the support that the pope's visit represented. And the U.S. ambassador to the United Nations, Madeleine Albright, called it a 'real boost.'

"'The pope gave a confidence vote to the United Nations, although recognizing its shortcomings,' Archbishop Martino said. He added that, 'U. N. Delegates did not see the papal appearance merely as a ceremonial event but recognized and responded to the substantive nature of his address.' Martino went on to say, 'a meeting of the pope with U. N. Secretary-General Boutros Boutros-Ghali was also more than ceremonial and involved substantive discussion.' He said he could not comment on their talks, but he said they covered the 'hottest' issues" (Catholic News Service, Oct. 12, 1995).

When the pope actually addressed the United Nations General Assembly he expressed the significance of the event by stating, "It is an honor for me to have the opportunity to address this international assembly and to join the men and women of every country, race, language and culture in celebrating the 50th anniversary of the founding of the United Nations Organization. In coming before this distinguished assembly, I am vividly aware that through you I am in some way addressing the whole family of peoples living on the face of the earth. My words are meant as a sign of the interest and esteem of the Apostolic See and of the Catholic Church for this institution" *(Make Room for the Mystery of God*, p. 18).

Pat Robertson Meets the Pope

Several news organizations reported that the pope declined requests by Robert Dole and Newt Gingrich for audiences with him. However, a number of sources, including the Catholic News Service, reported that Pat Robertson, leader of the Christian Coalition, was on the altar platform with the pope during the celebration of the Mass in Central Park in New York City. Robertson was described on the invitation list as head of the Christian Broadcasting Network. A Vatican spokesman said Robertson "up until now" has been known as a preacher. "He has not been in Congress. . . . He is being treated as a religious leader, not a politician." Following the Mass, Robertson was invited to a meeting with the pope at the residence of Cardinal O'Connor.

Christianity Today reported on this meeting under the title "Top Evangelicals Confer With Pope." "Pope John Paul II greeted several prominent American evangelicals during his five-day East Coast trip in October. Broadcaster Pat Robertson, Prison Fellowship founder Chuck Colson, and Don Argue, head of the National Association of Evangelicals, were among the 25 Christian leaders who met with the pontiff October 7 at the residence of Cardinal John O'Connor of New York.

"Robertson found the meeting 'very warm' and called the 75-year-old leader of the Roman Catholic Church 'a humble and caring servant of the Lord.' He [Robertson] also pledged, through a hand-delivered, three-page letter to the pontiff, to work for Christian unity between Catholics and evangelicals."

The article goes on to relate, "Joan Brown Campbell, general secretary of the National Council of Churches and the only woman at the meeting with the pope, also praised the Polish pontiff's call for Christian unity by the year 2000" *(Christianity Today*, Nov. 13, 1995).

The Christian Coalition mentioned this meeting in an article in their publication titled "The Crucial Catholic Vote," saying, "During his recent trip to the U.S., one of Pope John Paul's primary messages was that Catholics and Protestants should work together for the common good, despite theological differences. A symbol of that unity took place at the New York residence of Cardinal John O'Connor, when the pope met with leaders from several Protestant religions. Included in the group was Pat Robertson, president and founder of the Christian Broadcasting Network and the Christian Coalition. Each participant spent a few minutes with the pope" *(Christian American,* Nov./Dec. 1995).

The most striking of all the news accounts of this meeting was the news release from the Public Relations Division of the Christian Broadcasting Network on October 7, 1995. The release was headed, **"Pat Robertson Meets With Pope, Pledges Christian Unity and World Evangelization."** The text of the release, in part, read,

> "(New York, N.Y.)—Religious broadcaster Pat Robertson said tonight his meeting with His Holiness Pope John Paul II was 'very warm' and, through a personal letter hand-delivered to the Pontiff, pledged to work for Christian unity between Evangelicals and Catholics.

> " 'I think this meeting was historic,' said Mr. Robertson who joined with other Christian religious leaders in greeting the Pope at the New York residence of His Eminence John Cardinal O'Connor. 'I am hopeful this meeting will result in a new openness and harmony between Evangelicals and Catholics in this country and around the world.'

> "Mr. Robertson, who is the founder and chairman of the Christian Broadcasting Network, called the Pope 'a humble and caring servant of the Lord.' At the conclusion of his brief time with the Pope, Mr. Robertson presented a three-page letter to the Pontiff underscoring Mr. Robertson's commitment to work for Christian unity and world evangelization.

> "Mr. Robertson also wrote that he was 'encouraged' by the Pope's recent encyclical on Christian unity, *That All May Be One,* and praised the Pontiff for his recent call to Catholics to 'be more committed to prayer for Christian unity' in the Pope's 1994 Apostolic letter, *As the Third Millennium Draws Near.* In Mr. Robertson's words: 'I call on Evangelical Christians to lift up their voices in prayer for unity and world evangelization as well.'

"This meeting with the Pope came just hours after Mr. Robertson participated in an Ecumenical Procession at the Papal Liturgy in New York's Central Park on Saturday morning."

Papal Visit Impressions

The pope was scheduled to conduct a two-hour Mass in Giants' Stadium, in East Rutherford, New Jersey, on October 5, 1995. Because of the heightened security and the virtual gridlock on the highways after the pope arrived, those who were able to get tickets to attend the stadium Mass had to arrive several hours before the program started. The infield was fitted with additional chairs and a record 83,000 people jammed into the stadium. The weather didn't cooperate with the event as it rained, sometimes quite heavily, for most of the waiting period. The Catholic News Service reported that "Thousands of people showed their colors and their loyalties as they waited hours in the rain. . . . Lucky ones in the lower levels were sheltered from the weather by the overhang of the tiers above, but most sat out in the open for hours. The rain problems were worsened by the fact that umbrellas were prohibited in the stadium for security reasons."

When the pope visited Central Park in New York the estimated crowd of nearly 130,000 included thousands of representatives of area youth groups and "West Point cadets in their grey dress uniforms."

Catholics worldwide are being encouraged to pray the rosary to Mary. They believe that she is speaking through apparitions in many places around the world. Note the report by the CNS of the pope's visit to St. Patrick's Cathedral. "Pope John Paul II united Catholics around the world with thousands in St. Patrick's Cathedral to pray the rosary on the annual feast day of the Marian prayer. . . . The pope drew himself and his congregation into a spirit of deep and quiet meditation. The pope, even before he spoke, offered the rosary to busy Catholic families as an occasion for quiet time with each other and with the mother of God."

The pope visited Baltimore because it is "the birthplace of the Catholic Church in the United States." He "urged U.S. Catholics to bring the values of their faith to their social and political involvement."

Associated Press religion writer David Briggs reported that on the occasion of the papal visit "Joyous nuns emerged from convents after decades of isolation." He went on to say, "The most lasting impressions of the Pope's visit were not his words—but his gentle presence: a stoop-shouldered 75-year-old man believed by many in his 60 million-member U.S. flock to be the vicar of Christ on Earth." Briggs concluded his impressions of the papal visit by saying, "The speeches are not what Ramon Danian will remember most about the pope's visit. Damian, a Mexican immigrant, and his wife and two children were among the 20 people sharing a chicken casserole with the pope Sunday at Our Daily Bread soup kitchen. His reaction to the pope? 'God came to me today.'"

As the pope left New Jersey for Baltimore, Associated Press writer Victor L. Simpson reported, "Among those saying farewell to the pope at the airport was police officer Ward Foggin, whose 2-year-old daughter, Caitlin, was blessed by the pontiff. 'We've been waiting for the pope's visit for the last two years,' said Foggin, holding his neurologically impaired daughter. 'I feel so holy. We're on sacred ground right now on Newark Airport.'"

The Vice President Says Goodbye

As part of this very historic event the president of the United States welcomed the pope to the United States and the vice president bid him farewell. The Catholic News Service, Oct. 9, 1995, reported that, "Before departing for Rome from Baltimore-Washington International Airport, the pope met briefly with Vice President Al Gore for talks about Bosnia-Herzegovina, China, Vietnam and other world trouble spots. . . . Gore told pope John Paul that he and President Clinton were 'grateful' for the pope's peace efforts in Bosnia, especially his planned Oct. 17 meeting at the Vatican with all the Catholic bishops of the former Yugoslavia. 'We are optimistic,' the vice president said. 'The peace process will be difficult. There is more work to be done, but we are moving in the right direction.'

"In his farewell address to the pope, Gore thanked him for 'blessing the people of the United States with his Oct. 4-8 visit.'"

In his parting statements, the pope acknowledged the prominence of the United States in the past cold war and then added, "I say this too, to the United States to America: today, in our world as it is, many other nations and peoples look to you as the principal model and pattern for their own advancement in democracy."

And so ended the historic visit of the pope to the United States. Many books, magazines, and newspapers have discussed the five-day tour. But to those who are familiar with the outline of history as portrayed in *The Great Controversy* this visit has serious prophetic and eschatological significance as well. How could Ellen White have known that this would happen when in her day the papacy was still suffering the effects of the deadly wound?

In the weeks following the papal visit the Clinton Administration was urging the use of American forces to assist in the NATO peace plan for Bosnia. There was stiff opposition to the plan from some in Congress. On November 27, 1995, in an attempt to generate support for the troop deployment plan, President Clinton broadcast a live 20-minute televised address from the Oval Office. In concluding his remarks he made this appeal: "A few weeks ago, I was privileged to spend some time with His Holiness John Paul II when he came to America. At the very end of our meeting, the Pope looked at me and said, 'I have lived through most of this century. I remember that it began with a war in Sarajevo. Mr. President, you must not let it end with a war in Sarajevo'" (New York *Times*, Tuesday, November 28, 1995).

This was the first time in my memory that a sitting president has quoted the pope in a public speech. The speech was effective. The troops went to Bosnia.

CHAPTER 7

The Catholic Campaign for America

C atchy title, isn't it? Perhaps you think I made it up? Then think again. I first heard about the Catholic Campaign for America from literature at the Christian Coalition's 1995 Road to Victory Conference and Strategy Briefing the weekend after Labor Day. The brochure stated, "The Board of Directors of the Catholic Campaign for America invites you to join us at the First Annual National Convention to be held in Washington, D.C., November 17, 18, 1995." I accepted the invitation and made plans to attend.

The brochure went on to explain, "[The] Catholic Campaign for America was founded in 1991 with the mission to activate Catholic citizens, increase the Catholic electorate's influence in formulating policy, and focus the public's attention on the richness and beauty of Catholic teaching. The National Convention is one more step on the road to achieving our mission. Our goal is to attract 1,500 Catholics from across America to join together in this unique Catholic experience."

The list of 15 board members include familiar names like William Bennett, former U.S. Secretary of Education and "Drug Czar"; Mary Ellen Bork, writer and lecturer on Catholic life, former religion teacher as a Sacred Heart Nun and now wife of Judge Robert Bork; Hugh Carey, former governor of New York; Thomas Melady, former U.S. ambassador to the Holy See; Thomas Monaghan, owner of Domino's Pizza; and Frank Shakespeare, former U.S. ambassador to the Holy See. Their National Ecclesiastical Advisor is "His Eminence John Cardinal O'Connor," Archbishop of New York. It is obvious that there is power, influence, and money behind this organization.

Because It's Time . . .

These words are the theme words of the Catholic Campaign for America and occur regularly throughout its literature. The words remind me of the statement in *The Great Controversy*, p. 580: "Marvelous in her shrewdness and cunning is the Roman Church. She can read what is to be. <u>She bides her time,</u> seeing that the Protestant churches are paying her homage in their acceptance of the false sabbath and that they are preparing to enforce it by the very means which she herself employed in bygone days. Those who reject the light of truth will yet seek the aid of this self-styled infallible power to exalt an institution that originated with her. How readily she will come to the help of Protestants in this work it is not difficult to conjecture. Who understands better than the papal leaders how to deal with those who are disobedient to the church?"

She bides her time. But now she says, "It's Time!" Another current Catholic cliché is "Seizing the Catholic Moment." Catholic Campaign organizers state: "The Catholic Campaign for America is just that—a Catholic Campaign for America." They say, "We are building the greatest coalition of Catholic leaders in American History and recruiting these leaders from every part of the country and from every walk of life."

The goals of the CCA have been stated in four short sentences in the membership recruiting brochure:

Initiate . . . The recruitment of the greatest coalition of Catholic leaders in American History through an unprecedented mobilization of Catholic leaders at the national, state, and local levels.

Activate . . . Catholic Citizens that have never been activated before and <u>train them to serve in leadership capacities at the local level.</u>

Educate . . . The American public regarding the Catholic perspective through earned media opportunities and <u>a national radio, television, and print campaign</u> and defend the Church when it is under attack.

Create . . .   Opportunities for <u>Catholics to demonstrate to policy mak-
ers the power of an organized Catholic constituency.</u>

Former governor of New York and Catholic Campaign board member, Hugh Carey, has stated: "There is a reason why 58 million
Americans identify themselves as Catholics—because it is a church that
teaches and a church that stands for something. <u>It is time that we demonstrate our Catholic vitality</u> and engage in the public policy debate. **We
have the power and the people to embark on this movement—a
movement that will benefit all Americans."** Apparently, whether we
want it or not we will see changes that "are for our own good."

The promotional brochure concludes by saying, "Catholic
Americans are uniquely positioned to bring their influence to bear on
society. We are the largest denomination in America. We believe it is
time that we give a voice to countless Catholic Americans like you
who yearn for a more moral America."

The First Annual Convention of the Catholic Campaign for
America took place on November 17, 18, 1995, at the Renaissance
Hotel in Washington, D.C. The registration materials came in a large
glossy folder with the stars and stripes of the American flag on the front
and full-color picture of the pope on the back. The meeting began a few
minutes late—not because the executive director, Michael Fergeson,
wasn't ready, but rather because the first Speaker, the honorable Henry
Hyde of the U.S. House of Representatives, was delayed in his arrival
from the House. While waiting, Fergeson mentioned Vatican II and the
resulting "user friendly" Catholic Church. He also paid tribute to the
"Holy Father" [Pope John Paul II] and the "Blessed Virgin Mother."

During his introduction, Henry Hyde was noted as the Catholic
Layman of the Year 1994 by the Christian Coalition. Hyde noted that
"the Catholic Campaign for America is long overdue. We now have
128 Catholics in the House and 21 in the Senate. **If we had the
Catholics behind us we would always carry the day."**

Richard John Neuhaus, for 17 years a Lutheran minister before
converting to Roman Catholicism, was baptized and later ordained to
the priesthood by John Cardinal O'Connor of the New York diocese.
Since becoming a Catholic, Neuhaus has been a champion for
Catholicism and working for ecumenism with Protestants. He and

Protestant Chuck Colson were the primary architects of the historic document *Evangelicals and Catholics Together.*

Neuhaus was a speaker at the Catholic Campaign for America Conference. His remarks were quite pointed. "We [Catholics] belong in America in order to change the way things have been done in America for so long. Catholics have a distinct responsibility because of their size and mission. The bride of Christ is not for hire. We cannot be bound by other coalitions. There would be no pro-life movement were it not for Catholic Americans. The great question is truth—moral truth. Truth is determined by the majority as we are told by John Paul II in his encyclical *Centisemus Annus.* " He concluded his remarks by saying, "Likely, two generations from now this pope will be known as 'John Paul the Great.' This pontificate has set forth the Catholic faith."

The Catholic Campaign Conference took place just about six weeks after the papal visit to the United States. Accordingly, many of the speakers either quoted or praised "The Holy Father" in their speeches. The other hot topic was abortion. William Bennett called abortion the "culture of death"—a term coined by the pope.

When Thomas Melady, the U.S. ambassador to the Holy See from 1989 to 1993, spoke he reported on the phenomenal growth of the Catholic Church in the United States. In 1776 there were only 30,000 Catholics in the United States—1.4 percent of the population. Today there are 57 million—26 percent of the population. Melady, who has been involved in the Catholic educational system, said that the Catholic educational system includes two million students in 7,189 elementary schools; 623,000 students in 1,271 high schools; 660,000 students in 226 colleges and universities.

Melady's most striking statements came in his concluding remarks. They were so striking I could hardly believe I was hearing them. Here are his exact words from an audiotape of the address: "Catholic laypeople have an obligation to campaign for the incorporation of basic Catholic teachings within the legal, institutional, and legislative rules, traditions, and laws of the country. The papal advice written in that beautiful encyclical *[Evangelium Vitae]* can now be simply translated for American Catholics. Laypeople shall be active, should be active, in the electoral process at the local, state, and federal levels. Their influence should be to influence public policy so it is as close to Catholic teachings as possible." There can be no question, with words like these, about the aims of the papacy in the United States. The most unusual thing about the current climate is that Evangelical Protestants are prepared to help them do it. Revelation 13 is being fulfilled before our very eyes!

The Catholic Campaign's Plans for the Future

While waiting for Congressman Christopher Smith to make his appearance and presentation, Michael Fergeson outlined some of the future plans for the Catholic Campaign for America. The CCA will sponsor large meetings in cities across America to rally the Catholic faithful. There will be local chapter development. Aware of the Catholic voting block of 26 percent, polls will be taken among Catholics and then sent to the president [of the U.S.], the cabinet, the senators, the U.S. representatives, and church leaders.

In his basically pro-life speech, Congressman Smith called President Bill Clinton "the Abortion President." He pointed out, as did Ralph Reed of the Christian Coalition in his comments, that every U.S. president since John Kennedy has won the election by receiving the Catholic vote. Even Bill Clinton won a "plurality" though not the majority of the Catholic vote. Smith noted that President and Mrs. Clinton were in Newark to greet the pope on his arrival to the U.S. the first week of October 1995, and that they attended the Catholic services with the pope at the Sacred Heart Cathedral. Smith told the audience at the Catholic Campaign Conference that "Clinton outdid the Catholics at the service and received a standing ovation by the congregation as he departed." But then Smith said, "We can't let him back in again!"

It is obvious that if the CCA is successful in rallying the Catholic faithful to vote together for "Christian Values" in the 1996 election, the next president will not be pro-abortion. Congressman Smith did say that, unfortunately, of the 149 Catholic members of Congress most are pro-abortion. He indicated, as the pope does in *Evangelium Vitae*, that Catholic political leaders should vote like Catholics.

Ralph Reed Speaks to the Catholic Campaign

Ralph Reed, the executive director of the Christian Coalition of which Pat Robertson is the president, was a featured speaker at the Catholic Campaign Conference. His presentation was to express sorrow for the "bigotry" expressed to Catholics in the past and to encourage the CCA to work with the Christian Coalition in the 1996 election. Like Ambassador Melady, his remarks were very significant.

"I believe that the emerging alliance, the emerging partnership of Catholics and Evangelical Protestants, is going to be the most powerful force in the electorate in the 1990's and beyond—and anybody that ignores that alliance is going to make a big mistake.

"We are at an historic time in our nation and in our relationship as Protestants and Catholics.

"The change we are seeing in America is not just a political change. It is more deeply a spiritual shift that is shifting the plates of the American political landscape. And Catholics have been at the very center of that. According to exit polls taken after the 1994 election, for the first time in American history Roman Catholics, a majority of them—56 percent of church-attending Catholics and 51 percent of all Catholics—voted Republican in an off-year election.

"And I believe that, just as the Evangelicals have become the base vote of the Republican party, Catholics are now today the swing vote in American politics. Any candidate who wins the Catholic vote will be able to govern America. No president has been elected since John F. Kennedy was elected president in 1960 without winning the Catholic vote. Richard Nixon won it in 1968 and 72, Jimmy Carter barely carried it in 1976, Ronald Reagan and George Bush carried it throughout the 80's, and Bill Clinton carried a plurality—not a majority—but a plurality of the Catholic vote in 1992. The Catholic vote holds the key to the future of America. And I believe that if they can unite—if Catholics can unite with the Evangelical Christians—the Protestants, who share their views on the sanctity of innocent human life, on the need for religious liberty and school choice and common sense values—I believe if Catholics and Evangelicals can unite there is no person who runs for office in any city or any state in America that can't be elected and there is no bill that can't be passed in either house of Congress or any state legislative chamber anywhere in America. It is the emerging force in the electorate today.

"And how historic that truly is, because I don't need to tell you that there was a time in American history when major political parties in the 19th century actually had anti-Catholic planks in their political platforms.

"It was not until 1928 that a Catholic was nominated by either major political party and he was defeated in a campaign in which bigots made his Catholic religion the main issue.

"The truth my friends is this. Catholicism never has been, is not today, and never will be a threat to American democracy. It was and remains the most colorful and the most vibrant thread running through the tapestry of American democracy.

"Cardinal Gibbons said this: he said, No constitution is more in harmony with Catholic principles than the American constitution, and no religion is more in accord with that constitution than the Catholic religion.

"I want you to know that as Evangelicals we stand shoulder to shoulder with you in insuring that never again will bigotry be directed against Catholics and their religion be used to try and silence them and drive them from the public square. You ought to be welcomed into the political life of our nation. Faith in God is not what is wrong with America, it is what is right with America. We ought to be encouraging people with faith in God to get more involved instead of ridiculing them and attacking them in the media, in the culture, and in our political discourse.

"I think you know that we have recently launched a division of the Christian Coalition called the Catholic Alliance, which is designed to formalize and continue to build bridges in our partnership with Roman Catholics. The Catholic Alliance, like the Catholic Campaign, will be a lay movement.

"The fact is that already today, 16 percent—250,000—of the members of the Christian Coalition are Roman Catholic.

"My chief lobbyist here in Washington, Brian Lapena, is a Roman Catholic. Maureen Roselli, who is the director of the Catholic Alliance, is here, and of course she is Catholic. Brian's top deputy and our number 2 lobbyist here in Washington is a Roman Catholic. And the person who drafted and wrote and edited our Contract With the American Family is a Roman Catholic who graduated from Notre Dame University.

"The truth is, you and I are uniting. Why are we uniting? We are uniting because the darkness has become so pervasive that the light must come together. We are coming together because whatever theological differences there are, there is far more that unites us and brings us together than divides us and separates us.

"There is no denying that we have been separated as people of faith by a centurylong chasm of distrust and suspicion. The good news is that chasm is being bridged and that those walls are crumbling. I believe that this is not the work of any man. I believe that it is the work of God. I believe that He is ushering in a new work.

"And that is why we were so thrilled to join with Charles Colson and Richard John Neuhaus and John Cardinal O'Conner and Bill Bright with Campus Crusade for Christ in supporting the Evangelicals and Catholics uniting together project. It is bringing us together to work on the things that we care so deeply about.

"My friends, we have a lot of work to do. Let's go out and do it and let's do it with arms locked—united." Ralph Reed's remarks to the Catholic Campaign for America were indeed historic and, while he may not realize it, prophecy-fulfilling statements.

Deal Hudson, editor of *Crisis* magazine, a former Southern Baptist minister and a convert to Roman Catholicism, in his presentation to the CCA conference stated in part, "The greatest power in all the earth is in the Eucharist" (the mass in which it is believed that the actual body and blood of Christ is present). He went on to say, "Ralph Reed welcomed us to the public sector. It is a shame we haven't been there already. We have so much more to offer than others. Ralph [Reed] told me that *Evangelium Vitae* [a papal encyclical translated in English as The Gospel of Life] is being devoured by evangelicals. He envies our 'Natural Law' philosophy."

Then in the only mention of the Catholic persecutions of the past, Hudson stated, "When someone asks you about the inquisition just say, 'we made mistakes, but what about our universities, hospitals, and charities?'" In closing his remarks he challenged the conference attendees, "We must renew our faith by reading the Pope. Read his books!"

Most interesting were the remarks of John M. Hass, the John Cardinal Krol Professor of Moral Theology at St. Charles Borremeo Seminary of the Archdiocese of Philadelphia. He asked, "How can we tell our fellow Americans that they have nothing to fear from us? The Pope says, 'Do not be afraid.'"

So what is the significance of the Catholic Campaign for America? Its former executive director, Thomas Wykes, Jr., explained, "We see this [the first annual convention] as something that's really going to be a big annual convention on par with the Christian Coalition's Road to Victory." Wykes said that while CCA is focused on 1996 (the federal election), it's making long-range plans for the year 2000 and what the pope has said will be "a great Catholic Golden Age" *(National Catholic Register*, March 26, 1995).

Printed on the application form to join the Catholic Campaign for America is a quotation from the Second Vatican Council—Decree on the Apostolate of Lay People: "Catholics will make the weight of their convictions so influential that laws will accord with moral precepts and the common good."

Why are these things happening so fast and so boldly in America? "Because it's time!"

CHAPTER 8

Sunday's Coming!

The Bible predicts a time of religious intolerance at the very end of time—in the near future for us. Seventh-day Adventists have understood that this intolerance, and eventual persecution, will involve the object and manner of worship. In short, we believe that crucial to the chain of events just before Jesus comes will be a law requiring all to worship on Sunday.

This in itself will not be a great problem for us, because we can use the day for Bible study, Christian fellowship, and witnessing. The real problem will come, we believe, when the law is broadened to prohibit worship on Sabbath.

You might ask, "Do we see any evidence that such a law is desired by the antichrist power today and is it supported by a religio/political power in America?" **The answer to both questions is Yes!**

Some of our critics suggest that in studying eschatology—end-time events—we see a Sunday law behind every rock and every bush. There is a tendency, they say, to "create evidence" where no such evidence exists. I will let you be the judge of that as we examine what I see as unmistakable evidence that the climate in the United States today is ripe for just such a law.

Some of the more conservative believe that there is a national Sunday law already drafted and those supporting it are just waiting for the right time to spring it on the American people. More "liberal" thinkers, on the other hand, think and talk as though a Sunday law in America is a long way off. They point to the fact that our laws protect the civil and religious rights of citizens and in fact we are a watch dog country for civil and religious rights around the world.

The true situation is probably somewhere between those two positions. I believe we are so close to the end of time that we should be seeing the beginning stages or the foundation upon which a Sunday law will rest. We already see the players who will push for it, and we are already beginning to see the power and intolerance of those who will support it.

There have been serious Sunday laws in the United States before. Sunday blue laws, as they were called, existed in America from Colonial days. But it was not until the late 1880s and early 1890s that Sunday laws became a widespread issue in the United States. During that period 17 of the 48 states with Sunday laws were actually using them to prosecute Sabbath keepers. Arkansas and Tennessee were the worst. In fact, in the two years of 1895 and 1896 "no less than 76 Seventh-day Adventists were prosecuted in the United States and Canada under existing Sunday laws. Of these, 28 served terms of various lengths in jails, chain gangs, etc., aggregating 1,144 days" (*American State Papers*, p. 562; see also, Warren L. Johns, *Dateline Sunday, U.S.A.*, pp. 43-57).

From the beginning the devil has actively tried to subvert the kingdom of God and His Sabbath sign of commitment. In Old Testament times there was the ever-present sun worship to distract mankind from the worship of God Himself.

In New Testament times, with the "conversion of Constantine," many pagan rituals came into the Christian church—including the first historically recorded Sunday law that I am aware of. Enacted by the Roman Emperor Constantine in 321 A.D., it reads as follows:

"Let all judges and all city people and all tradesmen rest upon the venerable day of the sun. But let those dwelling in the country freely and with full liberty attend to the culture of their fields; since it frequently happens that no other day is so fit for the sowing of grain or the planting of vines; hence the favorable time should not be allowed to pass, lest the provisions of heaven be lost.

"Given the seventh of March, Crispus and Constantine being consuls, each for the second time (321)" (*"Codex Justin,"* lib. iii, tit. xii, 1, 3).

It is interesting to note that this first Sunday law was obligatory only on the city people.

America's First Sunday Laws

Many of the early settlers in America arrived from European countries seeking religious liberty. But even they had to learn the hard lesson of what religious liberty is all about. "In short, religious liberty as we understand the concept today existed nowhere in colonial America outside of William's Rhode Island. Citizens were usually taxed to support religion. Strict Sunday laws were strictly enforced. Blasphemy was a capital offense. Some colonies were flat-out theocracies; others came very close to it" (Robert Boston, *Why the Religious Right Is Wrong*, pp. 53, 54).

The old *Present Truth* magazine printed an article about Sunday laws in its February 1, 1930, issue. The article listed several of the Sunday laws from the Colonial period. While many later Sunday laws had a somewhat secular flavor, it is easy to see in these early Sunday laws an overt religious connotation.

VIRGINIA
America's First Sunday Law
1610

Every man and woman shall repair in the morning to the divine service and sermons preached upon the Sabbath day, and in the afternoon to divine service, and catechizing, <u>upon pain for the first fault to lose their provision and the allowance for the whole week following; for the second, to lose the said allowance and also be whipt; and for the third to suffer death.</u>

This interesting law primarily required church attendance upon pain of financial loss, public whipping, and on the third offense—death. Remember, all of these laws were written and enforced in the Colonies before the U.S. Constitution and the Bill of Rights were established.

MASSACHUSETTS
1650

Further bee it enacted that whosoever shall prophane the

Lord's day by doeing any servill worke or any such like abuses, <u>shall forfeite for every such default tenn shillings or be whipte.</u>

CONNECTICUT
1656

Whosoever shall profane the Lord's day, or any part of it, either by sinful servile work, or by unlawful sport, recreation, or otherwise, whether wilfully or in a careless neglect, <u>shall be duly punished by fine, imprisonment, or corporally,</u> according to the nature, and the measure of the sin, and offence. But if the court upon examination, by clear, and <u>satisfying evidence find that the sin was proudly, presumptuously,</u> and with a high hand committed against the known command and authority of the blessed God, such a person therein despising and reproaching the Lord, <u>shall be put to death, that all others may feare and shun such provoking rebellious courses.</u>

MARYLAND
1692-1715

Forasmuch as the sanctification and keeping holy the Lord's Day commonly called Sunday, hath been and is esteemed by the present and all the primitive Christians and people, to be principal part of the worship of Almighty God, and the honor due to His holy name; Be it enacted, . . . That from and after publishing of this law, no person or persons whatsoever within this Province, shall work or do any bodily labor or occupation upon the Lord's Day, commonly called Sunday, . . . (the works of absolute necessity and mercy always excepted) . . . nor shall abuse or profane the Lord's Day by drunkenness, swearing, . . . And if any person or persons . . . shall offend in any or all of these premises, <u>he . . . shall forfeit and pay for every such offence the sum of one hundred pounds of tobacco.</u>

This is just a sampling of the many such laws enacted in the Colonies, there being no central government at that time. The later persecution resulting from Sunday laws in 1895 and 1896 was again tied to the violation of state Sunday laws.

One of the most interesting and significant Sunday agitations in American history to date was the introduction in 1888 by Senator H. W. Blair of New Hampshire of a proposed national Sunday law. It was quite significant to Adventists for two reasons. First, because 1888 was a very pivotal year in Adventist history, and second, because the proposed law would have national force and not just be a matter of state law. The proposed law was quite comprehensive and attracted the attention and opposition of Adventists. A. T. Jones wrote an account of his presentation before the Senate Committee on Education and Labor on December 3, 1888. Jones states that his presentation was interrupted repeatedly by questions from Senator Blair so the 192-page book he wrote is written as though each question received a proper answer. He noted that "I was interrupted by the Chairman alone, *one hundred and sixty nine times in ninety minutes,* as may be seen by the official report of the hearing." Jones includes a copy of the Blair Bill in the book. It reads as follows:

THE BLAIR BILL
"50th CONGRESS}
              } S. 2983.
    1st SESSION}

"In the Senate of the United States, May 21, 1888, Mr. Blair introduced the following bill, which was read twice, and referred to the Committee on Education and Labor:

"A bill to secure to the people the enjoyment of the first day of the week, commonly known as the Lord's day, as a day of rest, and to promote its observance as a day of religious worship.

"Be it enacted by the Senate and House of Representative of the United States of America in Congress Assembled, That no person, or corporation, or the agent, servant, or employee of any person or corporation, shall perform or authorize to be performed any secular work, labor, or business to the disturbance of others, works of necessity, mercy, and humanity excepted; nor shall any person engage in any play, game, or amusement, or recreation, to the disturbance of others, on the first day of the week, commonly known as the Lord's day, or during any part thereof, in any territory, district, vessel, or place subject to the exclusive jurisdiction of the United States; nor shall it be lawful for any person or corporation to receive pay for labor or service performed or rendered in violation of this section.

"SEC. 2. That no mails or mail matter shall hereafter be transported in time of peace over any land postal route, nor shall any mail matter be collected, assorted, handled, or delivered during any part of the first day of the week: *Provided*, That whenever any letter shall relate to a work of necessity or mercy, or shall concern the health, life, or decease of any person, and the fact shall be plainly stated upon the face of the envelope containing the same, the postmaster-general shall provide for the transportation of such letter.

"SEC. 3. That the prosecution of commerce between the States and with the Indian tribes, the same not being work of necessity, mercy, or humanity, by the transportation of persons or property by land or water in such way as to interfere with or disturb the people in the enjoyment of the first day of the week, or any portion thereof, as a day of rest from labor, the same not being labor of necessity, mercy, or humanity, or its observance as a day of religious worship, is hereby prohibited; and any person or corporation, who shall willfully violate this section, shall be punished by a fine of not less than ten or more than one thousand dollars, and no service performed in the prosecution of such prohibited commerce shall be lawful, nor shall any compensation be recoverable or be paid for the same.

"SEC. 4. That all military and naval drills, musters, and parades, not in time of active service or immediate preparation therefore, of soldiers, sailors, marines, or cadets of the United States, on the first day of the week, except assemblies for the due and orderly observance of religious worship, are hereby prohibited, nor shall any unnecessary labor be performed or permitted in the military or naval service of the United States on the Lord's day.

"SEC. 5. That it shall be unlawful to pay or to receive payment or wages in any manner for service rendered, or for labor performed, or for the transportation of persons or of property in violation of the provisions of this act, nor shall any action lie for the recovery thereof, and when so paid, whether in advance or otherwise, the same may be recovered back by whoever shall first sue for the same.

"SEC. 6. That labor or service performed and rendered on the first day of the week in consequence of accident, disaster, or unavoidable delays in making the regular connections upon postal routes and routes of travel and transportation, the preservation of perishable and exposed property, and the regular and necessary transportation and delivery of articles of food in condition for healthy use, and such transportation for short distances from one State, district, or Territory, into another State, district, or Territory as by local laws shall be declared to be necessary for the public good, shall not be deemed violations of this act, but the same shall be construed, so far as possible, to secure to the whole people rest from toil during the first day of the week, their mental and moral culture, and the religious observance of the Sabbath day."

The bill, vigorously opposed by Jews, Seventh Day Baptists, Seventh-day Adventists, and other groups, was defeated in 1888 and also the amended 1889 version was likewise defeated. Of particular interest to those concerned with Sunday laws today is the counsel of Ellen White during this proposed legislation and also during the persecutions of 1895 and 1896. She continued to warn against such laws and even into the next century counseled to be vigilant in this area. She firmly believed that a national Sunday law would highlight the final events in the great controversy. It is my belief that the counsel she gave then will apply as well to the time when the final Sunday agitation arises.

It is axiomatic that in the end-time/Sunday law scenario Protestants in the United States will join with Roman Catholics to bring about a Sunday law in America. Remember Ellen White's prediction: "Through the two great errors, the immortality of the soul and Sunday sacredness, Satan will bring the people under his deceptions. While the former lays the foundation of spiritualism, the latter creates a bond of sympathy with Rome. The Protestants of the United States will be foremost in stretching their hands across the gulf to grasp the

hand of spiritualism; they will reach over the abyss to clasp hands with
the Roman power; and under the influence of this threefold union, this
country will follow in the steps of Rome in trampling on the rights of
conscience" *(The Great Controversy,* p. 588).

"Protestants of the United States," she stated. Who hasn't heard of
Chuck Colson, coauthor of *Evangelicals and Catholics Together,* discussed in chapter 5? And what about Pat Robertson's letter to the pope
and visit with him in New York? And who hasn't heard of Ralph Reed,
of the Christian Coalition and its auxiliary organization, the Catholic
Alliance? To me, these men and their activities are a
direct fulfillment of the predictions of *The Great Controversy!*

Note "the threefold union" mentioned above. Anglican
Charismatic leader Michael Harper in 1986 sent a message to Pope
John Paul II, saying, "We're with you for a united evangelization of
Europe." He has been very active in ecumenism. He has spoken of his
own ecumenical pilgrimage in terms of " 'the three major spiritual in-
fluences in the contemporary church.' In his book, *This Is the Day,*
Canon Harper speaks of three sisters whose names are Evangeline,
Charisma, and Roma, representing the Evangelical and Charismatic
movements and the Roman Catholic Church, 'which was once anathema to him, but in which he has found a deepening of profound, loving commitment to Christ and God'" (Michael Semlyen, *All Roads
Lead to Rome,* p. 30).

The establishment of diplomatic relations between the United
States and the Holy See, the escalating progress of the ecumenical
movement, the pope's visit to the U.S., and the Catholic Campaign for
America show clearly that the predictions of Ellen White and the tradi-
tional Adventist interpretation of Revelation 13 and 17 are proving to
be very correct. But what is it all leading to? We turn again to *The Great
Controversy* for the answer: "In the movements now in progress in the
United States to secure for the institutions and usages of the church the
support of the state, Protestants are following in the steps of papists,
Nay, more, they are opening the door for the papacy to regain in
Protestant America the supremacy which she has lost in the Old World.
And that which gives greater significance to this movement is the *fact*
that the principal object contemplated is the enforcement of Sunday ob-
servance—a custom which originated with Rome, and which she claims

as the sign of her authority" *(The Great Controversy*, p. 573).

We are going to examine evidence that the foundation for Sunday enforcement is being established now. But why aren't we seeing it mentioned prominently? Here is an answer.

"While men are sleeping, Satan is actively arranging matters so that the Lord's people may not have mercy or justice. <u>The Sunday movement is now making its way in darkness.</u> The leaders are concealing the true issue, and many who unite with the movement do not themselves see whither the under-current is tending. Its professions are mild, and apparently Christian; but when it shall speak, it will reveal the spirit of the dragon" (Ellen G. White, *The Watchman*, paragraph 11, Dec. 25, 1906).

Another similar statement points out the hidden nature of the Sunday movement. "Prophecy [Rev. 13] represents Protestantism as having lamb-like horns, but speaking like a dragon. Already we are beginning to hear the voice of the dragon. <u>There is a satanic force propelling the Sunday movement, but it is concealed.</u> Even the men who are engaged in the work, are themselves blinded to the results which will follow their movement." With this in mind, Ellen White goes on to counsel, "Let not the commandment-keeping people of God be silent at this time, as though we gracefully accepted the situation. There is the prospect before us, of waging a continuous war, at the risk of imprisonment, of losing property and even life itself, to defend the law of God, which is being made void by the laws of men. This Bible text will be quoted to us, 'Let every soul be subject unto the higher powers. . . . The powers that be are ordained of God'" *(Advent Review and Sabbath Herald*, Jan. 1, 1889).

So, apparently, initially we are not going to see a lot of overt action on the Sunday law, though behind-the-scenes steps are clearly being taken. In 1991 Pat Robertson, founder and president of the Christian Coalition, authored a book titled *The New World Order*. (My paperback edition states on the cover that it was on the New York *Times* best-seller list.) Robertson's main thrust is that the "secular humanists" are trying to take over the world and provide a "new world order." As citizens of "God's world order" Christians have several obligations. One is: "'Remember the Sabbath day, to keep it holy,' is a command for the personal benefit to each citizen. Our minds, spirits, and bodies demand a regular time of rest. Perhaps God's greatest gift to mankind's earthly existence is the ability to be free from work one day a week. Only when people are permitted to rest from their labors, to meditate on God, to consider His way, to dream of a better world can there be progress and genuine human betterment.

"Galley slaves and coolies forced to work seven days a week became no better than beasts of burden. Higher civilizations rise when people can rest, think, and draw inspiration from God. Laws in America [blue laws] that mandated a day of rest from incessant commerce have been nullified as a violation of church and state. . . . What idiocy our society has indulged in by refusing to acknowledge the wisdom of God."

Robertson concludes his "Sabbath" admonition by quoting Scripture and making a commitment. "I never gave the issue of a day of rest much thought until I read God's Word spoken through the Prophet Isaiah on the subject:

If you turn away your foot from the Sabbath,
From doing your pleasure on My holy day,
And call the Sabbath a delight,
The holy day of the Lord honorable, . . .
(Not) finding your own pleasure,
Nor speaking your own words,
Then you shall delight yourself in the Lord;
And I will cause you to ride on the high hills of the earth,
And feed you with the heritage of Jacob your father.

Isaiah 58:13, 14

"Since exaltation and promised rewards came from one day of rest and worship, I determined to remake my **Sundays** according to the biblical model" (Pat Robertson, *The New World Order*, pp. 236, 237).

The Christian Coalition's "Religious Liberty" department is headed up by Catholic attorney Keith Fournier. His recent book, *A House United,* with a foreword by Pat Robertson, applauds the work of Protestants and Catholics in uniting together. Remember both Robertson and Fournier were signers of the *Evangelicals and Catholics Together* document. In his book Fournier subtly states that Jesus kept Sunday: "The Son did not become man simply to be religious on Sundays or to do religious things" *(A House United,* p. 107). He also states, without any biblical support, of course, that the apostles kept Sunday. I quote, "All Christians also shared the same core beliefs, which came to them from the apostles and was first memorialized in creeds, The earliest creedal statements show up in the New Testament. These creeds predate the writing of the New Testament books in which they are cited. . . . All of these early creeds, probably formulated between AD 30 and 50, focus on the Person and work of Jesus of Nazareth. They show what even the pre-New Testament apostolic church was taught and believed about the central Figure of the faith. These core beliefs included twelve historical facts. [I will quote only his points 9 and 10] . . . As a result of this preaching, (9) the church was born and grew, (10) with **Sunday** as the primary day of worship" *(ibid.,* p. 165). This statement is of course absolutely false. There simply is no historical or biblical support for believing that the apostolic church kept Sunday, yet thousands who read Fournier's book will blindly believe they are reading truth!

Believe it or not, there is more to this book than his praising the *Evangelicals and Catholics Together* document and strongly supporting the ecumenical movement. Fournier apparently believes that Christians can get back together faster if they get back to the "core beliefs of the New Testament church." Accordingly, he tries to lead his readers to conclude that Jesus and the disciples kept Sunday as their day of rest. He goes on to discuss the church at the time of the early church fathers. This period is after the apostles had passed away but before the Council of Nicea in 325 A.D. Fournier states, "When one looks at the early church, one cannot divorce practice from values. For the most part, Christians conducted their lives according to their moral convictions and religious beliefs, even if it meant losing their possessions and their lives. One of the most revealing observations of this fact is conveyed by an early Roman governor, Pliny the Younger.

"Pliny's description of some of the practices and values of the early Christians corresponds to those taught by Jesus, the apostles, and other New Testament writers. Pliny's list also finds parallels in the writings of the church Fathers. What all of these show is that Christians met on the same day for worship—Sunday" *(ibid.,* pp. 170, 171). Fournier's point here is that if we want to get together today and be unified as the early church was, then we would also have the same common day of worship—Sunday.

Another indication of the way Christians are thinking about Sunday laws is recorded in the papers written for the Massachusetts Council of Churches that was printed in Boston, January 1993. The articles were written under the title **SUNDAY CLOSING LAWS REVISITED, A Biblical, Ethical, and Sociological Study of a Common Day of Rest.**

Bradley Googins, Ph.D., of Boston University writes, "Clearly the need for family time is more dire than ever. Yet the battle over Blue laws is a fierce one. At its most basic level, the attempt to repeal the laws is a manifestation of the dominance of the economic order and the perception that we have no choice but to follow the drumbeat of commercialism if we are to survive economically as a state and as a country." He then makes a "Call for Action." "Where then is all of this leading? In 'Chicago's' lyrics, 'Does anybody know what time it is?' is followed by 'Does anybody really care?' From what I have seen, there is an increasing concern that the fabric of life is unraveling around us. What can we do about our deteriorating families and communities? How can we protect our children? These questions are being raised with growing frequency and urgency as we confront increasing violence, stress, addiction and other signs of community and family breakdown.

"Up until now, groups in favor of repealing Blue Laws have been very successful in getting their agenda before the public and gaining a fair degree of acceptance. For the other side, however, there has been no strong voice or organized movement arguing for a time out to reflect on the problems afflicting our lives. Unless a broad constituency is formed to fight for this alternative, the L. L. Bean model [open 24 hours a day 365 days a year in Freeport, Maine] will soon be here, resulting in an even more materialistic society and frenetic Sundays.

"It seems to me that it is up to the clergy and others among us concerned with the quality of life to speak out strongly for a value system which is supportive of our families and communities. We must articulate a vision of life which values family time, reflective time and communities built on caring and mutual support. Only by framing the Sunday closing laws in this manner do we have a chance for insuring a basic quality of life for our families and communities."

Dr. Barbara Darling-Smith wrote the article "The Meaning of Sabbath Rest in the World of Commerce" for the series. She wrote that "The benefits of Sabbath for humans and our environment are too precious to be left to the vagaries of the marketplace, to the luck of where one finds employment, or to the good intentions of one's employer. Like the question of family leave, a basic human need of this sort needs legislative support; otherwise workers will be exploited."

But what about those who do not worship on Sunday such as Muslims, Jews, and Seventh-day Adventists? David M. Barney, of the Trinity Episcopal Church in Concord, MA, gives his answer to that question in his article "A View From a Parish." He asks, "In the face of these two considerations, the rights of minorities and the commandment to keep the Sabbath, what grounds have we for supporting Sunday closing laws?" His answer, "In America, Sunday remains our common day of rest for want of any practical alternative. Naturally it suits the Christian majority, but other religious and non-religious communities have adapted to it more or less happily. I cannot foresee having two or more days in which closing laws would be enforced. Since we have to choose one day in order for the whole community to enjoy it together, I see no alternative to Sunday.

"My impression is that the owners of businesses and employers generally oppose Sunday closing laws while the workers generally support closing laws. I always sleep better at night when I take the side of the workers against owners.

"The benefits of the workers' and community's time of rest also outweighs the benefits of increased profits. As a matter of justice, let our Commonwealth set some limit to the demands made on working people."

In concluding a Council of Churches session Dr. Ruy Costa stated, "Only with a renewed vision, with a statewide grassroots effort, and, with the will to be political in defense of the Sunday laws, will common day of rest advocates in this Commonwealth be able to persevere against the tremendous odds faced in defense of the current Sunday Closing laws."

The Catholic Perspective on Sunday Laws

Pope Leo XIII, in an encyclical letter, *Rerum Norarum*, released on May 15, 1891, gave a reflection on the meaning of the Sabbath that views it as "intrinsic and fundamental to our common human dignity." He stated in part:

"Here follows necessary cessation from toil and work on Sundays and Holy Days of obligation. Let no one, however, understand this in the sense of greater indulgence of idle leisure, and much less in that kind of cessation from work, such as many desire, that encourages vice and promotes wasteful spending of money, but solely in the sense of a repose from labor made sacred by religion. Rest combined with religion calls man away from toil and the business of daily life to admonish him to pay his just and due homage to the Eternal Deity. This is especially the nature, and this is the cause of the rest to be taken on Sundays and Holy Days of Obligation, and God has sanctioned the same in the Old Testament by a special law: 'Remember thou keep holy the Sabbath Day,' and He Himself taught it by His own action: namely the mystical rest taken immediately after He had created man: 'He rested on the seventh day from all His work which He had done.' "

Here the pope is using Sabbath texts to promote Sunday rest. This is of necessity, of course, because there is no biblical indication that Sunday is holy, or set apart, as anything but a common working day.

Exactly 100 years after Pope Leo's encyclical, Pope John Paul II issued an encyclical titled "ON THE HUNDREDTH ANNIVERSARY OF RERUM NOVARUM." Then he gives his letter the subtitle of *"Centesimus Annus."* Pope John Paul in reviewing Leo's letter affirms the right of the working man to have time for rest and to receive a just wage. Then referring directly to the former encyclical he says, "He [Leo] affirms the need for Sunday rest so that people may turn their thoughts to heavenly things and to the worship which they owe to Almighty God. No one can take away this human right, which is based on a commandment; . . . and consequently, the State must guarantee to the worker the exercise of this freedom. . . . In this regard, one may ask whether existing laws and the practice of industrialized societies effectively ensure in our own day the exercise of this basic right to Sunday rest."

Apparently, he believes that the state should have laws that provide the "basic right to Sunday rest."

In a recent *Adventist Review* article (October 12, 1995) pastor Wellesley Muir reported a shocking discovery. "While preparing for a

Revelation Seminar not long ago, I came across a new Catholic cate-chism and turned to the section dealing with the Sabbath. I was shocked by what I found. Under the heading 'Cooperation by the Civil Authorities Regarding This Commandment,' I read as follows: 'The civil authorities should be urged to cooperate with the church in main-taining and strengthening this public worship of God, and to support with their own authority the regulations set down by the church's pas-tors.' The next paragraph added, 'For it is only in this way that the faithful will understand why it is Sunday and not the Sabbath day that we now keep holy.'

"The Roman Catechism (1985), from which the above statement was taken, is no fly-by-night document, either! John Paul II called it 'a work of the first rank as a summary of Christian teaching.' And Silvio Cardinal Oddi, prefect of the Sacred Congregation of the Clergy, wrote concerning it as follows: 'The United States of America holds a spe-cial place in our heart, and we believe that *The Roman Catechism* will contribute to give the faithful in this great country a true *summa* of the main truths of the Catholic faith.' "

I had a similar shock when I read the new 1994 edition of the *Catechism of the Catholic Church.* This is the first fully revised and up-dated edition of the official catechism of the Catholic Church since 1566—Reformation era. In addition, the church says that this is the first unabridged edition of the Catechism ever translated and printed in English. The new Catechism is 800 pages in length and has the "impri-matur" of the Vatican. In the first six months of circulation the Catechism sold 2.3 million copies in the United States and 10 million copies worldwide.

On the upper-left corner of the first page of this new Catechism I read, "Imprimi Potest—Joseph Cardinal Ratzinger." Ratzinger? Somehow that name rang a bell. Then I remembered the *Time* maga-zine article I read (and saved) from the December 6, 1993, issue.

Reopening the Office of the Inquisition

The article titled "Keeper of the Straight and Narrow" had a subti-tle, "The Pope's chief enforcer of doctrine and morals, **Joseph Cardinal Ratzinger,** is the most powerful prince of the Church and one of the most despised." The *Time* article was three full pages. I will share just part of the first paragraph to let you know how significant it is that Ratzinger's name appears with the imprimatur.

"The world's most powerful cardinal lives a stone's throw from St. Peter's Square, above the terminus of the No. 64 bus, a line infamous for pickpockets. Each morning he sets off on foot at a brisk pace, crossing over cobblestones to arrive at 9:00 a.m. at the palazzo that once bore the title of the Roman and Universal Inquisition. Soft spoken and courteous, Joseph Cardinal Ratzinger, 66, looks too benign to be an inquisitor. But his Congregation for the Doctrine of the Faith is the Roman Inquisition's latest incarnation, and as the Catholic Church's chief enforcer of dogma, the Cardinal stands in direct succession to the persecutors of Galileo and the compilers of the index of banned books. The weight of history is borne in the attention that Ratzinger receives." Pope John Paul II named his friend Ratzinger to this position in 1981, just three years after he began his pontificate.

I was interested to see what the new catechism would say about the fourth commandment—the Sabbath commandment. By using the index I found the section that dealt with the Ten Commandments. I turned to the fourth commandment and read, "Honor your father and your mother . . ." Nothing has changed, I mused. Since the second commandment is dropped from the ten by Catholicism the fourth becomes the third, etc. Then in order to make ten, the "tenth" commandment is divided to make nine and ten.

So back I went to the third commandment. It started out great— "Remember the sabbath day, to keep it holy, Six days you shall labor, and do all your work; but the seventh day is a sabbath to the Lord your God; in it you shall not do any work." Then follows a page and a half of high praise for the biblical Sabbath including, "God entrusted the sabbath to Israel to keep as a *sign of the irrevocable covenant.*"(Italics in the Catechism.) Then somewhat mysteriously paragraph (they are all numbered) number 2175 states—**"Sunday—fulfillment of the sabbath.** Sunday is expressly distinguished from the sabbath which it follows chronologically every week; for Christians its ceremonial observance replaces that of the sabbath." The section summary states in number 2190: "The sabbath, which represented the completion of the first creation, has been replaced by Sunday which recalls the new creation inaugurated by the Resurrection of Christ."

The most significant paragraphs with regard to the scope of this book are numbers 2187 and 2188 on page 528. Number 2187 states in part, "Sanctifying Sundays and holy days requires a common effort. . . . In spite of economic constraints, public authorities should ensure citizens a time intended for rest and divine worship. Employers have a similar obligation toward their employees." Several points in this statement jump out at me. First, how does one "sanctify Sunday"? Only God can sanctify or make holy—something that He did not do with respect to Sunday. Second, who are "public authorities" that "should ensure citizens a time intended for rest and divine worship"? Public authorities are not church leaders—they are civil leaders, law makers, law enforcers. Here the Catechism states that civil authorities should ensure citizens a time for rest and worship. How could they do that? Only by passing a law!

Paragraph 2188 is the most revealing of the papal strategy. "In respecting religious liberty and the common good of all, <u>Christians should seek recognition of Sundays and the Church's holy days as legal holidays.</u> Note the key words here. "Religious Liberty"—to the Catholic mind this means the right to believe as a Catholic. "The common good of all"—this wording is similar to the preamble to the U.S. Constitution. In addition it sounds much like the words of the Catholic Campaign for America: "It is time that we demonstrate our Catholic vitality and engage in the public policy debate. <u>We have the power and the people to embark on this movement</u>—**a movement that will benefit all Americans.**

"Christians should seek recognition of Sundays . . . as legal holidays." Who makes things legal? For example, who made Martin Luther King day a "legal holiday"? The Congress of the United States, that's who. In common language this statement says Christians should encourage or pressure the civil authorities to make Sunday a legal holiday by passing a Sunday law! This will give you a clue as to how the Sunday law will be enacted—by pressure from the people. This is exactly how Ellen White said it would happen. In this way Catholicism defeated Communism in Eastern Europe. By orders of the Vatican and local bishops literally thousands upon thousands of people took to the streets in 1989 to demand a change in government—and as we all know it worked.*

The Catholic plan for urging a Sunday law from the grass roots, outlined in the new Catechism, has literally gone out to millions and millions of homes in the United States and around the world. The Catechism is even being advertized to Protestant clergy in the pages of *Christianity Today*—so that they can be informed regarding *"the richness and beauty of the Catholic faith."*

Ponder this short insight from Ellen White on how the Sunday law will come about and compare this with what you have just learned from the new Catechism. <u>"To secure popularity and patronage, legislators will yield to the demand [from Christian citizens] for a Sunday law.</u> **On this battlefield comes the <u>last great conflict</u>** of the controversy between truth and error" *(Testimonies for the Church*, vol. 5, p. 451).

Here's an illustration from current life that demonstrates the power of the people over leaders. **"Chicago's public schools can close on Good Friday**, a federal judge said. U.S. District Judge Ann Williams ruled last summer that the schools could not do so because it was a religious holiday. But last month the school system said a survey showed that 90 percent of its teachers would not work on Good Friday. [Judge] Williams provided a loophole: officials have the power to close schools for non-religious reasons on any day, she said. The officials reclassified Good Friday as an emergency closing day that will not have to be made up at the end of the year" *(National & International Religion Report*, Vol. 9, No. 8, p. 5, April 3, 1995).

Are you beginning to get the picture? Everything is in place for the Sunday law. Religio-political leaders writing in favor of a Sunday law; Evangelicals and Catholics, who together make up over 50 percent of the U.S. population, are organizing at the grass roots— precinct level for voting in the national elections; and U.S. leadership positions at all levels, Executive, Legislative, Judicial, occupied by activist Roman Catholics.

If the millions of readers of the new Catechism follow its counsel and urge a Sunday law in America, what could be the result? Many years ago we were told that "When our nation, in its legislative councils, shall enact laws to bind the consciences of men in regard to their religious privileges, enforcing Sunday observance, and bringing oppressive power to bear against those who keep the seventh-day Sabbath, the law of God will, to all intents and purposes, be made void in our land; and national apostasy will be followed by national ruin" *(Maranatha,* p. 193).

---

* For more information about how Catholicism in a "holy alliance" with the U.S. defeated Communism, see chapter five and the appendix to chapter five in my book *Even at the Door.*

CHAPTER 9

Countdown to Sunday

Perhaps the greatest joy to a studying Christian is to be rewarded with a greater understanding of truth. Many times those attending an Adventist evangelistic meeting or Prophecy seminar will report—"This makes so much sense to me now. I never could understand why there was a need for a resurrection if folks went straight to their eternal reward at death." Bible truths complement one another and fit together so well. The same is true of prophetic understanding. If you understand how God makes predictions and then see them fulfilled precisely on time it gives you more confidence in God.

How do we know <u>for certain</u> that there will be a "Sunday Law" before the Second Coming as part of the final events scenario? "The history which the great I AM has marked out in His word, uniting link after link in the prophetic chain, from eternity in the past to eternity in the future, tells us where we are today in the procession of the ages and what may be expected in the time to come. <u>All that prophecy has foretold as coming to pass, until the present time, has been traced on the pages of history, and we may be assured that all which is yet to come will be fulfilled in its order</u>" *(Education,* p. 178). Yes—Sunday is coming!

Much of the remarkable success in our evangelism worldwide is because many who have heard our message in the past are now seeing with their own eyes prophecy fulfilling. God does not want us to have to face any surprises at the end. He has given information, that if heeded, will save us from a lot of stress and grief later on. "God has revealed what is to take place in the last days, that His people may be prepared to stand against the tempest of opposition and wrath. Those who have been warned of the events before them are not to sit in calm expectation of the coming storm, comforting themselves that the Lord will shelter His faithful ones in the day of trouble. We are to be as men waiting for their Lord, not in idle expectancy, but in earnest work, with unwavering faith. It is no time now to allow our minds to be engrossed with things of minor importance. While men are sleeping, Satan is actively arranging matters so that the Lord's people may not have mercy or justice. The Sunday movement is now making its way in darkness. The leaders are concealing the true issue, and many who unite in the movement do not themselves see whither the undercurrent is tending. Its professors are mild and apparently Christian, but when it shall speak it will reveal the spirit of the dragon." Then Ellen White outlines how to prepare:

"It is our duty to do all in our power to avert the threatened danger.

"We should endeavor to disarm prejudice by placing ourselves in a proper light before the people.

"We should bring before them the real question at issue, thus interposing the most effectual protest against measures to restrict liberty of conscience.

"We should search the Scriptures and be able to give the reason for our faith. Says the prophet [Daniel]: The wicked shall do wickedly: and none of the wicked shall understand; but the wise shall understand" *(Testimonies for the Church,* vol. 5, p. 452).

Ellen White had a lot to say about Sunday laws when there was agitation for such near the turn of the last century.[1] Her comments apply very much today, as we face a similar challenge. "Sooner or later Sunday laws will be passed." She wrote in 1905, "But there is much for God's servants to do to warn the people" *(Review and Herald,* Feb. 16, 1905).

Many who become involved in the pro-Sunday law movement are apparently very sincere and conscientious Christians who are simply exasperated with world conditions. They believe with all their hearts that by "getting back to God" many of the problems that are evident in society will get better, and they will be able to offer hope for their children's future.

To His followers Jesus gave this warning, "They will put you out of the synagogues; yes, the time is coming that whosoever kills you will think that he offers God service" (John 16:2). It was in such a setting that Saul, at the stoning of Stephen, thought he was doing God service. No doubt the testimony of Stephen's life and death helped convict "Paul," leading directly to his own martyrdom for the cause of God.

We are told that, "There are many, even of those engaged in this movement for Sunday enforcement, who are blinded to the results which will follow this action. They do not see that they are striking directly against religious liberty" *(Testimonies for the Church,* vol. 5, p. 711).

Apparently the Sunday legislation will be encouraged from the grass roots up rather than being the work of bureaucrats in Washington trying to make it hard on civilians. In fact, we are told, "Plans of serious import to the people of God are advancing in an underhand manner among the clergymen of various denominations, and the object of this secret maneuvering is to win popular favor for the enforcement of Sunday sacredness. If the people can be led to favor a Sunday law, then the clergy intend to exert their influence to obtain a religious amendment to the Constitution, and compel the nation to keep Sunday" *(Review and Herald,* Dec. 24, 1889).

The Law Will Get Progressively Worse

Evidently those agitating for Sunday laws do not truly anticipate the reaction of those who choose to remain true to the law of God and honor the Bible Sabbath as the sign of their allegiance to God. Accordingly, the law at first is very mild with perhaps only fines for failure to comply. Then follow harsher penalties—loss of property, economic pressure (can't buy or sell), and finally the death sentence (see Revelation 13:15, 16).

"The time will come when men will not only forbid Sunday work, but they will try to force men to labor on the Sabbath. And men will be asked to renounce the Sabbath and to subscribe to Sunday observance or forfeit their freedom and their lives" *(The Southern Work,* p. 69).

"In the last conflict the Sabbath will be the special point of controversy throughout all Christendom. Secular rulers and religious leaders will unite to enforce the observance of the Sunday; <u>and as milder measures fail, the most oppressive laws will be enacted.</u> It will be urged that the few who stand in opposition to an institution of the church and a law of the land ought not to be tolerated" *(Maranatha,* p. 188).

Political Pressure

There are currently 149 Catholic members of Congress. Some observers choose to believe that these individuals are not influenced by the Church and therefore there is no significance in their large number. This may have been true in the past, but not now, as recent statements from Catholic leaders, including the pope, have indicated. Things have indeed changed.

Catholic attorney Keith Fournier, executive director for the Christian Coalition's American Center for Law and Justice, says, "It is the role of the lay faithful, according to Catholic theology, to 'renew the temporal order.' This is why it was second nature for a devout Catholic such as [U.S. Representative] Henry Hyde to bring his Christian convictions into the political arena. <u>It is simply *not Catholic* to privatize your faith.</u> Thus, the modern aberrations being proposed by certain Catholic politicians about their private convictions versus their public life are not only nonsense, but un-Catholic" (Keith Fournier, *A House United*, p. 32).

In Pope John Paul II's encyclical *"Evangelium Vitae"* (The Gospel of Life), issued on April 6, 1995, the pope states that the abortion culture is the "culture of death." He goes on to imply that Catholic politicians will be held responsible for their votes on the abortion question. "Catholic politicians who back abortion, even reluctantly, bear a greater responsibility before God than do women who undergo the procedure, Vatican leaders said. The question of whether they should be excommunicated is open to debate they suggested. They made their comments in a news conference in Rome after the release of Pope John Paul II's new encyclical *Evangelium Vitae* (The Gospel of Life). The 194-page document brands abortion and euthanasia as evils that no law can justify. It called for nonviolent opposition to both. . . . The encyclical dismissed claims by politicians who say they oppose abortion, but are compelled by their position to uphold laws allowing it.

'Politicians cannot renounce their consciences when they take on legislative duties,' the pope said" *(National & International Religion Report*, April 17, 1995).

Cardinal O'Connor of New York has stated that political figures that do not vote as Catholics do risk excommunication. To a non-Catholic or one not familiar with Roman Catholic theology the term excommunication may need some explanation. Remember, much of Catholic theology is based on fear. Even though there are those who may take a different view on some topics or issues than the pope, the bottom line is that very few feel so strongly about an issue that they are willing to risk excommunication.

According to Catholic theology, very few people, with the possible exception of a few popes and some saintly people, go straight to heaven when they die. Instead they go first to Purgatory (not a biblical term or place) where they are "purged" of their sins. This may require a great deal of suffering by the one in Purgatory and a great many prayers and much money from the living relatives to get the person out of Purgatory.

An excommunicated person doesn't "get" to go to Purgatory. He first of all loses all rights of church membership and is excluded from any fellowship with the church and cannot participate in the rites of the church. He cannot receive "last rights" before he dies or be buried in a church cemetery. At death he is simply banished straight to hell, to burn throughout the ceaseless ages of eternity—with no hope of ever going to heaven. How would you react to the possibility of such a fate?

Concerning this Ellen White stated, "The Roman Catholic Church, with all its ramifications throughout the world, forms one vast organization under the control, and designed to serve the interests, of the papal see. Its millions of communicants [now nearly 1 billion—that's a thousand million], in every country on the globe, are instructed to hold themselves as bound in allegiance to the pope. Whatever their nationality or their government, they are to regard the authority of the church as above all other. Though they may take the oath pledging their loyalty to the state, yet back of this lies the vow of obedience to Rome, absolving them from every pledge inimical to her interests" *(The Great Controversy*, p. 580).

What if a congressman wanted to just vote by secret ballot so no one would know how he voted on a particular issue? That is not a possibility as every vote is public—on the record. In fact, the Christian Coalition prints information as to how every member of Congress votes on issues of interest to them—i.e. family values. The higher percentage you have in votes to the liking of the Christian Coalition the greater are your chances of getting reelected.

Is there any power in the Christian Coalition's grassroots organization? The best way to tell is to take a quick look at the 1994 mid-term elections.

Arguably one of the most powerful men in Washington, Bob Dole, as this book goes to press, has just clinched the Republican nomination for president of the United States. He has been in politics since 1951. A story of Bob Dole and the Republican candidacy of Oliver North for U.S. Senator from the state of Virginia during the 1994 mid-term elections shows how pressure groups influence politicians. I'll let *Newsweek* tell the story. "You could hear tires screaming on the pavement last week as Bob Dole swerved into a political U-turn. On CBS's 'Face the Nation' he first refused to endorse Oliver North, whom Virginia Republicans had chosen as their nominee for the Senate. Instead, Dole said he would meet with Republican Marshall Coleman, who may run as an 'independent' this fall. Soon Dole was having second thoughts—and apoplectic advisers were sending him urgent messages to change course. By the next day, Dole said he would meet with North, too. The day after that he said he would endorse North. The day after that he brought Ollie into his Senate office, promised to campaign hard for him—and wrote him a $5,000 check.

"Why the turnaround? Simple enough: Dole covets the GOP presidential nomination. The way to get it is to win support from religious conservatives—the same voters who form the core of North's angry, anti-Washington campaign. 'Dole can count,' dryly observes Ralph Reed, director of Pat Robertson's Christian Coalition. With increasing sophistication, the religious right has been working to take over the GOP at the grass roots" *(Newsweek,* June 20, 1994). So there you have it. Obviously, Dole did not want to support North, but he did so to win the support of the Christian Coalition!

While speaking to the South Carolina chapter of the Christian Coalition the day before their Republican primary, Dole held up the

Christian Coalition's Congressional Voter Guides for the past three years and stated, "You have given me a one hundred percent rating over the past three years. You can't get much better than that." He won the South Carolina primary and went on to take a complete sweep of the eight primaries on "junior Tuesday." This was the turning point in the Republican primary. Dole recognizes the power of the Christian Coalition.

Things are changing in Washington—rapidly! Take the 1994 midterm elections, for example. The well respected Kiplinger Washington Letter in its June 10, 1994, issue tried to predict the outcome of the fall elections. "Religious right will gain more clout in the Republican party. . . . The religious right will have a big impact on midterm elections. . . . The [Republican] party has a shot at picking up 20 to 30 House seats and winning control of the Senate." Kiplinger correctly predicted taking the Republican takeover of the Senate but thought that the control of the House was out of reach for the Republicans because they would have to gain at least 40 seats when he thought the most they would gain would be 30 seats.

However, when the votes were counted after the November 8, 1994, election, not only did the Republicans win control of the Senate, making Bob Dole the majority leader, but instead of the 40 seats they needed to win control of the House they won a whopping 56 seats, making Newt Gingrich the Speaker of the House! It was reported as the largest political ideological shift in the twentieth century!

Two other factors are of considerable significance. Over 120 of the new members of Congress say they owe their seats to the Christian Coalition! Guess how they will vote? And, the number of Catholic members of Congress increased from 136 to 149! This gives the Catholics almost 28 percent of the voting power of the entire Congress! No wonder the Catholic Campaign people think that their time has come.

It's certain that when the Sunday law is proposed many of the lawmakers will not personally be in favor of it, but apparently they vote in favor in order to keep their positions. "Political corruption is destroying love of justice and regard for truth; and even in free America, rulers and legislators, in order to secure public favor, will yield to the popular demand for a law enforcing Sunday observance. Liberty of conscience, which has cost so great a sacrifice, will no longer be respected" *(The Great Controversy*, p. 592).

One can easily see how powerful the Christian Coalition and now the Catholic Campaign for America have become. The most powerful politicians seek their support. Ellen White might have been commenting directly from today's trends when she wrote: "To secure popularity and patronage, legislators will yield to the demand for Sunday laws. But those who fear God, cannot accept an institution that violates a precept of the Decalogue. On this battlefield will be fought the last great conflict in the controversy between truth and error" *(Prophets and Kings,* p. 606).

Legislators "will yield to the demand for Sunday laws." Now the statement in the new Catechism takes on greater significance, doesn't it? The command of the Roman Church is, "Christians should seek recognition of Sundays . . . as legal holidays." A ground swell of popular support will trigger the Sunday law. Apparently, fear of financial collapse, declining moral standards, and natural disasters motivate the people to ask for a law to appease "an angry God." Some folks talk about judicial action, others talk about constitutional amendment, others talk about executive orders. A personal study of the topic in the Spirit of Prophecy shows that the Sunday law will be enacted as a panic reaction to deteriorating world affairs. Much like the 1973 National Gas Station Sunday Closing law was a panic reaction to the Arab oil embargo, pressure tactics will be used by Satan to encourage Sunday law support.

Countdown to Sunday
Number 1
Financial Problems

Any thinking person recognizes the precarious economic situation in the United States today.[2] One could use the expression "out of control" and not exaggerate. Politicians have actually "stopped the government" in Washington twice in the past few months just to discuss what to do about deficit spending! And this addresses only the annual budget deficit, not the tremendous five trillion dollar national debt. Now we learn the Medicaid program will soon be out of money! Thousands are losing their jobs every week, and the Federal Reserve has continued to lower interest rates to try to get the debt-ridden American families to spend more. Yet in spite of all this the stock market continues to escalate to record levels. It seems that a madman is in charge. No wonder most experts predict that there will be a major "correction" in the market soon.

In commenting on this aspect of life in America, Ellen White wrote, "Those who hold the reins of government are not able to solve the problem of moral corruption, poverty, pauperism, and increasing crime. They are struggling in vain to place business operations on a more secure basis" *(Testimonies for the Church*, vol. 9, p. 13). But what does this have to do with the Sunday law? Note the following: "It will be declared that men are offending God by the violation of the Sunday—sabbath, that this sin has brought calamities which will not cease until Sunday observance shall be strictly enforced, and that those who present the claims of the fourth commandment, thus destroying reverence for Sunday, are troublers of the people, preventing their restoration to divine favor and **temporal prosperity**" *(The Great Controversy*, p. 590).

Attempts to appease God and restore temporal prosperity will be one of the motivations for the Sunday law.

Number 2
Moral Corruption

There is an almost complete breakdown of society in America today. Ellen White described conditions in our day very precisely, "Those in the world, having lost their connection with God, are making desperate, insane efforts to make centers of themselves [mass murderers and hostage takers]. This causes distrust of one another, which is followed by crime. The kingdoms of this world will be divided against themselves [Bosnia]. Fewer and fewer will become the sympathetic cords which bind man in brotherhood to his fellow man. The natural egotism of the human heart will be worked upon by Satan. He will use the uncontrolled wills and violent passions which were never brought under the control of God's will.

"Every man's hand will be against his fellow man [every man for himself]. Brother will rise against brother, sister against sister, parents against children [Susan Smith], and children against parents [the Menendez brothers]. All will be in confusion. Relatives will betray one another. There will be secret plotting to destroy life [Oklahoma City bombing]. Destruction, misery and death will be seen on every hand" *(Selected Messages*, vol. 3, p. 418). I have given a few illustrations in brackets. The situation is much worse than a few illustrations can convey. During the Susan Smith trial (she drowned her two little boys) the Washington *Post* reported that for each of the past three years running, over 2,000 children under the age of 5 were killed by their parents or guardians. Most were terribly abused before being killed!

Bill Bennett's best-selling *Book of Virtues* is an attempt to restore decency in society, and yet what has changed? It has merely highlighted the problem. And so we are told, "This very class [those who are sick and tired of the way things are going] put forth the claim that the fast-spreading corruption is largely attributable to the desecration of the so-called 'Christian sabbath,' and that the enforcement of Sunday observance would greatly improve the morals of society" *(The Great Controversy*, p. 587).

This indeed is the view of many people today. Take this letter to the editor of the Bakersfield *Californian* (Friday, May 5, 1995) following the tragic Oklahoma City bombing. "Being witness to the recent horror in Oklahoma City and mourning its losses, I am prompted to think about what has gone so wrong that Americans are now doing these things against themselves.

"And while watching the Sunday memorial, I remembered how I spent my growing up years every Sunday, going to church and being involved with my family, all day long, each week on that day.

"My idea is that we can return to that part of our past, and it would be so simple.

"The reason that Sunday worked then, with my family worshiping and playing together, was that every business was closed on that day to honor the Sabbath.

"We could do that now, and with all retail businesses closed, including movie theaters, we would then have no choice but to invent ways to enjoy the Sunday time we have, with our family and friends.

"Our families need to make Sunday 'a family activity day.' With all businesses closed, we would have no other choice.

"There is wisdom in the Commandment, 'Honor the Sabbath, to keep it holy.'"

David Rhea, Bakersfield

And just in case men have not thought of the moral corruption problem themselves, "Communications from the spirits will declare that God has sent them to convince the rejecters of Sunday of their error, affirming that the laws of the land should be obeyed as the law of God. They will lament the great wickedness in the world and second the testimony of religious teachers that the degraded state of morals is caused by the desecration of Sunday" *(The Great Controversy,* pp. 590, 591).

God's true followers will be blamed for the moral problems in society. "Those who honor the Bible Sabbath will be denounced as enemies of law and order, as breaking down the moral restraints of society, causing anarchy and corruption, and calling down the judgments of God upon the earth. Their conscientious scruples will be pronounced obstinacy, stubbornness, and contempt of authority" *(ibid.,* p. 592).

Number 3
Natural Disasters

Who would argue against the increasing prevalence of natural disasters worldwide? Major volcanic eruptions, major earthquakes, devastating floods are an ever more common occurrence. In January and February of 1996 the United States experienced record-breaking floods, record-breaking snowfall, and record-breaking cold. Apparently the devil not only causes these disasters but he also blames them on those who keep God's Sabbath.

"Satan has control of all whom God does not especially guard . . . While appearing to the children of men as a great physician who can heal all their maladies, he will bring disease and disaster, until populous cities are reduced to ruin and desolation. Even now he is at work. In accidents and calamities by sea and by land, in great conflagrations, in fierce tornadoes, and terrific hailstorms, in tempests, floods, cyclones, tidal waves, and earthquakes, in every place and in a thousand forms, Satan is exercising his power. He sweeps away the ripening harvest, and famine and distress follow. He imparts to the air a deadly taint, and thousands perish by the pestilence. These visitations are to become more and more frequent and disastrous . . . And then the great deceiver will persuade men that those who serve God are causing these

evils . . . It will be declared that men are offending God by the violation of the Sunday Sabbath" *(The Great Controversy,* pp. 589, 590).

Many who are involved in the Sunday movement are convinced by
Satan that they are doing God a service by establishing Sunday laws.
"Satan puts his interpretation upon events, and they [leading men]
think, as he would have them, that the calamities which fill the land are
a result of Sunday-breaking. Thinking to appease the wrath of God,
these influential men make laws enforcing the Sunday observance.
They think that by exalting this false rest-day higher, and still higher,
compelling obedience to the Sunday law, the spurious sabbath, they
are doing God service" *(Maranatha,* p. 176).

Number 4
Bribery

The enforcement of Sunday worship is directly contrary to the
principles of our Constitution and religious liberty. And, yes, there is
absolutely no Scriptural support for Sunday exaltation. So naturally,
those who point out these major problems will be approached with
bribes to comply. "The dignitaries of church and state will unite to
bribe, persuade, or compel all classes to honor the Sunday. The lack of
Divine authority will be supplied by oppressive enactments. Political
corruption is destroying love of justice and regard for truth; and even
in free America, rulers and legislators, in order to secure public favor,
will yield to the popular demand for a law enforcing Sunday observance" *(The Great Controversy,* p. 592).

In another statement Ellen White predicts, "As the movement for
Sunday enforcement becomes more bold and decided, the law will be
invoked against commandment keepers. They will be threatened with
fines and imprisonment, and some will be offered positions of influence, and other rewards and advantages, as inducements to renounce
their faith. But their steadfast answer is: 'Show us from the word of
God our error.'. . . Those who are arraigned before the courts make a
strong vindication of the truth, and some who hear them are led to take
their stand to keep all the commandments of God. Thus the light will
be brought before thousands [maybe on C-Span or courtroom TV cov-
erage] who otherwise would know nothing of these truths"
(Maranatha, p. 186).

Number 5
Appeal to Reasoning and Compromise

Since Sunday is "kept" by most Christians today it is the "logical" choice for a day of rest, worship, and family time. We can't have two rest days, some say. We must unite and work together to reverse the problems on society. Besides, aren't Christians supposed to be model citizens and uphold the law? How can you guys be right when the majority see things another way? The real kicker is when the Sunday law is mixed with other good reforms, such as temperance and morality. In fact, we can agree with most of what the Christian Coalition stands for. The problem is that they are preparing to "legislate" morality—which is contrary to Scriptural principles. When this happened in the former Sunday law crisis, Ellen White counseled, "The fact that a movement to establish error is connected with a work which is in itself good, is not an argument in favor of error. We may disguise poison by mingling it with wholesome food, but we do not change its nature. On the contrary, it is rendered more dangerous, as it is more likely to be taken unawares. It is one of Satan's devices to combine with falsehood just enough truth to give it plausibility. The leaders of the Sunday movement may advocate reforms which the people need, principles which are in harmony with the Bible; yet while there is with these a requirement which is contrary to God's law, His servants cannot unite with them. Nothing can justify them in setting aside the commandments of God for the precepts of men" *(The Great Controversy,* pp. 587, 588).

Ellen White was given a vision of how ridicule and mockery would also be used to try to persuade God's people to conform to the Sunday law. "The time of trouble was upon us. I saw our people in great distress, weeping and praying, pleading the sure promises of God, while the wicked were all around us mocking us and threatening to destroy us. They ridiculed our feebleness, they mocked at the smallness of our numbers, and taunted us with words calculated to cut deep. They charged us with taking an independent position from all the rest of the world. They had cut off our resources so that we could not buy or sell, and they referred to our abject poverty and stricken condition. They could not see how we could live without the world. We were dependent on the world, and we must concede to the customs, practices, and laws of the world, or go out of it. If we were the only people in the world whom the Lord favored, the appearances were awfully against us" *(Selected Messages,* vol. 3, pp. 427, 428).

We are all under tremendous pressure to conform. We call it peer pressure. While most young people "know" that tobacco and drugs are bad for them and really don't want to spend the money and waste their lives, many get involved to be like their friends. Other young people drift into various kinds of sexual immorality because of the tremendous peer pressure.

This pressure to conform is evident in the Christian world as well. Many of us were startled by the January 1995 announcement by Joseph Tkach, Sr., the leader of the Worldwide Church of God, that "it was no longer mandatory to observe a seventh day sabbath, Old Testament Holy Days, or to tithe." *Christianity Today* welcomed the WCG into the mainstream of Protestantism, saying that the Protestant world applauded them for efforts to shift from Levitical legalism to evangelical orthodoxy. (See *Christianity Today,* April 24, 1995, p. 53, and July 17, 1995, p. 63.)

The *Adventist Review* (Jan. 16, 1996) in a follow-up report on this incident, commented that "Joseph Tkach, Sr., introduced doctrinal changes to <u>bring the church more in line with the Protestant mainstream.</u>

"The changes included dropping the Sabbath, observance of the annual feasts, and the distinction between clean and unclean meats. The WCG has declared the practices to be part of the old covenant and no longer obligatory for its members. As a result, nearly 50,000 members [out of a total of 100,000] and 500 pastors have left the denomination." As you can see there is tremendous pressure to conform. The good news side of this particular incident is that many of these people are contacting Adventists to learn more about us. Dr. George Reid, director of the General Conference Biblical Research Institute, and Dr. Samuele Bacchiocchi, professor of theology and church history at Andrews University, were recently invited to make presentations to a gathering of 400 non-Adventist Sabbathkeepers.

Number 6
Miracles and Mariology

We are told that this will be one of the main avenues the devil uses to bolster support for the Sunday law.

Ellen White mentions that, "Papists, who boast of miracles as a certain sign of the true church, will readily be deceived by this wonder working power. And Protestants, having cast away the shield of truth, will also be deluded. Papists, Protestants, and worldlings will alike accept the form of godliness without the power, and they will see in this union a grand movement for the conversion of the world and the ushering in of the long-expected millennium" *(The Great Controversy,* pp. 588, 589). The most amazing fulfillment of this statement is that today Catholics believe that the miracles of God are happening now!

Malachi Martin, author of *Keys of This Blood*, wrote the foreword to *The Thunder of Justice,* currently a best-selling book in the Catholic bookstores. Here are his amazing words: "Only a very distracted and unaware Christian of today could have avoided receiving at least a fleeting impression . . . that for a number of years now there has been a steady build-up of events—in the broadest sense of that word—all of which indicate that humanity as a whole and the Holy Roman Catholic Church in particular have reached a fateful threshold beyond which lies a new condition of human affairs.

"Literally, every decade of this one century alone has piled one on the other, what Christ called 'the signs of the times.' (Matt. 16:1-4).

"In a general way of speaking, it is quasi-impossible to have totally escaped any awareness of these events, and the clamor of the claimant participants. Visions. Appearances. Messages. Predictions. Warnings. Interpretations. Weeping statues and bleeding icons. Miraculous spring waters. Spontaneous cures. Spinning dances of the sun, and eclipses of the moon. Little children telling the future. Uneducated men and women instructing popes and presidents. Nationwide publicity tours by bearers of special revelations. Throughout all of this, an obvious emphasis on the singular role of the Blessed Virgin Mary of Nazareth as the Queen of Heaven, Mother of All Living, and—not surprisingly—as the Mediatrix of All Graces is pervasive" (Malachi Martin, in the foreword to *The Thunder of Justice,* by Ted and Maureen Flynn).

What a list of current miracles and capped off by the exaltation of the virgin Mary. The whole of the 400-page book is devoted to the "Apparitions"—visits and messages—of the virgin Mary. And what is "Mary" saying? When "Our Lady appeared to a local farmer, Michael

O'Donnell. She told him, 'preserve Sunday for prayer' " (Flynn, *The Thunder of Justice*, p. 30).

It's startlingly plain. It's a direct fulfillment of prophecy. Another indication that Sunday's coming!

Eccl. 9: 10, 5, 6.

Number 7
Psa 115: 17   1 Thess. 4: 16-18
Messages From the Dead *Isa 26: 19, 52, 53*

As part of the continuing barrage of lying wonders Satan "will bring back the dead" in an attempt to seduce the faithful into dishonoring God and joining the Sunday movement. "Those who would stand in this time of peril must understand for themselves the testimony of the Scriptures. Many will be confronted by the spirits of devils personating beloved relatives or friends and declaring the most dangerous heresies. These visitants will appeal to our tenderest sympathies and will work miracles to sustain their pretensions. We must be prepared to withstand them with the Bible truth that the dead know not anything and that they who thus appear are the spirits of devils" *(The Great Controversy,* pp. 559, 560). This statement doesn't mention what those who "return" say except that they declare "the most dangerous heresies." A few pages later we are told, "Through the two great errors [heresies], the immortality of the soul and Sunday sacredness, Satan will bring the people under his deceptions" *(ibid.,* p. 588).

Already the devil is preparing people to accept this dangerous deception of visits from the dead. *The Christian Ministry* magazine, published by the Christian Century Foundation, recently featured an article titled "Looking for Angels." In the article the author, a pastor, stated, "My advice is to keep a look out for angels, but not to be myopic [a narrow view of something]. Angels take many forms—the current interest is too focused on the two-winged, haloed sort. Here are some other places to look for them. [The author lists five places—only number four is relevant here.] . . . Fourth, look for angels in the form of loved ones who have died" *(The Christian Ministry,* May-June 1995, p. 9).

Number 8
The "Return of the Apostles" *John 8: 44*

The Scriptures are the primary source of support for God's people, giving the standard by which they live and determine truth. Naturally the devil works to undermine the Scriptures and therefore eliminate its defense against his heresies such as the Sunday law. "The apostles, as personated by these lying spirits, are made to contradict what they wrote at the dictation of the Holy Spirit when on earth. They deny the divine origin of the Bible, and thus tear away the foundation of the Christian's hope and put out the light that reveals the way to heaven. Satan is making the whole world believe that the Bible is a mere fiction, or at least a book suited to the infancy of the race, but now to be lightly regarded, or cast aside" *(The Great Controversy,* p. 557).

A similar statement in *Early Writings* gives an additional perspective. "He who is the father of lies, blinds and deceives the world by sending forth his angels to speak for the apostles, and to make it appear that they contradict what they wrote by the dictation of the Holy Ghost when on earth. These lying angels make the apostles to corrupt their own teachings and to declare them to be adulterated. By so doing, <u>Satan delights to throw professed Christians and all the world into uncertainty about the Word of God</u>" *(Early Writings,* p. 264).

This revisionist view of the Bible is already current. Too many, perhaps even some in our ranks, see the Bible as an archaic book, more suited to, and shaped by, "the infancy of our race." What will be the reaction from those who think this way when spirit visitants appear and endorse their views?

Number 9
Evil Angels Appear as Good Angels

In the increasing pressure to push acceptance of Sunday worship the devil will send his angels to appear among men with the Sunday message. "They [the wicked] declared that they had the truth, that miracles were among them; <u>that angels from heaven talked with them and walked with them,</u> that great power and signs and wonders were performed among them, and that this was the temporal millennium they had been expecting so long. <u>The whole world was converted and in harmony with the Sunday law,</u> and this little feeble people stood out in defiance of the laws of the land and the law of God, and claimed to be the only ones right on the earth" *(Selected Messages,* vol. 3, p. 428).

"The miracle-working power manifested through spiritualism will exert its influence against those who choose to obey God rather than men. <u>Communications from the spirits [evil angels] will declare that God has sent them to convince the rejecters of Sunday of their error,</u> affirming that the laws of the land should be obeyed as the law of God. They will lament the great wickedness in the world and second the testimony of religious teachers that the degraded state of morals is caused by the desecration of Sunday. <u>Great will be the indignation excited against all who refuse to accept their testimony</u>" *(Maranatha,* p. 167).

Even the devil when he finally personates Christ "declares that those who persist in keeping holy the seventh day are blaspheming his name by <u>refusing to listen to his angels sent to them with light and truth</u>" *(The Great Controversy,* p. 624).

Number 10 *Matt. 24:23,24,5,22*
The Almost Overmastering Delusion

So far we have looked at nine aspects that put pressure on God's people to accept the Sunday law. Now Satan himself gets into the act by trying to make it appear that he is Christ—come again. Ellen White calls this the "strong, almost overmastering delusion."

"<u>As the crowning act in the great drama of deception, Satan himself will personate Christ.</u> The church has long professed to look to the Saviour's advent as the consummation of her hopes. <u>Now the great deceiver will make it appear that Christ has come.</u> In different parts of the earth, Satan will manifest himself among men as a majestic being of dazzling brightness, resembling the description of the Son of God given by John in the Revelation. Revelation 1:13-15. <u>The glory that surrounds him is unsurpassed by anything that mortal eyes have yet beheld.</u> The shout of triumph rings out upon the air: 'Christ has come! Christ has come!' The people prostrate themselves in adoration before him, while he lifts up his hands and pronounces a blessing upon them, as Christ blessed His disciples when He was upon the earth. His voice is soft and subdued, yet full of melody. In gentle, compassionate tones he presents some of the same gracious, heavenly truths which the Saviour uttered; he heals the diseases of the people, <u>and then, in his assumed character of Christ, he claims to have changed the Sabbath to Sunday, and commands all to hallow the day which he has blessed.</u> He declares that those who persist in keeping holy the seventh day are blaspheming his name by refusing to listen to his angels sent to them with light and truth. <u>This is the strong, almost overmastering delusion</u>" (*The Great Controversy*, p. 624).

And so he will look like Jesus, sound like Jesus, dress like Jesus, act like Jesus, and to most of the world <u>he will be Jesus.</u> How will the faithful ones realize that it isn't Jesus? There are only two ways.

The first identifying factor is the manner of his coming. The Bible says, "For as the lightning comes from the east and flashes to the west, so also will the coming of the Son of Man be" and "Behold He is coming with clouds, and every eye will see Him" (Matthew 24:27; Revelation 1:7). Ellen White adds, "This coming there is no possibility of counterfeiting. It will be universally known—witnessed by the whole world" *(ibid.,* p. 625). The second element to enable identification of the counterfeit is the sure Word of God. "Only those who have been diligent students of the Scriptures and who have received the love of the truth will be shielded from the powerful delusion that takes the world captive. <u>By the Bible testimony these will detect the deceiver in his disguise</u>" *(ibid.,* p. 625).

Do we know and love the Bible so well that we will be able to trust it over our senses? Have we been too busy with life's burdens to take time to study and memorize Scripture? God's Messenger to the Remnant asks, "Are the people of God now so firmly established upon His word that they would not yield to the evidence of their senses? Would they, in such a crisis, cling to the Bible and the Bible only?" She warns, "Satan will, if possible, prevent them [God's people] from obtaining a preparation to stand in that day. He will so arrange affairs as to hedge up their way, entangle them with earthly treasures, cause them to carry a heavy, wearisome burden, that their hearts may be overcharged with the cares of this life and the day of trial may come upon them as a thief" *(ibid.,* pp. 625, 626).

After digesting the startling information presented so far, maybe you are beginning to see that things are in place for the very final events. My purpose is not to alarm you, but rather to help you prepare for the challenge ahead. Spiritual things are of the utmost importance—eternal life or death is the real issue here. We need to know what we may expect in the weeks and months ahead and realize that we have been told these things before they happen. We each need to be spiritually secure and prepared to remain faithful.

In one long sentence we read the final scenario. "When Protestantism shall stretch her hand across the gulf to grasp the hand of the Roman power, when she shall reach over the abyss to clasp hands with spiritualism, when, under the influence of this threefold union, our country shall repudiate every principle of its constitution as a Protestant and republican government, and shall make provision for the propagation of papal falsehoods and delusions, <u>then we may know that the time has come for the marvelous working of Satan</u> [his personation of Christ discussed above] <u>and that the end is near"</u> *(Maranatha,* p. 190).

What an exciting time to be alive.

---

[1] Section 55 in volume 3 of *Selected Messages* contains 50 pages of very timely counsel. I would highly recommend the entire section. The chapter titles are: "Lessons From Meeting the Sunday Law Crisis of the Late 1880's and Early 1890's"; "As We Near the End"; and "The Last Great Struggle." The trustees of the White Estate give a short introduction to this section in which they state: "Agitation for Sunday legislation gradually waned, but in succeeding years Ellen White kept the issues of the final conflict before church leaders. Times might have changed, so far as actual persecution for Sabbath observance was concerned, but the issues and the principles involved remained the same. Since Ellen White's death further changes have taken place, but we believe that the same principles and the same issues will be revived in the coming conflict, present appearances to the contrary not withstanding" *(Selected Messages,* vol. 3, p. 381).

[2] In *Even at the Door* I dedicated an entire chapter "Economic Armageddon" to this topic.

CHAPTER 10

Spiritualism Joins the Church

The Bible and the Spirit of Prophecy both describe a threefold union that works together at the end of time. The Bible calls this trio the dragon, the beast, the false prophet. "And I saw three unclean spirits like frogs coming out of the mouth of the dragon, out of the mouth of the beast, and out of the mouth of the false prophet. For they are the spirits of demons, performing signs" (Revelation 16:13, 14). Some Bible students have called these powers the "Satanic trinity." The Spirit of Prophecy also gives an identification of this trio of powers. "Through the two great errors, the immortality of the soul and Sunday sacredness, Satan will bring the people under his deceptions. While the former lays the foundation of spiritualism, the latter creates a bond of sympathy with Rome. The Protestants of the United States will be foremost in stretching their hands across the gulf to grasp the hand of spiritualism; they will reach over the abyss to clasp hands with the Roman power; <u>and under the influence of this threefold union,</u> this country will follow in the steps of Rome in trampling on the rights of conscience" *(The Great Controversy,* p. 588).

Adventist expositors agree with the identification of the "dragon," the "beast," and the "false prophet" as modern spiritualism, or paganism, the papacy, and apostate Protestantism. This trio or trinity of religious powers together constitute the latter-day "great Babylon."

Here we have an amazing development. We have noted how the papacy and the United States are beginning a cooperation that will bring about worldwide support for the beast. Satan will use both the papacy and the United States (in its "speaking like a dragon" role) to push for Sunday support in violation of God's law. But now—at the very end—the devil himself becomes personally involved in the great controversy. The miracles of spiritualism are said to be "signs." The devil will use them to authenticate his false message and to attest to the power and authority of his false religious system.

The third frog of Revelation 16 is spiritualism. It is Satan at work in a dramatic way.

We have seen how cooperation between the papacy and the United States is moving toward the Sunday law. The evidence is overwhelming that the stage is set for such action. But doesn't spiritualism come in here somewhere? Indeed it does. It is working now.

Remember the evidence that spiritualism will play a major role in the pressure to conform to Sunday worship? The devil will work through "those who have died," "evil spirits," "the apostles," and finally "in person." If the end is near, we should be seeing the beginnings of spiritualism now.

There are literally hundreds of books on the topic of the "New Age" beliefs. In fact, by far the most dominant topic in the religion section of bookstores today is New Age type material. A number of books, such as Dave Hunt's *The Seduction of Christianity,* have been written on this topic and its acceptance by many Christian groups.

The Great Controversy chapters 31 through 34 discuss this topic. Ellen White points out how "Satan has long been preparing for his final effort to deceive the world. The foundation of his work was laid by the assurance given to Eve in Eden: 'ye shall not surely die.' 'In the day ye eat thereof, then your eyes shall be opened, and ye shall be as gods, knowing good and evil.' Genesis 3:4, 5. Little by little he has prepared the way for his masterpiece of deception in the development of spiritualism. He has not yet reached the full accomplishment of his designs; but it will be reached in the last remnant of time. Says the prophet: 'I saw three unclean spirits like frogs; . . . they are the spirits of devils, working miracles, which go forth unto the kings of the earth and of the whole world, to gather them to the battle of the great day of God Almighty.' Revelation 16:13, 14. Except those who are kept by the power of God, through faith in His word, the whole world will be swept into the ranks of this delusion. The people are fast being lulled to a fatal security, to be awakened only by the outpouring of the wrath of God" *(The Great Controversy,* pp. 561, 562).

In this heaven-sent warning, Ellen White gives the length of Satan's experience and his plans for the last advance of error. She begins chapter 32 by pointing out, "The great controversy between Christ and Satan, that has been carried forward for nearly six thousand years, is soon to close; and the wicked one **redoubles his efforts** to defeat the work of Christ in man's behalf and to fasten souls in his snares. To hold the people in darkness and impenitence till the Saviour's mediation is ended, is the object which he seeks to accomplish" *(ibid.,* p. 518).

"Little by little," we are told, Satan will make advances. Now all around us spiritualism is evident—in television advertisements and programing, and in the movies. Webster defines spiritualism as "a belief that spirits of the dead communicate with the living." This supposed communication is taking place today. But in addition to personating the dead (former living human beings), the devil also uses evil angels to personate holy angels and finally Jesus Himself. And the devil will use this spiritualistic phenomenon to bring the papacy and apostate Protestantism together, along with "the whole world." We are now seeing the beginning of this, the last act of Satan.

The notion seems to be prevalent today that all we need is to develop a love relationship with Jesus. From what I have studied in the Bible and the Spirit of Prophecy the only way to meet the devil in this last great conflict is with a "Thus saith the Lord; It is written." You must know your Bible to be able to stand! Proof texts are important! Knowing what the Bible teaches, for example about the condition of man in death, gives us a defense against Satan's final spiritualistic deceptions.

The Bible Teaching About Man's Condition in Death

Adventists believe that at Creation man had conditional immortality. That is, as long as he was faithful to God's commands he would have access to the Tree of Life and therefore could live on and on. Since the fall of man, however, we no longer have access to the Tree of Life, and are "subject to death." Our hope of eternal life is in Christ. He "died for us"—the second death—therefore though we may die now—it is only a sleep. At the second coming of Christ, there will be a general resurrection of the righteous who have lived down through the ages. They will awake to newness of life—immortality—to live with Christ forever.

Entire books have been written on Christian anthropology—the study of the nature of man. But here we will keep our focus on the "intermediate state" between natural death and the resurrection.

Bible Readings for the Home devotes nine sections to Christian anthropology—exactly 50 pages! The book is largely in question-and-answer form—with the answers being given in Bible texts. The following excerpt will help the reader to see that the Bible is clear on this topic and that its teachings should form our belief and understanding of it.

What Death Is Like
By what figure does the Bible represent death?

"But I would not have you to be ignorant, brethren, concerning them which are *asleep,* that ye sorrow not, even as others which have no hope." 1 Thessalonians 4:13. (See also 1 Corinthians 15:18, 20; John 11:11-14.)

Note.—In sound sleep one is wholly lost to consciousness; time goes by unmeasured; and mental activity is suspended for the time being.

Where do the dead sleep?

"And many of them that *sleep in the dust of the earth* shall awake." Daniel 12:2. (See also Ecclesiastes 3:20; 9:10.)

How long will they sleep there?

"So man lieth down, and riseth not: *till the heavens be no more*, they shall not awake, nor be raised out of their sleep." Job 14:12.

Thoughts and Feelings of the Dead
What does one in this condition know about his family?

"His sons come to honor, and *he knoweth it not*; and they are brought low, but *he perceiveth it not of them*." Job 14:21.

What becomes of man's thoughts at death?

"His breath goeth forth, he returneth to his earth, *in that very day his thoughts perish."* Psalm 146:4.

Do the dead know *anything?*
"For the living know that they shall die: *but the dead know not any thing."* Ecclesiastes 9:5.

Do they take part in earthly things?
"Also their *love,* and their *hatred,* and their *envy,* is now *perished; neither have they any more a portion for ever in any thing that is done under the sun."* Verse 6.

Note.—If one remained conscious after death, he would know of the promotion or dishonor of his sons; but in death one loses all the attributes of mind—love, hatred, envy, etc. Thus it is plain that his thoughts have perished, and that he can have nothing more to do with the things of this world. But if, as taught by some, man's powers of thought continue after death, he *lives;* and if he lives, he must be *somewhere.* Where is he? Is he in heaven, or in hell? If he goes to either place at death, what then is the need of a future judgment, or of a resurrection, or of the second coming of Christ? If men go to their rewards at death, before the judgment takes place, then their *rewards* precede their *awards.*

How much does one know of God when dead?
"For in death *there is no remembrance of Thee."* Psalm 6:5.

Note.—As already seen, the Bible everywhere represents the dead as *asleep,* with not even a remembrance of God. If they were in heaven or hell, would Jesus have said, "Our friend Lazarus *sleepeth"?* John 11:11. If so, calling him to life was really robbing him of the bliss of heaven that rightly belonged to him. The parable of the rich man and Lazarus (Luke 16) teaches not consciousness in death, but that riches will avail nothing in the judgment and that poverty will not keep one out of heaven. *(Bible Readings for the Home,* current hardcover ed., pp. 469, 470.)

Presently, leaders in Israel are laying plans for a great celebration during the year 2000 of the 3,000th-year anniversary of the 40-year reign of King David. Knowing of David's standing among the Jews, Peter mentions him twice in his sermon on the day of Pentecost. He declared, "Men and brethren, let me speak freely to you of the patriarch David, <u>that he is both dead and buried, and his tomb is with us to this day."</u> <u>"For David did not ascend into the heavens"</u> (Acts 2:29, 34).

Since the dead, according to the Bible, are asleep and don't know anything, then if someone claims to be speaking with the dead, he is either lying or speaking with the devil! For as Paul warned, "We do not wrestle against flesh and blood, but against principalities, against powers, against the rulers of the darkness of this age, against spiritual hosts of wickedness in heavenly [high] places" (Ephesians 6:12).

Ministers Are Setting Up the People for Deception

The church, where people expect to find spiritual wisdom, help, and protection, is being used by the devil to teach people to be open to spiritualism. Adventists understand that the Bible does not teach the conscious existence of man in death. However, the Catholic Church and now many Protestant churches are teaching the error that man has natural immortality and somehow lives on after death— either in the presence of God, in purgatory (being purified), or in the torments of hellfire.

Three very pointed statements from God's messenger to the remnant underscore the problem. <u>"The popular ministry cannot successfully resist spiritualism.</u> They have nothing wherewith to shield their flocks from its baleful influence. <u>Much of the sad result of spiritualism will rest upon ministers of this age;</u> for they have trampled the truth under their feet, and in its stead have preferred fables. The sermon which Satan preached to Eve upon the immortality of the soul—'ye shall not surely die'—they have reiterated from the pulpit; and the people receive it as pure Bible truth. <u>It is the foundation of spiritualism.</u> The word of God nowhere teaches that the soul of man is immortal. Immortality is an attribute of God only. 1 Timothy 6:16: 'Who only hath immortality, dwelling in the light which no man can approach unto; whom no man hath seen, nor can see; to whom be honor and power everlasting. Amen'" *(Testimonies for the Church,* vol. 1, p. 344).

<u>"Spiritualism is about to take the world captive.</u> . . . The foundation

for the success of spiritualism has been laid in the assertions that have been made from the pulpits of our land. <u>The ministers have proclaimed, as Bible doctrines, falsehoods that have originated from the arch-deceiver.</u> The doctrine of consciousness after death, of the spirits of the dead being in communion with the living, has no foundation in the Scriptures, and yet this theory is affirmed as truth. <u>Through this false doctrine the way has been opened for the spirits of devils to deceive the people representing themselves as the dead.</u> Satanic agencies personate the dead, and thus bring souls into captivity" (Ellen G. White, *Signs of the Times,* May 28, 1894).

These insightful statements help us to see how Satan has set up the world—even the professing Christian church—to be deceived by his spiritualistic endeavors. "The doctrine of man's consciousness in death [she also calls this "the doctrine of natural immortality"], especially <u>the belief that spirits of the dead return to minister to the living, has prepared the way for modern spiritualism.</u> If the dead are admitted to the presence of God and holy angels, and privileged with knowledge far exceeding what they before possessed, why should they not return to earth to enlighten and instruct the living? If, as taught by popular theologians, spirits of the dead are hovering about their friends on earth, why should they not be permitted to communicate with them, to warn them against evil, or to comfort them in sorrow?" *(The Great Controversy,* pp. 551, 552).

These three statements are being fulfilled right now. Prophecy is being fulfilled precisely as it was predicted—evidence that these writings are indeed inspired. Keeping the previous statements in mind, let's look at some current events for an exact match.

My research has uncovered dramatic evidence that the final working of Satan through spiritualism is about to begin. The fulfillments are very precise. While at the national conference of the Catholic Campaign for America I walked through the exhibit area to observe the various materials and services available. Knowing that I would include some of the material that I was learning that weekend in this book, I kept my eyes open for relevant material. It was while at that meeting that I subscribed to the journal *Inside the Vatican.* I also visited the *Our Sunday Visitor* booth. Our Sunday Visitor is both a publishing company and a magazine—much like the Review and Herald Publishing

Association and the magazine with a similar name. The booth had many different books and other publications available for sale but the "feature" of the booth was their hot new book, *Messengers,* with a sub-title *After Death Appearances of Saints and Mystics.*

At the time I visited the booth they were sold out of *Messengers,* but I did subscribe to the weekly publication, *Our Sunday Visitor.* I also was given a copy of the latest 48-page catalog of books and material available from Our Sunday Visitor Press. Featured as the only book on the cover of the catalog was *Messengers.* This book is really being pro-moted! In the January 7, 1996, issue of the *Our Sunday Visitor* maga-zine there was a full-page ad for *Messengers.* The text of the ad stated: "Celestial Couriers Reveal Heaven's Mysteries." "Since the days of the Old Testament, the holy dead have been sent to earth as God's celestial couriers." "This outstanding new work will fascinate and intrigue read-ers with its compelling glimpse into the reality of the afterlife as well as boost reader's faith in God who loves each of us individually."

I later purchased the hardbacked book of 352 pages at a Catholic bookstore. Much of the erroneous Roman Catholic theology and belief comes through in this book. For example, "Saints are also making after-death appearances *now*—that is, in whatever year you pick up this book. Nor are such appearances something new. Witnesses who spied on St. Francis of Assisi during prayer more than once saw dead saints—among them Peter, Paul, and John—speaking to him. After-death ap-pearances of the holy in western tradition go back, in fact, to the beginning of Christianity and beyond into Judaism. It was, after all, two dead, holy, Jewish men who appeared to Jesus on the Mount of Transfiguration" (Patricia Treece, *Messengers,* p. 14).

A little earlier we noted that on the day of Pentecost Peter stated that King David was in his grave and had not ascended into heaven. When David was about to die he told Solomon that he was going the way of all the earth. That is, like everyone else he would rest in his grave until the resurrection. The Bible says, "Then the days of David drew near that he should die, and he charged Solomon his son, saying: 'I go the way of all the earth; be strong, therefore, and prove yourself a man'" (1 Kings 2:1, 2). The Bible is clear that the three greatest patriarchs, Abraham, Isaac, and Jacob, along with their wives, Sarah, Rebekah, and Leah, are all buried in the Cave of Machpelah, where they are waiting the life giver. (See Genesis 49:29-50:14.)

If everyone, in the mortal course of events, finally dies and is buried and waits for the resurrection, then the only humans in heaven will be the ones the Bible specifically mentions in heaven as exceptions to the rule. For example, Enoch was taken to heaven, as is stated in Genesis 5:24. Elijah was also taken to heaven in the sight of Elisha, as is stated in 2 Kings 2:1-15. Moses died and was buried by God Himself in a place no one knew about. (Deuteronomy 34:5, 6.) Later Christ came and resurrected the body of Moses and took him to heaven. (Jude 9.) In addition, Matthew 27:52, 53 records that there was a group of people resurrected in connection with the death and resurrection of Christ. Again, this is pointed out in Scripture as an exception to the rule of resting quietly in the grave until the general resurrection.

So the Bible lists the exceptions. It is very specific. I repeat, everyone who dies, even Abraham, Isaac, Jacob, and David are all resting in their graves in a state of unconsciousness. The exceptions to this law of nature are specifically mentioned as Enoch, Elijah, and Moses. I mention all this to show that the Bible does not leave us in doubt or question about this matter. Ellen White in describing the transfiguration states, "Moses passed under the dominion of death, but he was not to remain in the tomb. Christ Himself called him forth to life. Satan the tempter had claimed the body of Moses because of his sin; but Christ the Saviour brought him forth from the grave. Jude 9.

"Moses upon the mount of transfiguration was a witness to Christ's victory over sin and death. He represented those who shall come forth from the grave at the resurrection of the just. Elijah, who had been translated to heaven without seeing death, represented those who will be living upon the earth at Christ's second coming. . . . Upon the mount the future kingdom of glory was represented in miniature,— Christ the King, Moses a representative of the risen saints, and Elijah of the translated ones" *(The Desire of Ages,* pp. 421, 422).

On a Bible basis it is easy to answer the erroneous teaching in the paragraph from *Messengers* quoted earlier. The Bible is consistent. A simple study of the Bible gives a clear picture on this topic. The author of *Messengers,* Patricia Treece, goes on to say, "*All* spiritual traditions [she later states that the other "spiritual traditions" in addition to Christianity include Buddhists, Muslims, Native Americans, Hasidic

Jews, and Hindus] make a place for important appearances of the dead . . . the idea of the dead returning to do God's work is not some weird Catholic notion, but a universal belief" *(Messengers,* p. 14).

Later when describing that a saint could come back to earth, Treece exposes the basic works orientation of the Catholic system. "Of course all in heaven, whether they achieved the purity during life to walk right in or entered following some after-death work [purgatory], are legitimately called saints" *(ibid.,* p. 15). In speaking of Mary, the mother of Jesus, she says, "Whenever a Catholic writes about saints, the question always comes up: what about the apparitions of the Virgin Mary? Having studied many reports, I believe that, after Jesus, no one gets around like his mother. The visits of the woman the Bible quotes as saying prophetically, 'all generations will call me blessed' are extremely frequent in the nineteenth and twentieth centuries, both to groups and to individuals" *(ibid.,* p. 16).

To whom do the dead "appear"? Treece says they primarily appear to family members and acquaintances. However, "Like angels, dead saints are spiritually equipped to serve as pure, loving messengers to whomever God sends them. So in addition to the appearances mentioned above [numerous appearances to family members and acquaintances], saints may appear to: 1) people they never knew; 2) people who never heard of them; or 3) those from whom they are separated by the widest barriers of culture, centuries, and of course— death" *(ibid.,* p. 24).

How does one know if the visit from the dead is authentic—that is, from heaven? Treece gives a list of "fruits" that authenticate a visit. She states: "Fortunately, when an after-death appearance is really God-sent, there are aftereffects which speak for its authenticity. Called 'the fruits of the apparition,' especially where the claimant's honesty and stability are established, one or more of these is a powerful confidence booster that something supernatural may really be happening here. These possible fruits are:

    1. Physical healing from serious, even terminal, illness.

    2. Emotional healing, often with visible radical personality improvement.

    3. Spiritual growth from egotism into greater other-centeredness.

    4. Rescue in a life-threatening situation from either a natural

peril such as fire or flood, or man-made such as enemy troops, or self-destruction.

    5. New direction in life, particularly regarding vocation.

    6. New acceptance—even joy—in carrying some burden.

    7. Resolution of spiritual questions or difficulties" *(ibid.,* p. 28).

    In this list the work of God through the Holy Spirit and the angels is relegated to the dead saints. Because I believe that these so-called "visits" from the dead are of the devil I will not quote from the hundreds of stories and experiences that are quoted in the book. However, the author's conclusion is very significant to the scope of this book. She states, in essence, that these visits from the dead—spiritualistic phenomenon from my perspective—are what will eventually bring all mankind together. Treece says, "As I see it, the major religions—Buddhism, Hinduism, Christianity, Judaism, and Islam—are each divided into two camps: *thinkers*, who find God more readily through reasoning, reflection, and virtuous 'rational' models like St. Thomas More, and *feelers*, who see God more easily in signs, wonders, and models like Padre Pio. Every religion, I believe, needs both types, just as every person is fully developed only when both tendencies are in balance. . . .

    "Seeing after-death experiences universally acknowledged I hope will buttress your faith in the reality of life after life. . . . I see the Holy Spirit working, to varying degrees, in and through all faiths and present in all people of good will. . . .

    "When I speak of saints like Buddha, Mohammed, the Torah's holy men and women, holy Hindus, and certain shamanistic sages, I do so comfortably with the hope of hastening the day when all of us who believe in supernatural realities and moral imperatives change our world through our love for each other and for God Who, as Hindu priest Narasimha Bhattar of the Southern California Hindu Temple says, is 'One' even if our mode of praying and religious beliefs are different" *(ibid.,* pp. 288, 289).

    In concluding her book that is being so widely promoted by the Catholic Church, Treece reflects, "In writing these pages, I have dipped my pail in a mere hundred seventy-five years of the stream of time. Its living waters rush on, filled with the universe's abundant life—including after-death appearances of saints and mystics. May such visits remind us not only that there is a greater life after life but that it is God's love which makes this so and sends us His messengers" (*Messengers*, p. 343).

After reading this book I am reminded of the words of Isaiah, "And when they say to you, 'Seek those who are mediums and wizards, who whisper and mutter,' should not a people seek their God? Should they seek the dead on behalf of the living? To the law and to the testimony! If they do not speak according to this word, it is because there is no light in them" (Isaiah 8:19, 20). It is very easy to see that the great final working of Satan through the work of his evil angels is beginning and generating a lot of interest in the "Christian" world. But the most influential and open spiritualistic phenomenon is happening with even greater recognition and deception.

The Marian Apparitions

I want the readers of this book to understand at the outset that I emphatically believe that just like Abraham, Isaac, Jacob, King David, and other noted individuals of Scripture, Mary, the mother of Jesus, is resting in her grave today, in a state of unconsciousness, waiting for the return of Jesus and the resurrection. I believe that while the so-called apparitions of Mary are genuine supernatural events, they are satanic deceptions. Accordingly, prayers to Mary, as in the rosary, and contact with Mary is really contact with Satan who is personating the concept of Mary in a grand deception that the real Mary knows nothing about. Unless you have been reading about this topic recently you will be amazed to discover that spiritualism is rapidly growing within the Catholic Church and other groups through the contacts of Mary at places all over the earth—including the United States.

During the fall of 1995 *The Thunder of Justice* was one of the best-selling books in the Catholic bookstores. During that time, on a visit to a Catholic bookstore in Wheaton, Maryland, I asked a clerk whether or not the church had any books on the time of the end, or the book of Revelation. The young clerk told me that one of the older men on the staff was a specialist in that area and he was called to serve me. The older gentleman showed me an area of books, perhaps 50 or so, that dealt with end times and the book of Revelation. I told him my reading time was limited, so I would appreciate his recommendation as to which of all the books was the best one. He quickly stated that *The Thunder of Justice* would be his choice, and that they could hardly keep copies of the book in the store. He told me that the most exciting thing happening in the church today was the apparitions of Mary. He offered to get tickets for me to travel with the bus caravan that would be traveling from the Washington, D.C., area to Conyers, Georgia, where on the thirteenth of each month the "Blessed Virgin Mother" comes in an apparition. Thanking him for the offer, I bought the book and went on my way. What I found in the book was 416 pages of spiritualism. Over 90 percent of it deals with the messages Mary has given to prepare the world for the second coming of Christ! The gentleman at the store also told me of the visits of Mary to Gianna Talone Sullivan at St. Joseph's Catholic Church in Emmitsburg, Maryland, not far from my home. I have since noted that on the Catholic forum on CompuServe there is a weekly posting of the messages of Mary from Emmitsburg!

The Thunder of Justice was written by Ted and Maureen Flynn, with a foreword written by Malachi Martin, the "former Jesuit" author of *Keys of This Blood*. The Flynns begin their book, "The Twentieth Century is witnessing a phenomenon that has simply grown too big for any reasonable person to ignore. The supernatural explodes in our midst on a near-daily basis. . . . Our Lady states that the reasons for her warnings are to prepare us for the Second Coming of Jesus Christ. It is being stated in very clear and concise terms. The Holy Trinity has sent Mary, the Mother of God, Mother of the Church, our mother, to warn us."

"The hardness of men's hearts makes it difficult to hear the trumpets of Heaven. Statues weep human tears and blood, the young prophesy, religious communities sprout up, messengers receive warnings, Mary raises up an army of the devout, and reported apparitions of Mary appear at a frequency never seen before in all of recorded history. . . . God is using apparitions (heavenly appearances) and locutions (interior messages) because other means have failed. . . . These apparitions have yielded a wealth of messages as well as remarkable fruits: millions of conversions world-wide, the reorientation of life towards the spiritual; and physical, mental, moral, and spiritual healings. An entire culture is arising spontaneously from the powerful shared experiences of those who have been touched by the unexpected and the supernatural. This culture is articulating itself through and by means of Marian centers, publishing houses, prayer groups, and alternative media networks. <u>Many persons come away convinced that in the eyes of God, they are forgiven and loved, and infinitely important for the fulfillment of Heaven's plan.</u>"

"Through the current deluge of apparitions and locutions, <u>the Blessed Virgin Mary is issuing a wake-up call.</u> . . . We are witnessing the intercession of the Blessed Virgin Mary, Queen of Heaven and true beacon for all Christians. It is now part of God's plan to have the 'Woman Clothed with the Sun' (Revelation 12:1) appear throughout the world, to offer people a safe haven in her Immaculate Heart" *(The Thunder of Justice,* pp. 3-5).

There are many Marian centers and shrines worldwide, reflecting a fascination that draws in many from pope to peasant. But to give you just an idea of the growing phenomenon, let's return to Flynn's book. "The messages given for the world originate with 'visionaries' from every part of the globe, from enormously varied educational backgrounds and social classes. For example, Italian priest Father Stefano Gobbi currently receives detailed locutions that have resulted in the formation of an international <u>55,000-member Marian Movement of Priests.</u>" Major centers around the world are visited by millions of "pilgrims" each year. Those of some note include Fatima, Portugal; Garabandal, Spain; and Medjugorje, [former Yugoslavia]. As an example of the interest, "In Medjugorje, in former Yugoslavia, six children (now young adults) in a rural village have been seeing Mary daily and receiving messages from the Blessed Mother since <u>1981. That remote village has been visited by an estimated 15 million pilgrims and 15,000 clergy.</u> It has been the hub of Marian devotion in these times. Whereas Fatima was the most significant apparition for the early part of the Twentieth Century, Medjugorje is meeting the spiritual needs of this generation in the latter part of this century. <u>His Eminence Joseph Cardinal Ratzinger</u> [remember he put his *imprimatur* on the new Catechism] has stated in *The Ratzinger Report,* 'One of the signs of our times is that the announcements of "Marian Apparitions" are multiplying all over the world' " *(ibid.,* pp. 7, 8).

In a rather strong ecumenical statement and at the same time a call to Rome, "Mary indicates, in various apparitions, that her messages are meant for all peoples, and not for Catholics alone. Mary says the Catholic Church has the fullest expression of the many gifts which have been given to mankind for salvation and the perseverance in battle against the devil's constant wiles; but she is the mother of everyone on earth" *(ibid.,* p. 9). From what we know of the prophecies about the little horn and the antichrist power, the fact that Mary supports the Catholic Church is indeed indication that "she" is really a satanic spirit. What's more she also is a medium for the dead to contact the living! The following experience is listed under the heading *"Father Ramon Andreu, S.J."* [Society of Jesus or Jesuit Order]:

"Father Ramon is the brother of the deceased Father Luis Andreu, the priest who saw the great miracle and later died of joy. Father Ramon received permission from his superiors to visit Garabandal. He also received authorization from the Apostolic Administrator of the diocese of Santander, Bishop Doreteo Fernandez. He was privileged to have witnessed more than 400 ecstasies. During his visits to the village, he kept a detailed record in his notebooks of everything he saw and heard. These notebooks represent some of the more valuable documentation, due to Father Ramon's keen analytical mind. The most startling event for Father Ramon was the revelation from the visionaries that they had conversed with his dead brother, Father Luis Andreu. Conchita's [one of the mediums or visionaries] diary entries of August 15, 16, stated the following.

"'A few days after Father Luis' death, the Blessed Virgin told us that we were going to talk to him . . . At eight or nine o'clock in the evening, the Blessed Virgin appeared to us smiling, very, very much, as usual. She said to the four of us, "Father Luis will come now and speak with you." A moment later, he came and called us one by one. We didn't see him at all but only heard his voice. It was exactly like the one he had on earth. When he had spoken for a while, giving us advice, he told us certain things for his brother, Father Ramon Maria Andreu. He taught us some words in French, German, and in English and he also taught us to pray in Greek.'

"Father Ramon was told precise details of his brother's funeral and details of his personal life that were unknown to anyone but himself. On another occasion, Father Luis gave a message for his mother: 'Be happy and content for I am in Heaven and I see you every day.' A message of great joy for his mother, who entered the convent, and a remarkable revelation about our loved ones who have gone to Heaven" *(ibid.,* pp. 166, 167).

This is big-time spiritualism—just as has been predicted in *The Great Controversy*. The Third Frog is taking giant leaps into end-time events.

Mary and Eschatology

Many times "Mary" has predicted that we are in the last decade of earth's history as we know it. She claims to be the Messenger of the Second Coming. And following this decade she predicts a long period of peace. Listen as she describes the shortness of time.

"Our Blessed Mother told us through Father Gobbi in a message given September 18, 1988, that we have a period of ten years—ten decisive years: 'In this period of ten years there will come to completion the time of the great tribulation, which has been foretold to you in Holy Scripture, before the Second Coming of Jesus" *(ibid., p. 12)*.

"Many Mariologists believe that the revelations of Our Lady of All Nations, also known as *Our Lady of All Peoples*, hold the key to these questions and foretell future events that the world will undergo before the year 2000" *(ibid., p. 51)*.

"On January 1, 1990, through Father Gobbi, Mary further stated she is the Mother of the Second Advent. '. . . I want to take you by the hand and accompany you on the threshold of this decade, which you are beginning precisely on this day. It is a very important decade. It is a period of time particularly marked by a strong presence of the Lord among you. During the last decade of your century, the events which I have foretold to you will have reached their completion" *(ibid., p. 56)*.

In another very interesting prediction Mary has used the lives of two very old people as time lines leading up to the Second Coming and the end of time.

"Fatima is perhaps the key apparition of the Twentieth Century. Many current messages from around the world are bringing our attention back to the Fatima events, most notably events in Russia. Mary, calling herself Queen of the Rosary, appeared to three shepherd children in the rural countryside of Portugal in 1917. This was the year of the Bolshevik revolution, and Mary entrusted vital messages for the people of the Twentieth Century to the three children, Lucia, Francesco, and Jacita. Before the Bolshevik revolution, she prophesied that Russia would 'spread her errors throughout the world.' She gave secrets to the children concerning the future of the Church and of mankind. <u>She told two of the children, Francesco and Jacinta, that they</u> <u>would soon be with her in Heaven (they died shortly thereafter) but</u> <u>that Lucia would live to see the fulfillment of all the messages. It</u> <u>should be noted that at the time of this writing [1993], Lucia is in her</u> <u>mid-eighties</u>" *(ibid.,* p. 24).

The Flynns continue with more details about Lucia—the only surviving child of the Fatima miracle. "Sister Lucia, as of this writing, is still alive. She has continued to receive messages from Our Blessed Mother. Lucia has been told that she will live to see the fulfillment of all the messages of Fatima. Lucy today [1993] is eighty-six years old." [Accordingly, in 1996 she is 89!]

The other time line is the life of the current pope, John Paul II. Conchita, one of the "visionaries" of Garabandal, Spain, has said, "After Pope John XXIII died, Our Lady told me, 'after Pope John, there will be three more Popes, one will reign only a short time, and then it will be the end of times.' When Pope Paul VI became Pope, Our Lady mentioned this to me again. She said 'Now there will be two more Popes and then it will be the end of times, but not the end of the world'" *(ibid.,* pp. 170, 171). It is interesting to note that most Catholics believe that when Christ comes the world will not be destroyed but rather enter into a long age of peace. As most readers well know, one of the last two popes, Pope John Paul I reigned only a short time, according to the prediction, from August 26, 1978, to September 28 of the same year—only 33 days! The current pope, John Paul II, is getting old and feeble—and he is the third pope since John XXIII!

Apparently, the devil is preparing the world for his personation of Christ just before the real Second Coming. But what about Sunday? Is Mary—the evil spirits—saying anything about the day of worship as we understand will happen just before the end? Remember the 10-point countdown?

Mary and the Day of Worship

Mary—remember she is really dead, so this is the devil speaking—is telling people to revere the Sunday sabbath. "One evening Our Lady appeared to a local farmer, Michael O'Donnell. She told him, <u>'preserve Sunday for prayer'</u>" *(ibid.,* p. 30).

In a series of apparitions from Lubbock, Texas, Mary said, " 'I did not come here to prepare you for the Feast of my Assumption but to prepare you for the coming of my Son, . . . for the final judgment. My dear little children, listen to me, your Mother' (July 11, 1988)."

Apparently bringing a message from God, she says, " 'I, the Lord God, shall make anew. . . . A new moon. . . . A new dawning and so forth, A new Sabbath. The old shall pass away as [will] their offenses against Me. Again the people will call Me their God and I shall have them again . . . and worship, once more. (August 1, 1988)' " *(ibid.,* p. 367).

And in a concluding chapter the Flynns list the central points of several of the Marian requests. She says, "This is the place where we see many of the root causes of our problems. It is the commandment of 'Keeping the Sabbath Holy.' In the Old Testament, not honoring this day was only one of several sins punishable by death. Although we are not living under the law of the Old Testament, there is widespread abuse all throughout the Christian Culture concerning the Sabbath. . . . And thus our problems have become so large we no longer even know where to start to find the solutions to our ills.

"God's intention for the Sabbath was a day of rest honoring God through worship, conversation, teaching and praise. Today if someone even bothers to go to church at all, Sunday will be an endless litany of recreation, television, athletic events, shopping, and errands all crammed together" *(ibid.,* p. 389).

The Popes and Mary

On November 1, 1950, Pope Pius XII made an allegedly infallible ex cathedra declaration in his Apostolic Constitution *Munificentissimus Deus* that "the immaculate Mother of God and ever Virgin Mary was at the end of her life assumed into heaven body and soul." In commenting on this, author Dave Hunt explains, "In the Constitution the pope claimed that the dogma of the assumption had been unanimously believed in the Church from the very beginning and that it was fully supported by Scripture. In fact, the dogma was unknown to the early church and is unsupported by Scripture. Such papal declarations simply responded to the popular sentiment of Catholics and contributed to the growing cult of Mary" (Dave Hunt, *A Woman Rides the Beast,* p. 444).

But what about the current pope? "No one is more convinced of the validity of the Fatima visitations than the present pope. Nor is anyone more devoted to Mary. John Paul II, who has 'dedicated himself and is Pontificate to Our Lady,' bears the M for Mary in his coat of arms; his personal motto, embroidered on the side of his robes in Latin, is *totus tuns sum Maria* (Mary, I'm all yours). The pope has unusual personal reasons for this special devotion. The assault upon his life occurred on May 13, 1981, the anniversary day of the Virgin's alleged first appearance on May 13, 1917, at Fatima, Portugal. In a vision during his convalescence she told him that she had spared his life for a special mission he must fulfill in bringing peace.

"Returning to the Vatican after his recovery, John Paul II prayed at the tombs of his immediate predecessors and declared, 'There could have been another tomb, but the blessed Virgin . . . has willed it otherwise.' He added gratefully and reverently, 'For everything that happened to me on that day, I felt that extraordinary Motherly protection and care, which turned out to be stronger than the deadly bullets.' Why, Hunt asks, would you need God when you have Mary's protection?

"The thankful pope made a pilgrimage to Fatima on May 13, 1982 [one year after the assassination attempt], where he 'prayed before the statue of Our Lady of Fatima. Thousands heard him speak and consecrate the world to Mary as she had requested' " *(ibid.,* pp. 458, 459).

It is interesting that nowhere in the Bible is there a prayer to Mary, not one instance of her miraculously helping anyone, nor any promises that she could or would. Yet "more Catholic prayers are offered to Mary and more attention and honor is given to her than to Christ and God combined. There are thousands of shrines to Mary around the world, with tens of millions of visitors annually, but only one small and scarcely known shrine to Christ located in Beauvoir, Quebec" *(ibid.,* p. 435).

Playing With Fire

God's messenger to the remnant was shown clearly the bewitching nature of spiritualism in the last days.

"There are few who have any just conception of the deceptive power of spiritualism and the danger of coming under its influence. Many tamper with it merely to gratify their curiosity. They have no real faith in it and would be filled with horror at the thought of yielding themselves to the spirit's control. <u>But they venture on the forbidden ground, and the mighty destroyer exercises his power upon them against their will.</u> Let them once be induced to submit their minds to his direction, and he holds them captive. <u>It is impossible, in their own strength, to break away from the bewitching, alluring spell. Nothing but the power of God, granted in answer to the earnest prayer of faith, can deliver these ensnared souls</u>" *(The Great Controversy,* p. 558). Sometimes those of us who have training and experience in the Scriptures have a desire to debate those who believe in spiritualism. Ellen White warns against this because in essence one then places himself in actual debate with the devil! She warns, "Men who bring these damnable heresies [the teachings of spiritualism] will dare those who teach the word of God to enter into controversy [debate] with them, and some who teach the truth have not had the courage to withstand a challenge from this class, who are marked characters in the word of God. [What should one do?] Some of our ministers have not had the moral courage to say to these men, 'God has warned us in His word in regard to you. He has given us a faithful description of your character and of these heresies which you hold.' <u>Some of our ministers, rather than give this class any occasion to triumph or to charge them with cowardice, have met them in open discussion.</u> **But in discussing with Spiritualists they do not meet man merely, but Satan and his angels.** They place themselves in communication with the powers of darkness, and encourage evil angels about them" *(Gospel Workers,* p. 194).

Early in our history as Adventists, one of our ministers, Moses Hull, decided to "straighten out" the spiritualists by engaging them in discussion. But Hull found himself fascinated by the power of spiritualism and was powerless to break away. Ellen White wrote to him, "Brother Hull, you were shown me under the soothing influence of a fascination which will prove fatal unless the spell is broken. You have parleyed with Satan, and reasoned with him, and tarried on forbidden ground, and have exercised your mind in things which were too great for you, and by indulging in doubts and unbelief have attracted evil angels around you, and driven from you the pure and holy angels of God. If you had steadfastly resisted Satan's suggestions and sought strength from God with a determined effort, you would have broken every fetter, driven back your spiritual foe, come closer to God, and triumphed in His name. I saw that it was presumption in you to go forth to meet a spiritualist when you were yourself enshrouded and bewildered by clouds of unbelief. You went to battle with Satan and his host without an armor, and you have been grievously wounded, and are insensible to your wound . . . If you do not arouse and recover yourself from the snare of the devil, you must perish" *(Testimonies for the Church,* vol. 1, p. 428). The final fate of Moses Hull is recorded by Arthur White, "The wavering and then the final apostasy of Moses Hull, a prominent evangelist who in the fall surrendered to the agents of Satan, was a difficult and sad experience. He preached an evangelistic sermon on the night of September 20, 1863, and then within a few weeks joined the forces of the Spiritualists" *(Ellen G. White Biography,* vol. 2, p. 53).

Over the years many have felt that the phenomenon associated with spiritualism could be explained as some cheap magic trick. However, the Bible indicates that the world is deceived by the signs which he [the second beast] had power to do. (Revelation 13:14) This is referring to the United States—the land beast—in its "dragon mode." "Many will be ensnared through the belief that spiritualism is a merely human imposture; when brought face to face with manifestations which they cannot but regard as supernatural, they will be deceived, and will be led to accept them as the great power of God" *(The Great Controversy,* p. 553).

When confronted with the supernatural many are inclined to accept it as of divine origin and accept the message given as of higher authority than scripture. (See *Patriarchs and* Prophets, p. 684.)

Spiritualism is the masterpiece of Satan's deceptions. It contacts people at their most vulnerable emotional level. "Evil angels come in the form of those loved ones [who have died], and relate incidents connected with their lives, and perform acts which they performed while living. In this way they lead persons to believe that the dead friends are angels, hovering over them, and communicating with them. These evil angels, who assume to be the deceased friends, are regarded with a certain idolatry, and with many their word has greater weight than the word of God" (Ellen G. White, *Signs of the Times,* August 26, 1889). The Bible predicts that people will reject the truth and give heed to seducing spirits and doctrines of devils (1 Timothy 4:1). The book *Messengers* notes that over the past 175 years these great events of contacts with the dead have occurred with increasing regularity. The Marian centers have become shrines to millions.

Spiritualism's Express Train to Hell

Apparently, the devil is trying to deceive the world and catch millions in his grasp before the latter rain and the loud cry are given. Ellen White was shown a vision of the rapid spread of spiritualism and the calmness of those who are deceived as they ride the devil's train. "I saw the rapidity with which this delusion [spiritualism] was spreading. A train of cars was shown me, going with the speed of lightning. The angel bade me look carefully. I fixed my eyes upon the train. It seemed that the whole world was on board. Then he showed me the conductor, a fair, stately person, whom all the passengers looked up to and reverenced. I was perplexed and asked my attending angel who it was. He said, 'It is Satan. He is the conductor, in the form of an angel of light. He has taken the world captive. They are given over to strong delusions, to believe a lie that they may be damned. His agent, the highest in order next to him, is the engineer, and others of his agents are employed in different offices as he may need them, and they are all going with lightning speed to perdition" (*Early Writings,* p. 263).

We need not be on the train to hell. God has made ample provision through His Word for us to know the truth. He has warned us about the devil and his deceptions. We can see that the devil is doing exactly what we were told he would do—use his evil angels to pretend to speak through the dead. And the world is falling for this deception in a big way. The train is filling up and about to leave the station for the last wild run. Don't get on that train. It's the wrong one!

CHAPTER 11

The Coming Millennium of Peace

Any examination of miracles and spiritualism in the Catholic Church takes on a new significance in association with the coming millennium. Great efforts are being made to bring about Christian unity by the year 2000. Sounding as fresh as if written by a contemporary commentator is this prediction given by Ellen White in *The Great Controversy:*

"The line of distinction between professed Christians and the ungodly is now hardly distinguishable. Church members love what the world loves and are ready to join with them, and Satan determines to unite them in one body and thus strengthen his cause by sweeping all into the ranks of spiritualism. Papists, who boast of miracles as a certain sign of the true church, will be readily deceived by this wonder-working power; and Protestants, having cast away the shield of truth, will also be deluded. Papists, Protestants, and worldlings will alike accept the form of godliness without the power, and they will see in this union a grand movement for the conversion of the world and the ushering in of the long expected millennium" *(The Great Controversy,* pp. 588, 589).

The World Looks to the Year 2000

The *Washington Post Magazine* of January 1, 1995, had a cover story titled "The End." The nine-page article by Peter Carlson discussed the growing agitation over the approach of the year 2000 and the turn of the decade, century, and millennium. Carlson quoted the special 1992 issue of *Time* magazine that discussed the millennium that "hyped the year 2000 as if it were, well, the Second Coming."

The January 1996 *Inside the Vatican* magazine listed the pope's travel plans for the year with trips to Central and South America, France, and other countries and noted that "There is an additional journey the Pope longs to make: to Jerusalem, in preparation for the Great Jubilee of the Year 2000. The trip would include stops in Nazareth, Bethlehem, Mt. Sinai and perhaps also in Cairo and Damascus.

"The Pope is also expected to fix the dates soon for three continental Synods of Bishops for the Americas, for Asia and for Australia. These gatherings are intended to prepare entire regions of the Church for the challenges of the coming millennium."

The article concluded by observing, "All in all, then, 1996 offers a very full schedule for a pontiff whose eyes are now focused on the year 2000, and on the final four years of preparations before the new millennium begins."

On Wednesday, January 17, 1996, while speaking at the weekly general audience, Pope John Paul II called on all Christians to undergo a change of heart and seek greater unity as the Jubilee Year 2000 approaches. That same day the pope met with Shimon Shetreet, the Israeli Minister for Religious Affairs. Shetreet said that his two-day visit to Rome was important both at the governmental and spiritual level. He spoke about his 20-minute audience with the "Holy Father" saying, "We expressed the great appreciation for the connection the Pope has made between Rome and Jerusalem in the celebrations of the Jubilee of the Year 2000, especially that Jerusalem will be included as a place of ceremonies in addition to Rome."

Shetreet extended an invitation to the pope to visit the Holy City of Jerusalem, saying he expects it could take place in 1997 and that "it will be viewed as an encouragement, as an act of dynamic influence in the peace process" *(Inside the Vatican,* February 1996).

Unity and Celebration

There are clearly two recurring themes in the pope's preparations for the Great Jubilee of the Year 2000. First is unity—not only among all Christians but also of the other world religions. The second is the great celebrations planned for Mount Sinai, Jerusalem, and Rome.

These two factors, along with the "miracles," need to be kept in mind as we look at a very significant vision given to Ellen White in the great controversy series. On Sunday, January 20, 1884, while spending a few days at the St. Helena Sanitarium, Mrs. White wrote a letter to two of the leading ministers of the denomination, George I. Butler, president of the General Conference, and S. N. Haskell, describing the vision that she had seen just two nights before. She recalled:

"I saw our people in great distress, weeping and praying, pleading the sure promises of God, while the wicked were all around us, mocking us, and threatening to destroy us. They ridiculed our feebleness, they mocked at the smallness of our numbers, and taunted us with words calculated to cut deep. They charged us with taking an independent position from all the rest of the world. They cut off our resources so that we could not buy or sell, and referred to our abject poverty and stricken condition. They could not see how we could live without the world; we were dependent upon the rest of the world, and we must concede to the customs, practices, and laws of the world or go out of it. If we were the only people in the world whom the Lord favored the appearances were awfully against us. They declared that they had the truth, that miracles were among them, that angels from heaven talked with them, and walked with them, that great power, and signs and wonders were performed among them, and **this was the Temporal Millennium,** which they had been expecting so long. **The whole world was converted and in harmony with the Sunday law,** and this little feeble people stood out in defiance of the laws of the land, and the laws of God, and claimed to be the only ones right on the earth" *(Maranatha,* p. 209). Do you realize that in this vision shared with the General Conference president, Ellen White puts the Sunday law at the beginning of the Millennium! Now you see why I believe that "Sunday is Coming!"

The Bible View of the Millennium

In the past, some have wondered why it was important to know what the Bible teaches about the millennium. Their reasoning was that it didn't make any difference because one could be saved either way. However, now you can begin to see why it is important to know what the Bible teaches: to have "proof texts," if you please. Having this biblical knowledge is the only way to keep from being deceived! So many today are teaching that the world will get better and better and that Christ will reign on the earth during the 1,000 years of peace. This is why the devil's personation of Christ will be so convincing to so many. The Bible, however, teaches that the second coming of Christ will be the end of this world as we know it. It will be desolate during that period of time—the wicked are dead and the righteous are in heaven with Christ.

"The millennium is a great sabbath of rest, both for the earth and for God's people. For six thousand years the earth and its inhabitants have been groaning under the curse of sin. The millennium, the seventh thousand, will be a sabbath rest and release; for, says the prophet concerning the land, 'as long as she lay desolate she kept *sabbath.'* 2 Chronicles 36:21.

"The millennium is the closing period of God's great week of time—a great sabbath of rest to the earth and to the people of God. It follows the close of the gospel age, and precedes the setting up of the everlasting kingdom of God on earth. It comprehends what in the Scriptures is frequently spoken of as 'the day of the Lord.' It is bounded on each end by a resurrection.

"Its beginning is marked by the pouring out of the seven last plagues, the second coming of Christ, the resurrection of the righteous dead, the binding of Satan, and the translation of the saints to heaven; and its close, by the descent of the New Jerusalem, with Christ and the saints, from heaven, the resurrection of the wicked dead, the loosing of Satan, and the final destruction of the wicked.

"During the one thousand years the earth lies desolate; Satan and his angels are confined here; and the saints, with Christ, sit in judgment on the wicked, preparatory of their final punishment.

"The wicked dead are then raised; Satan is loosed for a little season, and he and the host of the wicked encompass the camp of the saints and the Holy City, when fire comes down from God out of heaven and devours them. The earth will be cleansed by the same fire that destroys the wicked, and, renewed, becomes the eternal abode of the saints.

"The millennium is one of 'the ages to come.' Its close will mark the beginning of the new-earth state" *(Bible Readings for the Home,* current paper edition, p. 333).

I believe that one's relationship with Jesus is primary and that this relationship is enhanced by a study of Scripture to determine the will of God and the truth about His dealings with mankind. The world is rushing to prepare for the Great Jubilee of the Year 2000. The "spring-time" of earth's history—an age of peace when the righteous rule the earth. The place to be during the 1000 years—the millennium—is in heaven, not here. But, before that time, we have some work to do and some challenging experiences to go through.

CHAPTER 12

Preaching the
Sabbath More Fully

The great Protestant Reformation began the road back to biblical Christianity. Martin Luther and his fellow Reformers were almost to the last man Roman Catholic priests in their early lives. Coming as they did from the Roman Church, having themselves once believed and advocated her doctrines, it could hardly be expected that they would discern all of the errors of the church. It was their work to break the fetters of Rome, and to give the Bible to the world. There were many important truths which they failed to discover, and many errors which they failed to renounce. Most of them, for example, continued to keep Sunday as the day of worship. They did not regard it as possessing any divine authority, but they believed that it should be observed as a generally accepted day of worship.

So much progress in uncovering biblical truth has been made and yet at the same time, incredibly, many are taking the road back to the errors of Rome. But as we near the close of time the Bible states that a remnant will appear to keep the commandments and have the faith of Jesus. (See Revelation 12:17; 14:12.) The Bible calls the last message of God, given to the world through His faithful ones, "the three angels" of Revelation 14:6-12. The first angel calls in a loud voice with the everlasting gospel—the good news of righteousness by faith alone in the merits of Jesus Christ to all the world. It is a message restoring worship of the Creator-God. Of course God expects a loving response of obedience—including Sabbathkeeping.

The second angel warns that Babylon is fallen. Since the message is given at the end of time, the Babylon referred to is the anti-Christ power—the false religious system.

The third angel warns against the mark of the beast, gives a warning to avoid the seven last plagues, and states the fate of the wicked. He describes God's true saints as patient commandment keepers, who are full of faith in Jesus.

Then Revelation 18 reveals that the second and third angels' messages will be given again—just before Jesus comes. The message is described as being given with great power and lighting the earth with its glory. I believe that this Revelation 18 message is beginning to be given right now. But its full proclamation will be far beyond what we can even imagine now.

The message of Revelation 18 is so important that it is represented as being given with great authority by an angel from heaven.

"After these things I saw another angel coming down from heaven, having great authority, and the earth was illuminated with his glory. And he cried mightily with a loud voice, saying, 'Babylon the great is fallen, is fallen, and has become a dwelling place of demons, a prison for every foul spirit, and a cage for every unclean and hated bird!

" 'For all the nations have drunk of the wine of the wrath of her fornication, the kings of the earth have committed fornication with her, and the merchants of the earth have become rich through the abundance of her luxury.'

"And I heard another voice from heaven saying, 'Come out of her, my people, lest you share in her sins, and lest you receive of her plagues' " (Revelation 18:1-4).

Adventists have understood that this "great outpouring of God's Spirit" will come in the form of the latter rain that enables God's people to give the message of Revelation 18 with a loud voice. I wondered whether this chapter belonged after a discussion of persecution, because it seems that persecution brings the church to the place where it is ready to give the Revelation 18 message. The reason is very basic. When persecution comes, those who are not really rooted in God's Word or fully committed to Him will leave immediately. Those who remain are willing to suffer for God, if necessary, to give the message. Then God will pour out His Spirit in a manner never before experienced—greater than at Pentecost! But because there is a work for us now, even before the latter rain, this chapter and its message is important before the persecution comes.

The Power of Pentecost

The disciples prepared themselves for God's promised blessing. "Before the day of Pentecost they met together, and put away all differences. They were of one accord. They believed Christ's promise that blessing would be given, and they prayed in faith. They did not ask for a blessing for themselves merely; they were weighted with the burden for the salvation of souls. The gospel was to be carried to the uttermost parts of the earth, and they claimed the endowment of power that Christ had promised. Then it was that the Holy Spirit was poured out, and thousands were converted in a day.

"So it may be now. Instead of man's speculations, let the word of God be preached. Let Christians put away their dissensions, and give themselves to God for the saving of the lost. Let them in faith ask for the blessing and it will come" *(The Desire of Ages,* p. 827).

Studying the topic of the outpouring of the Spirit it is evident that there are two results or, even purposes, to it. One is to perfect of character of the individual recipient and the second is to equip the recipient to work more efficiently in the work of Christ. In fact we are told, "All who consecrate soul, body, and spirit to God will be constantly receiving a new endowment of physical and mental power. The inexhaustible supplies of heaven are at their command. Christ gives them the breath of His own spirit, the life of His own life. The Holy Spirit puts forth its highest energies to work in heart and mind. The grace of God enlarges and multiplies their faculties, and every perfection of the divine nature comes to their assistance in the work of saving souls. Through cooperation with Christ they are complete in Him, and in their human weakness they are enabled to do the deeds of Omnipotence" *(ibid.).*

Beyond Pentecost

My inspiration for this chapter is the understanding that at some point in time the work will explode around the world. We will then be able to give the message in a clear and articulate manner. Many who have heard it before as well as many who have never heard before will come under conviction.

But when will all this happen? We have been told, "I saw that God had children who do not see and keep the Sabbath. They have not rejected the light upon it. And at the commencement of the time of trouble, we were filled with the Holy Ghost as we went forth and <u>proclaimed the Sabbath more fully</u>" *(Early Writings,* p. 85).

Ellen White adds, "The work of this angel [of Revelation 18] comes in at the right time to join in the last great work of the third angel's message as it swells to a loud cry. And the people of God are thus prepared to stand in the hour of temptation, which they are soon to meet. I saw a great light resting upon them, and they united to fearlessly proclaim the third angel's message" *(ibid.,* p. 277).

As I have stated before, God wants people to know that His coming is near. The only ones taken by surprise will be those who will not listen to or believe the message. We are told in Amos that He will do nothing without revealing it to His servants the prophets. (Amos 3:7) God could use angels to finish the work, but He has chosen to use people with messages from angels. The description of their work is very inspiring. "Servants of God, with their faces lighted up and shining with holy consecration, will hasten from place to place to proclaim the message from heaven. By thousands of voices, all over the earth, the warning will be given. Miracles will be wrought, the sick will be healed, and signs and wonders will follow the believers. Satan also works, with lying wonders, even bringing fire down from heaven in the sight of men. Revelation 13:13. Thus the inhabitants of the earth will be brought to take their stand.

"The message will be carried not so much by argument as by the deep conviction of the Spirit of God. The arguments have been presented. The seed has been sown, and now it will spring up and bear fruit. The publications distributed by missionary workers have exerted their influence, yet many whose minds were impressed have been prevented from fully comprehending the truth or from yielding obedience. Now the rays of light penetrate everywhere, the truth is seen in its clearness, and the honest children of God sever the bands which have held them. Family connections, church relations, are powerless to stay them now. Truth is more precious than all besides. Notwithstanding the agencies combined against the truth, a large number take their stand upon the Lord's side" *(The Great Controversy,* p. 612).

There are several reasons why this message goes with such power and conviction and has the results described. First, time is short and God wants everyone to be ready for His return. Second, the people of God are eager to finish the work and meet their Saviour. And, third, when those who hear our message see that what we have been predicting for so many years is now actually taking place it will give great credence to our presentations. When Sunday law talk begins in a public way it will have a polarizing effect. "Heretofore those who presented the truths of the third angel's message have often been regarded as mere alarmists. Their predictions that religious intolerance would gain control in the United States, that church and state would unite to persecute those who keep the commandments of God, have been pronounced groundless and absurd. It has been confidently declared that this land could never become other than what it has been—the defender of religious freedom. But as the question of enforcing Sunday observance is widely agitated, the event so long doubted and disbelieved is seen to be approaching, **and the third message will produce an effect which it could not have had before**" (ibid., p. 605).

We all know that there are many people, many living in close proximity to our churches, who know nothing about us or our message. There are thousands who sincerely believe that Sunday is the Sabbath of the fourth commandment. Others don't really have a belief about the Sabbath because it was just not that important to them. As far as they are concerned, Sunday must be the right day of worship, just because most Christians have observed that day for hundreds of years. All these categories will hear a clear and concise presentation of the Sabbath as the sign of God's people.

The Loud Cry Message

Remember, the loud cry message has two distinct parts: Babylon is fallen and Come out of her My people. God still has people in the churches of Babylon and before the close of probation they must be called out so that they don't receive the wrath of God in the plagues. "When Jesus began His public ministry, He cleansed the Temple from its sacrilegious profanation. Among the last acts of His ministry was the second cleansing of the Temple. So in the last work for the warning of the world, two distinct calls are made to the churches. The second angel's message is, 'Babylon is fallen, is fallen, that great city, because she made all nations drink of the wine of the wrath of her fornication.' (Rev. 14:8) [cf. Rev. 18:2, 3]. And in the loud cry of the third angel's message a voice is heard from heaven saying, 'Come out of her, my people, that ye be not partakers of her sins, and that ye receive not of her plagues . . .' (Rev. 18:4, 5)" *(Selected Messages,* vol. 2, p. 118).

Speaking about the errors of another belief system is just not politically correct in today's society. However, for the sake of God's people who are caught up in erroneous churches, the message must be given in a positive and loving way. Some may think this message too divisive or that others may think they are prejudiced and refuse to give the message. But it will be given and the results will be awesome. "The message of the third angel will be proclaimed. As the time comes for it to be given with greatest power, the Lord will work through humble instruments, leading the minds of those who consecrate themselves to His service. The laborers will be qualified rather by the unction of His Spirit than by the training of literary institutions. Men of faith and prayer will be constrained to go forth with holy zeal, **declaring the words which God gives them. The sins of Babylon will be laid open.** The fearful results of enforcing the observances of the church by civil authority, the inroads of spiritualism, the stealthy but rapid progress of the papal power—**all will be unmasked.** By these solemn warnings the people will be stirred. Thousands upon thousands will listen who have never heard words like these. In amazement they hear the testimony that Babylon is the church, fallen because of her errors and sins, because of her rejection of the truth sent to her from heaven" *(The Great Controversy,* pp. 606, 607).

What kind of people will give this message? As ever in times of reform and spiritual danger, God uses humble men and women of faith and prayer. He does not need skillful debaters. "The world can only be warned by seeing those who believe the truth sanctified by the truth, acting upon high and holy principles, showing in a high, elevated sense, the line of demarcation between those who keep the commandments of God, and those who trample them under their feet. The sanctification of the Spirit signalizes the difference between those who have the seal of God, and those who keep a spurious rest day. When the test comes, it will be clearly shown what the mark of the beast is. It is the keeping of Sunday" (Ellen White, *Bible Training School,* December 1, 1903). It is interesting that part of the testimony at the end will be the character of the children of God. They act on high and holy principles. They do not desire to kill those who believe differently than they do. They have that quality that Jesus spoke of when He was on earth, "Love one another, as I have loved you" (John 15:12). They have a genuine, sincere interest in saving others. People will be able to discern the peace of God, the very light of heaven, shining in their faces.

Doors will be opened to present the truth about the Sabbath in high places. Back in the 1890s when the Sunday laws were being enforced in various states Ellen White stated, "The Lord is far ahead of us, He has permitted this Sunday question to be pressed to the front, in order that the Sabbath of the fourth commandment may be presented before legislative assemblies. The leading men of the nation are to have their attention called to the testimony of God's word in favor of the true Sabbath. If the testimony does not convert them, it is a witness that will condemn them. The Sabbath question is the great testing question for this time" *(Review and Herald,* February 7, 1893).

The Sabbath to Be Restored

Many Bible passages convey the promise of a remnant returning to the Lord. One of the things that the remnant will do is restore the Sabbath. "Those from among you shall build the old waste places; you shall raise up the foundations of many generations; and you shall be called Repairer of the Breach, the Restorer of Streets to Dwell In. If you turn away your foot from the Sabbath, from doing your pleasure on My holy day, and call the Sabbath a delight, the holy day of the Lord honorable, and shall honor Him, not doing your own ways, nor finding your own pleasure, nor speaking your own words, then you shall delight yourself in the Lord; and I will cause you to ride on the high hills of the earth, and feed you with the heritage of Jacob your father. The mouth of the Lord has spoken" (Isaiah 58:12-14).

Another version says, "You will partake of Jacob's heritage." What is the heritage of Jacob? Hebrews 11 gives the answer. Speaking of Abraham the Bible says, "By faith he sojourned in the land of promise as in a foreign country, dwelling in tents with Isaac and Jacob, the heirs with him of the same promise; **for he waited for the city which has foundations, whose builder and maker is God"**

(Hebrews 11:9, 10). What an awesome thought! Those who restore the Sabbath will inherit the city built by God!

It was a new thought to me that not only do we preach the Sabbath more fully but we also understand it better at the end. Because, "When the refreshing and latter rain shall come from the presence of the Lord and the glory of His power, we shall know what it is to be fed with the heritage of Jacob and ride upon the high places of the earth. Then shall we see the Sabbath more in its importance and glory." And apparently it continues to grow in importance and glory! "But we shall not see it in all its glory and importance until the covenant of peace is made with us at the voice of God, and the pearly gates of the New Jerusalem are thrown open and swing back on their glittering hinges, and the glad and joyful voice of the lovely Jesus is heard richer than any music that ever fell on mortal ear bidding us enter" *(Selected Messages,* vol. 3, p. 388).

And so when many Protestants are making their way back to Rome we have a message to give. "Let us show people where we are in prophetic history, and seek to arouse the spirit of true Protestantism, awakening the world to a sense of the value of the privileges of religious liberty so long enjoyed" *(Christian Service,* p. 163). We are to lift up Christ as the One altogether lovely. The One who has been revealed in the Old and New Testaments as the Saviour of the world.

Martin Luther changed the world with his pen at the very dawn of printing technology. The communication tools available today are capable of flashing the Word around the world in moments. Our options include: television, radio, telephone, computer, fax, e-mail, the Internet, satellites, and more. The devil knows that the work will be finished in a mighty way and so he works diligently to fill the technological pathways with garbage and diversions. Worst of all, however, is his attempt to deceive the honest seekers for truth with his false revival.

The False Latter Rain

We are counseled to be vigilant. Satan hopes to deceive, if possible, even the very elect. Listen to the warning: "I saw that God has honest children among nominal Adventists and the fallen churches, and before the plagues shall be poured out, ministers and people will be called out from these churches and will gladly receive the truth. Satan knows this; and before the loud cry of the third angel is given, he raises an excitement in these religious bodies, that those who have rejected the truth may think that God is with them. **He hopes to deceive the honest** and lead them to think that God is still working for the churches. But the light will shine, and all who are honest will leave the fallen churches, and take their stand with the remnant" *(Early Writings,* p. 261).

At the risk of being misunderstood I want to give what I believe could be an example of this happening now. I know from reading many articles about the Promise Keepers organization and movement and talking with individuals who have attended the meetings that "life-changing experiences" are taking place in their lives.

The idea of Promise Keepers began in the minds of University of Colorado head coach, Bill McCartney, and a few close friends in 1990. They had a dream of seeing a football stadium filled with committed Christian men who would honor Christ and uphold Christian principles. The dream began to come true in 1993 when over 50,000 men gathered at Folsom Field in Boulder, Colorado, for the first Promise Keepers rally. In 1994 there were similar rallies in six U.S. cities with 280,000 men in attendance. Since then Promise Keepers has grown into a 300-staff operation with a $64 million budget in 1995 and more than 725,000 men attended the 13 conferences in 1995. Ambitious plans are being laid to bring about "Biblical Unity" of denominations and races. Major stories about Promise Keepers have appeared in *Christianity Today* (Feb. 6, 1995), *Time* magazine (Nov. 6, 1995), and *Our Sunday Visitor* (Dec. 31, 1995).

The year 1996 started off with a gathering of nearly 40,000 ministers at the Promise Keepers conference in Atlanta's Georgia Dome on February 13-15. Over 20 conferences are planned in stadiums across the U.S. in 1996. In addition, leader Bill McCartney is calling for 1 million men with Christian commitments to go to a Washington, D.C., rally in September of 1997 to show their concern for the nation's spiritual condition. This all sounds great on the surface. What is my concern?

My concern is the major emphasis on "Biblical Unity" that overlooks individual and church interpretations of Scripture and the emphasis on the "verbal inspiration of the Bible." This is evident in promise number 6 and statement of faith number 2. With regard to the inspiration concern, it puzzles me how one can say that "every word is inspired by God" and reject His sign of allegiance—the Sabbath. There is great emphasis on love, but Jesus Himself said, "If you love Me, keep My commandments" (John 14:15). In addition, we know that, "To the law and to the testimony! If they do not speak according to this word, it is because there is no light in them" (Isaiah 8:20). I know that there are thousands of sincere and honest men involved with this organization, but these are the very ones whom the devil is seeking to deceive.

Let's consider some important aspects of this organization that is more than doubling every year. The February 19 and the March 4, 1996, issues of *The National and International Religion Report* both gave full front page coverage to the ministers' Promise Keepers meeting in Atlanta. A few excerpts follow: One of the largest gatherings of ministers in history—nearly 40,000, led Promise Keepers' founder Bill McCartney to say, "This is Biblical unity, this is historic stuff." "All the major denominations were represented, including the Catholic Church." "Many of the ministers who attended are describing the conference as a spiritual high-water mark for themselves and possibly a turning point for the church." One pastor said, "I've seen nothing like it in 35 years of ministry." Another said the conference was "a defining development in the life of the church." One speaker stated, "We are on the verge of the greatest spiritual revolution in the history of the church, and you are called to be a part of it."

"Preachers [were] on their knees after Chuck Swindoll's sermon on brokenness and repentance, a few face-down on the floor, weeping and praying." There were "sustained cheers and applause for Max Lucado's wall-razing treatise on biblical unity, 'Unity matters to God. It is a priority item for Him and should be for us,' he said." There was an entire emotional session healing racial tensions. And "Of equal concern to McCartney are denominational differences that impede unity. 'I am not saying that we should dismantle our denominations and ignore our distinctives, but we should concentrate on the 95 percent where we agree,' he told reporters . . . At the final session, he invited everyone who could partake in communion without violating his conscience to do so as a sign of unity in Christ. He noted the presence of Catholic priests and others in the assembly with views that might bar them from taking part. Hardly anyone left the building."

By mentioning the Promise Keepers organization, I in no way believe that anyone in the organization is other than a sincere and honest person with the highest motives and concern for the problems in the family and society at large. The fact remains, however, that it takes more than enthusiasm and emotional demonstrations to bring about true biblical unity. The unity Christ spoke of was led by His Spirit that would guide us "into all truth." Let's pray for these committed men that they will get into God's Word and find the Way everlasting. Let's pray that their commitment and the organization is not hijacked by the Christian Coalition or the ecumenical rush that covers gross error.

Our Challenge

"The end is near, stealing upon us stealthily, imperceptibly, like the noiseless approach of a thief in the night. May the Lord grant that we shall no longer sleep as do others, but that we shall watch and be sober. <u>The truth is soon to triumph gloriously, and all who now choose to be laborers together with God, will triumph with it.</u> The time is short; the night soon cometh when no man can work" *(Evangelism,* p. 692). Prayer and the study of God's Word is essential to prepare us to stand firm and true to the end.

CHAPTER 13

Standing Firm Through Persecution

O ne cannot study the topic of end times and Sunday laws without discovering that difficult times are just ahead. A few biblical examples include Daniel 12:1: "At that time Michael shall stand up . . . and there shall be a time of trouble, such as never was since there was a nation, even to that time. <u>And at that time your people shall be delivered, every one who is found written in the book.</u>" Another is Matthew 24:9-13: "Then they will deliver you up to tribulation and kill you, and you will be hated by all nations for My name's sake. And then many will be offended, will betray one another, and will hate one another. Then many false prophets will rise up and deceive many. And because lawlessness will abound the love of many will grow cold. <u>But he who endures to the end shall be saved.</u>" Matthew 5:11, 12 gives another insight: "Blessed are you when they revile and persecute you, and say all kinds of evil against you falsely for My sake. Rejoice and be exceedingly glad, <u>for great is your reward in heaven,</u> for so they persecuted the prophets who were before you." Revelation 2:10 encourages us, "Do not fear any of those things which you are about to suffer. Indeed, the devil is about to throw some of you into prison, that you may be tested, and you will have tribulation ten days. <u>Be faithful until death, and I will give you the crown of life.</u>"

It is interesting to note that each of these verses has two parts. The prediction by God that persecution would come and then the promise of God's care for the faithful ones. But still the questions persist. Why does God allow persecution? Why will there be greater persecution just before Jesus comes again? Why did faithful followers of God like Daniel and John the revelator have to endure persecution in their old age? Why? Why? Why? Where is God during all of this? And, yes, there are answers to these questions. We can know the whys of persecution and how to prepare for it.

Persecution in its various forms is the development of a principle which will exist as long as Satan exists, and Christianity has vital power. All who serve God will encounter great opposition from Satan and his hosts. And now the devil is even more determined "because he knows that he has a short time" (Revelation 12:12).

Some don't believe that there will be persecution at the end. However, God points out that "all who live godly in Christ Jesus shall suffer persecution" (2 Timothy 3:12). As we study the "when it will come" we need also the "how to prepare for it." Obviously, there are some questions as to the "why" of suffering and persecution that we will have to ask the Lord in heaven. Ellen White noted, "The mysterious providence which permits the righteous to suffer persecution at the hand of the wicked has been a cause of great perplexity to many who are weak in faith. Some are even ready to cast away their confidence in God because He suffers the basest of men to prosper, while the best and purest are afflicted and tormented by their cruel power. How, it is asked, can One who is just and merciful, and who is also infinite in power, tolerate such injustice and oppression? This is a question with which we have nothing to do. God has given us sufficient evidence of His love, and we are not to doubt His goodness because we cannot understand the workings of His providence" (*The Great Controversy,* p. 47).

As He looked to the future and saw that His beloved disciples would suffer trials and persecution, Jesus said, "Remember the word that I said to you, 'A servant is not greater than his master.' If they persecuted Me, they will also persecute you" (John 15:20). Jesus suffered terribly at the hands of His creatures. So when we suffer we are in excellent company because Jesus suffered for us. This may be one of the reasons that we are counseled to study the life of Christ, especially the closing scenes of His life. "There was never one who walked among men more cruelly slandered than the Son of man. He was derided and mocked because of His unswerving obedience to the principles of God's holy law. They hated Him without a cause. Yet He stood calmly before His enemies, declaring that reproach is a part of the Christian's legacy, counseling His followers how to meet the arrows of malice, bidding them not to faint under persecution" *(Sons and Daughters of God,* p. 308).

Christian Against Christian

To one not familiar with the issues in the great controversy it would seem reasonable that the persecution of God's faithful would come from the lower element—the real wicked—the hoodlums, criminals, gangs, drug dealers, and the mafia. But as history records in the past, the Bible predicts that the most severe persecution will come from other "Christians." "Christ forewarned His disciples of this, saying: 'These things have I spoken unto you, that ye should not be offended. They shall put you out of the synagogues; yea, the time cometh, that whosoever killeth you will think that he doeth God service. And these things will they do unto you, because they have not known the Father, nor Me. But these things I have told you, that when the time shall come, ye may remember that I told you of them.' It is not the world, who make no profession, from whom the persecution comes. It is those who profess to be doing God service who manifest the most bitter hatred" (Ellen White, *Signs of the Times,* September 2, 1897).

For several centuries during the time of the early church Satan persecuted the church through paganism. But when the church compromised with paganism, making a pretense of serving God, it became a more dangerous and cruel foe. The Roman Catholic Church believes that God has committed to it the right to control conscience and to define and punish heresy. This is one of the most deeply rooted of the papal errors. What will it be like at the end? "The persecutions of Protestants by Romanism, by which the religion of Jesus Christ was almost annihilated, will be more than rivaled when Protestantism and popery are combined" *(Maranatha,* p. 194).

The persecution predicted in the Bible and the Spirit of Prophecy is far more than just stress and anxiety. In some cases there will be torture and death. "As the defenders of the truth refuse to honor the Sunday—sabbath, some of them will be thrust into prison, some will be exiled, some will be treated as slaves. To human wisdom all this now seems impossible; but as the restraining Spirit of God shall be withdrawn from men, and they shall be under the control of Satan, who hates the divine precepts, there will be strange developments. The heart can be very cruel when God's fear and love are removed" *(The Great Controversy,* p. 608).

Some will lose property. Many will suffer want when it is decreed that God's Sabbathkeepers can no longer buy and sell. But "of all persecution the hardest to bear is variance in the home, the estrangement of dearest earthly friends" *(The Desire of Ages,* p. 357). Jesus predicted that this would happen to some. "A man's foes will be those of his own household. He who loves father or mother more than Me is not worthy of Me. And he who loves son or daughter more than Me is not worthy of Me" (Matthew 10:36, 37). We will have to make the decision right now that there is no possession or person worth trading for eternal life. Even if we face death, so what? Jesus said, "He who loses his life for My sake will find it" (Matthew 10:39).

The primary reason persecution will come is that God's faithful people will not conform to the command to violate the Sabbath of the Bible. "The time is coming when God's people will feel the hand of persecution because they keep holy the seventh day . . . But God's people are to stand firm for Him. And the Lord will work in their behalf, showing plainly that He is the God of gods" *(Christian Service,* p. 156). We can see that this time is not far away when we consider the evidence of cooperation between the United States and the Vatican that has been given in this book. And we know that "When the churches of our land, uniting upon such points of faith as are held by them in common, shall influence the State to enforce their decrees and sustain their institutions, then will Protestant America have formed an image of the Roman hierarchy. Then the true church will be assailed by persecution, as were God's ancient people" *(The Spirit of Prophecy,* vol. 4, p. 278).

We are also told that this time of trouble will not last for a long time. "We are standing on the threshold of great and solemn events. Prophecies are fulfilling. The last great conflict will be short, but terrible . . . . How long will it last? Only a little while" *(Selected Messages,* vol. 3, p. 419).

Why God Allows Persecution

A number of reasons could be cited for seeing the good side of persecution. It is actually turned back on the devil because of the positive effect it has on those who receive it and those who witness it. Note the following positive results.

Character building. "God, in His great love, is seeking to develop in us the precious graces of His Spirit. He permits us to encounter obstacles, persecution, and hardships, not as a curse, but as the greatest blessing of our lives. Every temptation resisted, every trial bravely borne, gives us a new experience, and advances us in the work of character building." In addition, "The soul that through divine power resists temptation, reveals to the world and to the heavenly universe the efficiency of the grace of Christ" *(Colporteur Ministry, p. 67).*

A witness to the world. "On every occasion when persecution takes place, those who witness it make decisions either for Christ or against Christ" *(The Desire of Ages, p. 630).* As the movement for Sunday enforcement moves forward some will be arrested and brought before courts. "Those who are arraigned before the courts make a strong vindication of the truth, and some who hear them are led to take their stand to keep all the commandments of God. Thus light will be brought before thousands who otherwise would know nothing of these truths" *(The Great Controversy, p. 607).* Recent televised trials have gripped the attention of millions. When God's faithful are dragged into court it may result in far more free air time for God!

To reveal God's grace. "Through trial and persecution the glory—the character—of God is revealed in His chosen ones" *(God's Amazing Grace, p. 280).* It must have been very clear to onlookers that God was with the martyrs who were tortured and killed. Many, instead of cursing or screaming, prayed or sang as they died. "These examples of human steadfastness bear witness to the faithfulness of God's promises—of His abiding presence and sustaining grace" *(Reflecting Christ, p. 357).* Why would God allow aged, faithful Daniel to be thrown to the lions? Apparently, as a testimony to God's protection and sustaining grace.

To put us in a place of service or blessing. "By permitting John to be banished to the Isle of Patmos, Christ placed His disciple in a position where he could receive the most precious truth for the enlightenment of the churches. . . . The persecution of John's enemies became a means of grace. . . . Never had he learned so much of Jesus. Never had he heard such exalted truth" *(Our High Calling, p. 315).*

To spread the gospel. People have a tendency to gather around institutions in colonies. But "the Lord desires that His people shall be dispersed throughout the earth. They are not to colonize. Jesus said, 'Go ye into all the world, and preach the gospel to every creature.' Mark 16:15. When the disciples followed their inclination to remain in large numbers in Jerusalem, persecution was permitted to come upon them, and they were scattered to all parts of the inhabited world" (*Testimonies for the Church,* vol. 8, p. 215).

It is evidence of following God. The devil is working hard to discourage God's people. Accordingly, the trials he sends are evidence that one is on God's side. "As men seek to come into harmony with God, they will find that the offense of the cross has not ceased. Principalities and powers and wicked spirits in high places are arrayed against all who yield obedience to the law of heaven. Therefore, so far from causing grief, persecution should bring joy to the disciples of Christ, for it is an evidence that they are following in the steps of their Master" (*Thoughts From the Mount of Blessing,* p. 29).

The Great Divider

The Bible indicates that when persecution comes those who are shallow and uncommitted will leave immediately rather than suffer for something that they really don't believe in that much. The parable of the sower is one illustration of this.

"Behold a sower went out to sow . . .

"Some fell on stony places, where they did not have much earth; and they immediately sprang up because they had no depth of earth.

"But when the sun was up they were scorched, and because they had no root they withered away . . .

[Biblical explanation]

"But he who received the seed on stony places, this is he who hears the word and immediately receives it with joy;

"Yet he has no root in himself, but endures only for a while. For <u>when tribulation or persecution arises because of the word, **immediately** he stumbles</u>" (Matthew 13:1, 5, 6, 20, 21).

In another story, or parable, Jesus illustrates the same point.

"But why do you call Me 'Lord, Lord,' and do not the things which I say?

"Whoever comes to Me, and hears My sayings and does them, I will show you whom he is like:

"He is like a man building a house, who dug deep and laid the foundation on the rock. And when the flood arose, the stream beat vehemently against that house, and could not shake it, for it was founded on the rock.

"But he who heard and did nothing is like a man who built a house on the earth without a foundation, against which the stream beat vehemently, <u>and **immediately** it fell.</u> And the ruin of that house was great" (Luke 6:46-49).

One of the most interesting statements I have found on this topic paints a very graphic picture of the great divide between the saved and the lost. "As the trials thicken around us, <u>both separation and unity will be seen in our ranks.</u> Some who are now ready to take up weapons of warfare will in times of real peril make it manifest that they have not built on the solid rock; they will yield to temptation. Those who have had great light and precious privileges, but have not improved upon them, will, under one pretext or another, go out from us. Not having received the love of the truth, they will be taken in the delusions of the enemy; they will give heed to seducing spirits and doctrines of devils, and will depart from the faith. <u>But on the other hand, when the storm of persecution really breaks upon us, the true sheep will hear the true Shepherd's voice.</u> Self-denying efforts will be put forth to save the lost, and **many who have strayed from the fold will come back to**

follow the great Shepherd. The people of God will draw together and present to the enemy a united front. In view of the common peril, strife for supremacy will cease; there will be no disputing as to who shall be accounted greatest" *(Maranatha,* p. 194).

Many who have joined with God's church in a time without persecution may appear solid, but when persecution comes it will take out a larger number than we now anticipate. "It is difficult to hold fast Christian integrity. The fact is, much which is current in our day as Christianity is indebted for its very existence to the absence of persecution. When the test of fiery trial comes, a great proportion of these who profess the faith will show that their religion was hollow formalism" *(That I May Know Him,* p. 352).

Fear of suffering will drive some from the ranks of God's people, but how could this light affliction compare with the second death?

In a very vivid picture Ellen White described the separation that persecution will bring. "When the testing time shall come, those who have made God's word their rule of life will be revealed. In summer there is no noticeable difference between evergreens and other trees; but when the blasts of winter come, the evergreens remain unchanged, while other trees are stripped of their foliage. So the falsehearted professor may not now be distinguished from the real Christian, but the time is just upon us when the difference will be apparent. Let opposition arise, let bigotry and intolerance again bear sway, let persecution be kindled, and the halfhearted and hypocritical will waver and yield the faith; but the true Christian will stand firm as a rock, his faith stronger, his hope brighter, than in days of prosperity" *(The Great Controversy,* p. 602).

Preparation for Persecution

Only the power of God will guide us through the trials ahead. Yet we can prepare by following His counsel to us. I have found a number of points we are encouraged to pay attention to.

Study God's Word. The Bible contains so many promises that should be committed to memory and claimed personally. My favorites are in the Psalms, Isaiah, the Gospels, and Philippians. Also Chapter 36 of *The Great Controversy,* "The Scriptures a Safeguard," gives good counsel. Two short statements there tell a lot. "None but those who have fortified the mind with the truths of the Bible will stand through the last great conflict" (p. 593). "It is the first and highest duty of every rational being to learn from the Scriptures what is truth, and then to walk in the light and encourage others to follow his example" (p. 598).

Spend time with God in prayer. Regular communion with God will enable one to maintain a relationship with Him. The chapter on prayer in *Steps to Christ* is very helpful. "What was the strength of those who in the past have suffered persecution for Christ's sake? It was union with God, union with the Holy Spirit, union with Christ. It is this fellowship with the Saviour that will enable God's people to endure to the end" *(The Faith I Live By,* p. 330).

Make friends with others. We need to get to know our neighbors and those of influence in our communities. This will help them to realize that we are sincere and honest people and not members of a cult or some wild-eyed kooks. It is also the best, grassroots way to witness to them. The counsel is, "As they approach the time of trouble, the followers of Christ should make every exertion to place themselves in a proper light before the people, to disarm prejudice, and to avert the danger which threatens liberty of conscience" *(The Great Controversy,* p. 616).

Help to advance the work of God. We know that what we do not accomplish in times of relative calm we will have to do in very difficult times. We should work, for the night is coming.

Learn the principles of health and how to help the sick. "As religious aggression subverts the liberties of our nation, those who would stand for freedom of conscience will be placed in unfavorable positions. For their own sake they should, while they have opportunity, become intelligent in regard to disease, its causes, prevention, and cure. And those who do this will find a field of labor anywhere. There will be suffering ones, plenty of them, who will need help, not only among those of our own faith, but largely among those who know not the truth" *(Medical Ministry,* p. 321).

Develop unity and fellowship with fellow believers. Hebrews 10:25 counsels us to get together more often and exhort one another as we see the day approaching. Over and over we are told to "press together." One of the characteristics of Christ's disciples after He returned to heaven was how they loved one another.

Learn to be self-sufficient. It was reported in the Washington

Post recently that over 95 percent of Americans subsist entirely on food from the store. Our counsel is to become more independent. "Privation may be the lot of every soul who now believes and obeys the truth. Christ has told us that we will have reproach. If persecution for the truth's sake is to come, it is important that every line of work become familiar to us, that we and our families may not suffer through lack of knowledge. We can and should have tact and knowledge in trades, in building, in planting, and in sowing. A knowledge of how to cultivate the land will make rough places much smoother. This knowledge will be counted a great blessing, even by our enemies" *(Manuscript Releases,* vol. 19, p. 26).

Get out of the cities. We have had this counsel for many years. It is no mystery to us now why this counsel was given. We can see the crime, overcrowding, violence, sickness, poverty, noise, and stress of city living. Read through the little booklet *Country Living* for more pertinent information on this topic.

God's Promised Protection

We can bank on the fact that God loves us, and that no matter what, He will be with us and see us through to the kingdom of glory. The stories of the Bible show us that God doesn't need a large army to win a battle. In fact He doesn't need an army at all. Remember that one angel destroyed Sennacherib's army and one angel scattered the soldiers guarding the grave of Jesus. Re-read the stories of Gideon, Jonathan, Elijah, and Elisha. God has given us the promises in His Word to be claimed. One such promise is Isaiah 41:10: "Fear thou not; for I am with thee: be not dismayed; for I am thy God: I will strengthen thee; yea, I will help thee; yea, I will uphold thee with the right hand of My righteousness."

We don't need to worry about the future, because God has promised to be with us. "The prospect of being brought into personal danger and distress, need not cause despondency, but should quicken the vigor and hopes of God's people; for the time of their peril is the season of God to grant them clearer manifestations of His power" *(Maranatha,* p. 194). "God's people are not to fear. Satan cannot go beyond his limit. The Lord will be the defense of His people" *(ibid.,* p. 191).

Ellen White has written much on the topic of what to do when the Sunday law is enforced. Devoting Sunday to missionary work will take the whip out of the hands of our enemies for a while. In addition, just because Sunday is not a holy day, we should not go out of our way to be noisy, like using our chain saw to cut firewood. We will not receive the mark of the beast by doing missionary work on Sunday.

The Abomination of Desolation

This unusual term is mentioned in Daniel 12 and Matthew 24. In her comments on these verses, Ellen White reports, "The time is not far distant, when, like the early disciples, we shall be forced to seek a refuge in desolate and solitary places. As the siege of Jerusalem by the Roman armies was the signal for flight to the Judean Christians, so the assumption of power on the part of our nation [the United States] in the decree enforcing the papal sabbath will be a warning to us. It will then be time to leave the large cities, preparatory to leaving the smaller ones for retired homes in secluded places among the mountains" *(ibid.,* p. 180).

God in His infinite wisdom will allow some to be laid to rest before the persecution comes so they won't have to bear it. "The Lord 'doth not afflict willingly nor grieve the children of men.' Lam. 3:33. 'Like as a father pitieth his children, so the Lord pitieth them that fear Him. For He knoweth our frame; He remembereth that we are dust.' Ps. 103:13, 14. He knows our heart, for He reads every secret of the soul. He knows whether or not those for whom petitions are offered would be able to endure the trial and test that would come upon them if they lived. He knows the end from the beginning. Many will be laid away to sleep before the fiery ordeal of the time of trouble shall come upon our world. This is another reason why we should say after our earnest petition: 'Nevertheless not my will, but Thine, be done.' Luke 22:42. Such a petition will never be registered in heaven as a faithless prayer" *(Counsels on Health,* p. 375).

"If God is for us, who can be against us?

"He who did not spare His own Son, but delivered Him up for us all, how shall He not with Him also freely give us all things?

"Who shall bring a charge against God's elect? It is God who justifies.

"Who is he who condemns? It is Christ who died, and furthermore is also risen, who is even at the right hand of God, who also makes intercession for us.

"Who shall separate us from the love of Christ? Shall tribulation, or distress, or persecution, or famine, or nakedness, or peril, or sword?

"As it is written: 'For Your sake we are killed all day long; we are accounted as sheep for the slaughter.'

"Yet in all these things we are more than conquerors through Him who loved us.

"For I am persuaded that neither death nor life, nor angels nor principalities nor powers, nor things present nor things to come, nor height nor depth, nor any other created thing, shall be able to separate us from the love of God which is in Christ Jesus our Lord" (Romans 8:31-39).

CHAPTER 14

The Revival Is Coming

As a church family we have been talking about the "latter rain" for many years. After much research on this topic, I am convinced that what we really need now is the power of the early rain—the power of Pentecost. While we are beginning to see that power being experienced in various parts of the world, even the true early rain/Pentecost experience is way beyond what we have experienced as a church today. The latter rain will come when the church is ready to give the loud cry of Revelation 18. Apparently this power will come after the Sunday agitation begins and the unconverted leave the church. Then those who are left will seek the power of God to finish the work.

The Bible is full of evidence that God is eager to pour out His Spirit and work with us both for our needs and to equip us to finish His work. God wants to reveal to us even more than we now know, to encourage and strengthen us. "Call to Me," He says, "and I will answer you, and show you great and mighty things, which you do not know" (Jeremiah 33:3). Ellen White gives the steps in this experience. "Strict integrity should be cherished by every student. Every mind should turn with reverent attention to the revealed word of God. <u>Light and grace will be given to those who thus obey God.</u> They will behold wondrous things out of His law. <u>Great truths that have lain unheeded and unseen since the day of Pentecost, are to shine forth in their native purity.</u> To those who truly love God <u>the Holy Spirit will reveal truths that have faded from the mind, **and will also reveal truths that are entirely new.**</u> Those who eat the flesh and drink the blood of the Son of God will bring from the books of Daniel and Revelation truth that is inspired by the Holy Spirit. They will start into action forces that cannot be repressed. The lips of children will be opened to proclaim the mysteries that have been hidden from the minds of men. The Lord has chosen the foolish things of this world to confound the wise, and the weak things of the world to confound the mighty" *(Fundamentals of Christian Education,* p. 473).

One of my favorite verses of Scripture expresses God's desire to work with us. "Sanctify yourselves, for tomorrow the Lord will do wonders among you" (Joshua 3:5). Ellen White called this sanctifying process a reformatory movement, and God showed her its results. "In visions of the night representations passed before me of a great reformatory movement among God's people. Many were praising God. The sick were healed and other miracles were wrought. A spirit of intercession was seen, even as was manifested before the great day of Pentecost. Hundreds and thousands were seen visiting families and opening before them the word of God. Hearts were convicted by the power of the Holy Spirit, and a spirit of genuine conversion was manifest. On every side doors were thrown open to the proclamation of the truth. The world seemed to be lightened with the heavenly influence. Great blessings were received by the true and humble people of God. I heard voices of thanksgiving and praise, and there seemed to be a reformation such as we witnessed in 1844" *(Counsels on Health,* p. 580).

What a list of blessings! What a day that will be. And it is coming! All around the world, in Asia-Pacific, in Europe, in Latin America, in Africa, and, yes, even in North America the power is coming. The preparation for and implementation of NET '96 gives all of us the opportunity to cooperate with God in an awesome experience.

One of the greatest promises in all the Bible, given as the words of God Himself, is, "Return to Me, and I will return to you" (Malachi 3:7). Speaking directly to people awaiting the Lord's coming the prophet outlines the steps for a revival that will result in overflowing blessings. It is very encouraging to me to see thousands of individuals and families taking God at His word, renewing their covenant with Him, and keeping faith with God in their tithe*—in spite of the devil's attacks on the remnant church! This was all predicted. "The remnant will return, the remnant of Jacob, to the Mighty God" (Isaiah 10:21).

God plans to work mightily on behalf of willing workers. We all

remember that for the most part, the disciples of Jesus were not edu-
cated men with perfect diction and large vocabularies. But after
Pentecost, "The language of the disciples was pure, simple, and accu-
rate in word and accent, whether they spoke their native tongue or a
foreign language. These humble men, who had never learned in the
school of the prophets, presented truths so elevated and pure as to as-
tonish those who heard them" *(The Story of Redemption,* p. 246).

Apparently, this will happen again near the end as part of the great
revival. "It is with earnest longing that I look forward to the time when
the events of the Day of Pentecost shall be repeated with even greater
power than on that occasion. John says, 'I saw another angel come
down from heaven, having great power; and the earth was lightened
with his glory.' Rev. 18:1. Then, as at the Pentecostal season, the people will hear the truth spoken to them, every man in his own tongue"
(Last Day Events, p. 202).

On the day of Pentecost thousands were assembled in Jerusalem
from all over the world. When the disciples preached these listeners
were "cut to the heart." Their hearts were touched with the great sacrifice of Christ, and 3,000 people were baptized and added to the church.
We are told this was just a foretaste of the last great revival. "The time
is coming when there will be as many converted in a day as there were
on the day of Pentecost, after the disciples had received the Holy
Spirit" *(Evangelism,* p. 692). But as we look around us today we ask,
"How will this ever happen?" The Bible gives the answer. "Behold, I
will send you Elijah the prophet before the coming of the great and
dreadful day of the Lord" (Malachi 4:5).

The Power of Elijah

A careful study of the work of Elijah, especially his stand for God
on Mount Carmel, will give us insights on how to prepare for the "falling
of the fire" at the end time. The Bible tells the story in 1 Kings 17 and
18. Chapter 17 primarily gives the setting for the great experience of
chapter 18.

It had been over 50 years since the heydays of Israel under Kings
David and Solomon. Fifty years of sliding backward—falling from for-
tune to famine. Israel had fallen from adoration of God to addiction to
Baal. Ahab's father, who had been one of the better kings of the north-

ern kingdom, made a political alliance with the Phoenicians, and as part of the deal his son Ahab married a Phoenician girl named Jezebel, a very wicked woman, who brought her false gods with her. To put it mildly, she was a very bad influence on Ahab and the nation. The Bible reports, "Now Ahab the son of Omri did evil in the sight of the Lord, more than all who were before him" (1 Kings 16:30). Elijah the Tishbite stepped into this evil society that Ahab had developed and began to take center stage.

Without so much as an appointment or a letter sent ahead to announce his coming, Elijah just marched right in, past the royal guard, and the royal courtiers, right into the king's throne-room. And before anyone could stop him he blurted out, "As the Lord God of Israel lives, before whom I stand, there shall not be dew nor rain these years except at my word" (1 Kings 17:1). As abruptly as he had entered, Elijah turned on his heels and left. He was not seen or heard for three years, though the local equivalent of the CIA and the KGB searched for him throughout the entire kingdom and even in the surrounding nations. We know he was at the brook Cherith and later in a foreign land with the widow of Zarephath—but that's another story.

Because of the wickedness of Ahab and the apostasy of the people, God brought a drought upon the northern kingdom. Conditions were terrible—crop failures, dust storms, lakes and rivers dried up—desert-like conditions. Things became so desperate that the king himself went out looking for some place to water the royal horses to keep them from dying. Then through Obadiah, Elijah met Ahab once more. And the "troubler of Israel" seemed alone against a terrible hatred of God's ways. But when the fire fell from heaven at the showdown on Mount Carmel everything changed. On Mount Carmel, after Elijah repaired the Lord's altar and prayed a fervent prayer, it says, "Then the fire of the Lord fell and consumed the burnt sacrifice" (1 Kings 18:38).

Focus for a moment on that phrase—"Then the fire of the Lord fell." Fire is synonymous with power, with God's presence. It is the only thing that will melt away dissension and pettiness. It is the only thing that will purify the carnal mind. It is the only thing that will empower us for evangelism. It is the difference between a church that changes lives for God and one that doesn't change. That fire must be a part of our lives as members of the Remnant Church.

John the Baptist was another type of Elijah, as you know. The Bible calls him "a burning and shining lamp" (John 5:35). He had knowledge and enthusiasm. He had light and fire. Light gives direction! Light gives illumination!

I hope and pray that this book gives light—so that people reading it will say, "Now I see how important these events are. It makes sense." I don't want fire without light. Fire without light just makes people hot. And we certainly don't want light without fire. That's what we have had for too long. Light without fire is the best description of the Laodicean condition. Spiritual couch potatoes. We know the truth, we have the light, but most are not doing anything with it. We have to have both heat and light and that equals power.

So the question for each of us is "When will the fire fall?" I have discovered some points or principles from the experience of Elijah that should give us a good indication as to the answer to this question.

1. The fire comes when we know our message is from God.

"Now it came to pass after many days that the word of the Lord came to Elijah, in the third year, saying, 'Go, present yourself to Ahab, and I will send rain on the earth" (1 Kings 18:1). The fire comes—the power comes into our lives when we know that God has given us something that we are to share with others. That we have in the three angels' messages—the last warning to a dying world.

2. The fire will fall when we stand for what is right regardless of the consequences.

On his way to meet the king, Elijah met Obadiah, a God-fearing servant of King Ahab. Obadiah had even hidden 100 of the Lord's prophets in caves and kept them with food and water. He immediately recognized Elijah and expressed his respect for God's prophet. Elijah told him to inform Ahab that he had found the prophet. Obadiah was very frightened and asked Elijah, "What if the Lord carries you away and I can't bring you to the king? He will kill me." But Elijah promised, "As the Lord of hosts lives, before whom I stand, I will surely present myself to him today" (1 Kings 18:15).

Let me ask you a very pointed question. Are you willing to stand by your position on the interpretation of Revelation 13? Or will you compromise in the face of cries of bigotry or prejudice. Will you opt for religio-political correctness or will you stick by the simple and true interpretation of Scripture?

3. The fire will fall when our need is the greatest.

Elijah was there on Mount Carmel representing the people of God. Standing before those who would kill him if they could. He was 100 percent dependent on God's miraculous power. He was outnumbered at least 450 to 1. The prophets of Baal needed God and knew their power was futile, but they were too stubborn to change. The mass of people who had come to watch the showdown had a decision to make. "And Elijah came to all the people, and said, 'How long will you falter between two opinions? If the Lord is God, follow Him; but if Baal, then follow him.' But the people answered him not a word" (v. 21). He was there alone—and God blessed him.

4. The fire will come when we take our message to the people.

The power of God will come when we minister to people in need. The power does not come to a waiting church but a working church. We don't need power if we don't have plans so big that only God's power can accomplish them.

When the message is given to the people, the power of God comes to make the message effective. We need wisdom and light from God as we prepare, but the real power comes when it is delivered to the people.

5. The fire falls—the power comes—when we bring people to a point of decision.

When the call is given, "Babylon is fallen, Come out of her My people," people will have to make a decision. And it's a life-or-death decision! We will need the power of God to speak with authority. That's when His power will be given with its greatest measure. Elijah told the people, "It's time to make a decision. How long are you going to halt between two opinions?"

6. The fire falls—the power of God comes—when we go back to the altar of the Lord to repair it and use it.

In a certain sense being filled with the Spirit does not so much mean that we receive more of God's Spirit than that we give Him more of ourselves. As we yield our lives to the Holy Spirit and are filled with His presence, He has greater freedom to work in and through our lives, to better exalt and glorify Christ. God is too great to be placed in a man-made mold. However, there are certain spiritual laws that are inviolate. When we meet the conditions, He responds. <u>The Holy Spirit will fill us with His power the moment we are fully yielded and working in tasks that need supernatural power!</u>

Elijah proposed that the prophets of Baal, who were 450 strong, and he prepare for a burnt offering, but that neither would put a fire under the wood. Then, he said, whichever god was the true God would send fire from heaven to burn the sacrifice. Immediately the people said, "It is well spoken,"—or as we would say—"That's a good idea." Since the people agreed, the priests had no choice but to proceed.

You remember the story of how the prophets of Baal jumped, danced, and shouted all day long around their altar—from morning, through noon, and on to the time of the evening sacrifice—and no fire came. The Bible says, "But there was no voice; no one answered, no one paid attention" (v. 29).

Then it was Elijah's turn. He called to the people to come near. He repaired the broken-down altar of the Lord. He used 12 large stones—one for each of the sons of Jacob. He did what he could. He repaired the altar.

7. The fire will fall when we have circumstances that only God's power will light.

Elijah dug a trench around the altar and placed the wood and the sacrifice on it. Then he said to the people, "Bring four water pots [barrels] of water and pour it on the sacrifice and the wood." Then he said, "Do it a second time" and they did. Then he asked them to do it a third time, and they did. Twelve barrels of water were poured on the sacrifice and the wood. The water filled the trench around the altar. Everything was soaked! Elijah wanted the people to know that the fire came from God.

Elijah knew a truth that we all need to know, and it is an awesome fact. God can light wet wood! We may feel that we have to have everything just right in order for God to work. But God doesn't need newspaper and dry kindling. God is not limited to the person who can speak the best, or say things just the right way. God just tells us that He can ignite wet wood. And when we are ready, He will light the fire. Do circumstances seem formidable where you are? That's no problem with God. No situation is too difficult for Him!

8. The fire will fall when we want God to receive the glory.

Elijah's prayer is awesome. It is only 63 well-chosen words. "Lord God of Abraham, Isaac, and Israel, let it be known this day that You are God in Israel and I am Your servant, and that I have done all these things at Your word. Hear me, O Lord, hear me, that this people may know that You are the Lord God, and that You have turned their hearts back to You again" (vs. 36, 37). We need to grasp the reality that God sends His power, His fire, to the people who want Him to receive the glory. When people see the fire, they recognize the power of God. And when the fire falls, people turn to God.

9. The fire will fall when we obey God's Word. Obedience brings power.

Elijah stated, "I have done all these things at Your word." He wasn't just showing off when he poured the 12 barrels of water on the sacrifice and the wood. He was following the command of God. He went out on a limb for God. He knew that if the fire hadn't fallen he would have been killed on the spot.

10. The fire falls when we desire to see other people return to God.

The fire, the power for spiritual working, will come into our lives when we have a heart that desires to see people return to God—when we have a love for souls. Elijah was concerned about two things: The glory of God and the revival of the people. When we desire to see people return to God, or find Him for the first time, and put forth efforts to that end, the fire will fall.

11. When we prevail in prayer, the fire will fall.

This story of God's miraculous power on Mount Carmel has been told down through the ages. I like the way James speaks of it in the New Testament. He says, "Elijah was a man with a nature like ours, and he prayed earnestly that it would not rain; and it did not rain on the land for three years and six months. <u>And he prayed again,</u> and the heavens gave rain, and the earth produced its fruit" (James 5:17, 18). That one phrase is so intriguing, "And he prayed again." When Elijah prayed on Mount Carmel, it wasn't the first time that he prayed. <u>In fact, he didn't even mention fire in his prayer.</u> He and God had this all worked out before.

Short prayers can be spoken at public events if we have prayed our long prayers before. We don't need to pray long, agonizing prayers at church. If we have prayed before we get there, God will come. Only 63 words and the fire fell. What a contrast to the priests of Baal.

Ellen White gives a very graphic account of the scene. "After the victim is laid upon the altar, he commands the people to flood the sacrifice and the altar with water, and to fill the trench round about the altar. He then reverently bows before the unseen God, raises his hands toward heaven, and offers a calm and simple prayer, unattended with violent gestures or contortions of the body. No shrieks resound over Carmel's height.

"A solemn silence, which is oppressive to the priests of Baal, rests upon all. In his prayer, Elijah makes use of no extravagant expressions. He prays to Jehovah as though He were nigh, witnessing the whole scene, and hearing his sincere, fervent, yet simple prayer. Baal's priests have screamed, and foamed, and leaped, and prayed, very long—from morning until near evening. Elijah's prayer is very short, earnest, reverential, and sincere.

"No sooner is that prayer uttered than flames of fire descend from heaven in a distinct manner, like a brilliant flash of lightning, kindling the wood for sacrifice and consuming the victim, licking up the water in the trench and consuming even the stones of the altar. The brilliancy of the blaze illumes the mountain and is painful to the eyes of the multitude. <u>The people of the kingdom of Israel **not gathered upon the mount** are watching with interest those there assembled. As the fire descends, **they witness it and are amazed at the sight.**</u> It resembles the pillar of fire at the Red Sea, which by night separated the children of Israel from the Egyptian host" *(Testimonies for the Church,* vol. 3, pp. 284, 285).

The Results

After witnessing this phenomenal sight the people immediately fell down and exclaimed, "The Lord, He is God; the Lord, He is God."

Elijah commanded the people to seize the priests of Baal and then he executed all 450 of them. Then he turned his attention to the speechless King Ahab and said in faith, "Eat something and refresh yourself, for there is the sound of abundance of rain."

Then while Ahab went to eat, Elijah went back to the top of the mountain and knelt down with his head between his knees and prayed for rain. After his prayer he sent his servant to look toward the sea to see if any clouds were on the horizon. The servant returned and said, "There is nothing." Seven times Elijah prayed and said, "Go look again." And after the seventh prayer the servant returned with a shout, "There is a cloud, as small as a man's hand, rising out of the sea." Quickly Elijah sent his servant to Ahab with the message "Prepare your chariot and go down before the rain stops you." Suddenly the sky became black with clouds and wind. The rain began to pour. It was dark and Ahab couldn't see the road that was then a torrent of water and mud. Then the Spirit of God came upon Elijah and he ran ahead of the horses, guiding them all the way to Jezreel.

Present Application

Very soon the words of the prophet Malachi will be fulfilled: "Behold I will send you Elijah the prophet before the coming of the great and dreadful day of the Lord" (Malachi 4:5). As we follow the faithful example of Elijah, the fire will fall again. This time it will not just light up a single mountain top. The Bible says that the whole earth will be illuminated!

Shortly after this someone will exclaim, "I see it, I see it. A small cloud, about half the size of a man's hand." But instead of getting darker, it will get brighter and brighter with the glory of God and the holy angels. That moment is close at hand. And the revival is coming!

~

Over the past couple of years I have had the privilege of serving on the Spiritual Life Task Force of the North American Division. After much prayer, study, and discussion we have prepared a statement that we hope receives wide circulation and implementation. With the permission of the committee chairman I have reproduced it below.

It's Time . . .

Prepared by the
North American Division
SPIRITUAL LIFE TASK FORCE

The prophetic implications of the three angels' messages of Revelation 14 are increasingly relevant. World conditions are deteriorating. Momentous events are taking place in the Christian church and the world. People are perplexed and full of anticipation and anxiety. Many are ready for a message of hope. This growing search for spiritual meaning demands that God's church must awake. It is "The Time for Revival." Now is the time to respond to the moving of the Holy Spirit and to prepare for the second coming of Christ.

The following is based on a conviction that 2 Chronicles 7:14 provides a needed sequence for God's call to revival.

If my people . . .

"Here is the patience of the saints; here are those who keep the commandments of God and the faith of Jesus." Revelation 14:12

"Seventh-day Adventists have been chosen by God as a peculiar people, separate from the world. By the great cleaver of truth He has cut them out from the quarry of the world and brought them into connection with Himself. He has made them His representatives and has called them to be ambassadors for Him in the last work of salvation. The greatest wealth of truth ever entrusted to mortals, the most solemn and fearful warnings ever sent by God to man, have been committed to them to be given to the world." *Last Day Events,* p. 45.

"If My people who are called by My name will humble themselves, and pray and seek My face, and turn from their wicked ways, then I will hear from heaven, and will forgive their sin and heal their land." 2 Chronicles 7:14

"A revival of true godliness among us is the greatest and most urgent of all our needs. To seek this should be our first work. There must be earnest effort to obtain the blessing of the Lord, not because God is not willing to bestow His blessing upon us, but because we are unprepared to receive it. Our heavenly Father is more willing to give His Holy Spirit to them that ask Him, than are earthly parents to give good gifts to their children. *But it is our work, by confession, humiliation, repentance, and earnest prayer, to fulfill the conditions upon which God has promised to grant us His blessing.* **A revival need be expected only in answer to prayer"** (1 SM, p. 121; emphasis added).

who are called by my name . . .

Boldness: Like Noah, Moses, Isaiah, John the Baptist, Jesus, the Disciples, the Reformers, and our Pioneers, we must proclaim the "Elijah message" with boldness. We must be willing to risk something—maybe everything—to advance the cause of Christ.

Leadership: The revivals of the past all had leaders—heroes—that gave direction to the Reformation. God calls upon leaders to place revival and spiritual leadership ahead of their heavy administrative responsibilities. Leaders in all areas of church responsibility are challenged to make revival and reformation the number one priority.

Support: The experience of Aaron and Hur in supporting the hands of Moses in the battle with Amalek provides a model for us today. Fellow leaders and church members are encouraged to support each other in prayerful and thoughtful ways so that the burdens borne by leaders will be carried by all.

will humble themselves . . .

Unity: We derive our unity from the headship of Christ and deplore all that separates us. Accordingly, the remnant church will be age, gender, and culture inclusive. The success of the great commission will come as we truly become one in Christ.

Simplicity: Historically, God has always used simple means to carry forward His work and to bring about revival. There is a need to study the models of revival and reformation of the past—from the great epochs of the Old Testament, the New Testament, the Reformation, and Early Adventism to determine the will of God in this matter. It will take great faith to be willing to utilize the simple ways He has used in the past.

Repentance: Repentance, the humbled heart before God, is so vital to a genuine and lasting revival and reformation. It is the result of coming to Christ and having the light of Christ shine upon us. The uplifted Christ brings to view the good news of the gospel. Thus our conscience is quickened and brings us to pray the prayer of David, "Create in me a clean heart, O God, and renew a steadfast spirit within me." (Ps. 51:10) By allowing Christ to do His work in our hearts we can welcome the outpouring of the Holy Spirit's power.

and pray and seek my face . . .

Prayer: Prayer has always preceded the spiritual renewal of God's people. The needed revival will come in response to focused, united, and persevering prayer. Communion with God in prayer is a powerful weapon in our warfare and assures victory.

Bible Study: Scripture contains the wisdom and power of Christ— power that we desperately need. Through the study and memorization of Scripture we discover the loveliness of Christ our Saviour. Seeing His goodness makes the adventure of systematic study and meditation a joy. Such Bible study also leads the student to satisfying answers to today's needs.

Commission: Our prayer, Bible study, revival and reformation leads us to one end—taking the unbelievably good news of Christ to our world. Therefore, Adventist Christians have a unique commission—giving to others what has been learned and experienced. Every person we contact is that one special soul Christ came to save. In doing this work we have the privilege of cooperating with the Holy Spirit and with angels. This work will soon lighten the whole world with the glory of God.

and turn from their wicked ways . . .

Lifestyle: Lasting revival will encourage the development of a devotional life. To "pray without ceasing" and to "be ready always to give a reason for the hope that is in you" is a model for Christian maturity. Our faith in the Word of God will be demonstrated in the management of our resources. Our belief in the soon coming of Christ will be evident in our lifestyle.

Attitudes: Considering the serious times in which we live one positive response is to replace strife, discord, and criticism with the positive qualities of kindness, respect, and affirmation. Then the fruit of the Spirit will be seen in our lives.

then I will hear from heaven,

God Hears: God never fails to respond to genuine contrition. He always makes good on His promises. Earth's serious plight calls for Heaven's intervention, and Scripture affirms God's willingness and ability to answer this entreaty. Hearing on God's part is not just an abstract perception of sound but a promise of responsive action. When God "hears" He acts. When we come to a realization of our personal and corporate need, and in confidence seek God, Heaven's response is guaranteed.

and will forgive their sin

God Forgives: Sin has infected the very core of human existence. Yet through Christ, God willingly extends deliverance, peace and power. The fact of forgiveness from Christ is as sure as one believes in His ability to do so. Jesus is eager to forgive our sins. None are so sinful that they cannot find strength, purity, and righteousness through the forgiveness that He offers. He promises to abundantly pardon and remember our sins no more. He then treats us as if we had never sinned.

and heal their land.

God Heals: God wants to heal the brokenhearted and there is no brokenness that He cannot heal. Every promise of God's presence, provision, protection and blessing is given for all His children. Whether for individual, family, church or nation—God's desire is for healing and restoration. Though ultimately full healing will occur in heaven, His provisions include our here and now. "But to you who fear My name the Sun of Righteousness shall arise with healing in His wings." Malachi 4:2

Our Response:
The urgency of the times demand that we communicate in every way possible that the time has come for revival and reformation and what God is doing now in His mighty acts for the advancement of His work. It is time for a concerted effort to "finish the work" that God has given us. This means that every meeting conducted, every article written, and every media presentation will emphasize our great need of revival and how to bring it about. They will focus on spiritual growth for

the individual and the church and our primary task—preparing for the soon coming of Christ.

God says, "If my people will . . . Then I will." 2 Chronicles 7:14
　　By God's grace I will accept the promise.

> I will . . . Seek Unity
> I will . . . Seek His Face
> I will . . . Humble Myself
> I will . . . Claim His Forgiveness
> I will . . . Accept God's Call for Revival
> 　　　　　 in My Life and in My Church.

Will you join us in that commitment right now?

---

* See Malachi 3:8-10.

CHAPTER 15

The God of
Abraham, Isaac, and Jacob

Two factors are motivating me to make a recommitment to God. First is the knowledge of God's great love for me, and the second is the certainty of the soon return of Christ. Surely there will be difficulties before we see our Saviour face-to-face, but claiming His promises we can look to the future with assurance. Prophecy indicates that the great day of God is right upon us. All heaven is astir, anticipating the rescue of God's faithful ones.

My confidence is in Christ as He is revealed in the Scriptures. "The Lord of hosts is with us; the God of Jacob is our refuge." Who is this God of Jacob? And why is He referred to as the God of Jacob? The Bible reveals a fascinating story in Genesis 28 that gives me great confidence in the care, love, and concern that God exercises toward us. Desiring the blessing of God and the birthright, Jacob, with the cooperation of his mother Rebekah, deceived his father Isaac into believing that he was his brother Esau. When Esau learned of this act of deception he declared, "My father will die soon and when the days of mourning are past I will kill Jacob."

When Jacob and Rebekah heard of Esau's plans they decided that Jacob must leave the family home and flee for his life to the homeland of Rebekah. In his last meeting with Jacob, his father charged him: "Don't take a wife from the daughters of Canaan. Go to Padan Aram— to the house of your mother's father and take yourself a wife." Isaac concluded his counsel to Jacob by saying, "May God Almighty bless you . . . and give you the blessing of Abraham."

And so Jacob fled from the wrath of Esau his brother. And as he literally ran for his life, somewhere between Beersheba and Haran he had an awesome experience with God. At the end of the second day of running—just as the sun was setting—Jacob realized that he must stop for the night and looked for a safe place to sleep. The Bible says that he found a large rock and placed it at the head of where he planned to sleep.

As the sun dropped behind the horizon no doubt he began to think, *What have I done? I have really messed up! My father is a wealthy man and I look like a deadbeat—two days' beard and clothes that look and smell like I have run in them for two days. Just look at me!*

He began to wonder: *What will become of me? Will I ever see Mom and Dad again? Will I ever see my homeland again? What have I done?* And he began to weep. Finally after picking over his hastily packed escape provisions he lay down to rest. Then, the Bible says, "He dreamed, and behold, a ladder was set up on earth, and its top reached to heaven; and there the angels of God were ascending and descending on it" (Genesis 28:12).

As a young person in Sabbath School I remember being quite impressed with the picture of that ladder. But I missed the best part. God was standing at the top of the ladder! We may be faced with all kinds of problems today. But let's not look around us to other people who may also have their own problems—maybe even worse than our own. Let's look up! God is at the top of the ladder!

Returning to Genesis 28:13-15 we read, "And behold, the Lord stood above it and said, 'I am the Lord God of Abraham your father and the God of Isaac." He apparently wanted to be Jacob's God too. And then God made some tremendous promises to Jacob. "The land on which you lie I will give to you and your descendants. Also your descendants shall be as the dust of the earth; you shall spread abroad to the west and the east, to the north and the south; and in you and your seed all the families of the earth shall be blessed." It was almost a word for word renewal of the promises by God made to Abraham in Genesis 12:1-3. God assured Jacob, "Behold, I am with you and will keep you wherever you go, and will bring you back to this land; for I will not leave you until I have done what I have spoken to you."

When Jacob woke from the dream he said to himself, "Surely the Lord is in this place and I did not know it." He was afraid and said, "How awesome is this place! This is none other than the house of God, and this is the gate of heaven!" Jacob rose early in the morning and took the stone on which he had laid his head and stood it up on end as a marker and poured oil on it and named the stone "Bethel"—meaning house of God. It was common in the days of the Old Testament to build a memorial as an honor to God when something great had happened. An example of this is when Israel crossed into the Promised Land, Joshua asked one man from each tribe to pick up a large stone in the dry Jordan riverbed and place it in a memorial structure to remember God's deliverance.

Another interesting example of this phenomenon is mentioned in the hymn *Come Thou Fount of Every Blessing*. The second stanza reads, "Here I raise my Ebenezer, Hither by Thy help I've come." I remember wondering as a child what an Ebenezer was. How could you raise it if you didn't know what it was? Of course the Bible has the answer. In 1 Samuel 7 is recorded the story of Israel's great victory over the Philistines. Following the battle "Samuel took a stone and set it up between Mizpah and Shen, and called its name Ebenezer, saying, 'Thus far the Lord has helped us'" (1 Samuel 7:12). So in this case the "Ebenezer stone" was just a reminder to Israel of God's great deliverance.

After Jacob set up his memorial stone he made a vow or promise to God: "If God will be with me, and keep me in this way that I am going, and give me bread to eat and clothing to put on, so that I come back to my father's house in peace, then the Lord shall be my God." And from that day on, as I will point out, God always refers to Himself as the God of Abraham, Isaac, and Jacob!

Tangible Evidence of the Vow

Jacob told God, "This stone which I have set as a pillar shall be God's house, and of all that you give me I will surely give a tenth to You" (Genesis 28:22). This vow of Jacob came as a natural, spontaneous response to the great promises of God. And that should characterize our response to God also. "He who gave His only-begotten Son to die for you has made a covenant with you. He gives you His blessings, and in return He requires you to bring Him your tithes and offerings" *(Counsels on Stewardship, p. 75).*

The tithe is the very foundation of our covenant relation with God and it is also the foundation of the financial success of our church. The devil, the great anti-Christ, wants neither your relationship with God nor the mission of the church to succeed. Those who state that they will not return their tithe for this and that reason are in actual fact listening to the devil and cutting off their nose to spite their face. If one does not maintain his loyalty to God in these relatively easy times and fails to uphold his covenant with God and stops his support of the remnant church of Bible prophecy—the one that keeps the commandments of God and has the testimony of Jesus—what will he do when the going gets tough? The answer is plain and simple. Having listened to the devil so long, such a one may finally believe the lie and sever his connection with God's church. Sadly, this is happening to many today.

As a part of my work I have had the opportunity to speak at many "workers' meetings" over the past several years. Did you know that as part of the great controversy the devil also has workers' meetings? During one of her visions in the great controversy series, Ellen White was given a view of one of these satanic workers' meetings. Listen! "As the people of God approach the perils of the last days, Satan holds earnest consultation with his angels as to the most successful plan of overthrowing their faith. . . . Says the great deceiver . . . 'We can separate many from Christ by worldliness, lust, and pride . . . Go make the possessors of lands and money drunk with the cares of this life. Present the world before them in its most attractive light, that they may lay up their treasure here and fix their affections upon earthly things. We must do our utmost to prevent those who labor in God's cause from obtaining means to use against us. Keep the money in our own ranks. The more means they obtain, the more they will injure our kingdom by taking from us our subjects [the whole point of the plan of salvation]. Make them care more for money than the upbuilding of Christ's kingdom and the spread of the truths we hate, and we need not fear their influence; for we know that every selfish, covetous person will fall under our power, and will finally be separated from God's people'" *(Testimonies to Ministers,* pp. 472-474).

Has the devil been successful in his plan to cut off support for God's church? He has been very successful! The recent report of the General Conference World Survey Commission in its report for the North American Division pointed out that on a given Sabbath, of the 860,000 members in our church in North America, only about half are in church, and of those who do attend, only 63 percent are faithful tithers! Unfortunately, these statistics will change dramatically when persecution begins.

Tithing was not invented by Ellen White, Jasper Wayne, or the General Conference Committee. Tithing was God's idea! The tithing principle goes all the way back to the Garden of Eden. We have scriptural evidence of tithing practice dating back 4,000 years to the days of Abraham, the father of the faithful (Genesis 14). Don't let the devil discourage you and turn you away from your vow of faithfulness to God.

Every time I see a baptism I remember my own. My older brother, Ken, and I were baptized together, along with a number of others many years ago in a farm pond north of Fort Bragg, California. The actual baptism was conducted in the afternoon, but during the morning worship service, the pastor called the candidates forward for our examination. As a typical pastor, he asked us 13 questions. I well recall the one which went something like this: "Do you believe that the Seventh-day Adventist Church is the remnant church of Bible prophecy, and is it your purpose to support it with your tithes and offerings?" When I said, "Yes," I didn't have my fingers crossed behind my back. I meant it then, and I still mean it today. That was part of my baptismal vow. That was a Bethel, an Ebenezer, experience for me! I still want God to know that He can count on me to be faithful in this regard.

But let's get back to the story of Jacob. After Jacob had served Laban for many years, God came to him, saying, "I am the God of Bethel, where you anointed the pillar and where you made a vow to Me. Now arise, get out of this land, and return to the land of your kindred" (Genesis 31:13). Of course, Jacob was thrilled! He excitedly told his family, and while Laban was away they started off on their journey home.

When Laban returned home and realized that Jacob was gone, he pursued him and after three days caught up with him. He chastised Jacob for leaving without saying goodbye, saying, "It is in my power to do you harm, but the God of your father spoke to me last night, saying, 'Be careful that you speak to Jacob neither good nor bad'" (Genesis 31:29). God was keeping His word with Jacob and protecting him on his way back home! Then Laban and Jacob made a "witness heap of stones—a pillar" and called it Mizpah: "The Lord watch between you and me when we are absent one from another" (v. 49).

Traveling on from Mizpah, Jacob was getting closer and closer to home and Esau. He engaged in earnest prayer that God would protect him. Then he sent messengers on before him to tell Esau that he was following them with gifts. Though Jacob had left Padan-aram in obedience to God's command, it was not without many misgivings that he made his way back home. Retracing his steps of 20 years before, his sin of deception was on his mind. He knew that his long exile from home was the direct result of that sin. As he saw the hills of home in the distance his heart was deeply moved. But with the memory of his sin came the memory of God's promises of Divine help and guidance.

We are told that while Jacob was thinking over these things, a host of heavenly angels met him and seemed to travel along with him.[1] This experience is so awesome because Jacob's time of trouble is given as an illustration of what God's people will go through at the very end. We will be eager to go home, but our past will come up before us. Though we have asked forgiveness and received God's forgiveness, we will think again of how unworthy we are of God's protection. The story of Jacob will surely bring comfort to God's faithful saints.

When the messengers sent on ahead to Esau returned, they reported that he was coming with 400 men, with no response to the gifts sent. Terror filled Jacob's camp. His company was unarmed and defenseless—completely unprepared for a hostile encounter. His reaction was simple. He did all in his power to atone for the wrong to his brother by sending gifts and apologies, and then in humiliation and repentance he pleaded for Divine protection.

Reaching the river Jabbok, Jacob sent his family across the ford while he remained behind alone. He decided to spend the night in prayer with God. "God could soften the heart of Esau. In Him was the patriarch's only hope" *(Patriarchs and Prophets,* p. 196).

And thus alone, he pled with God. All his family and his servants were at a distance from him across the river. Then in the middle of the night a strong hand was suddenly laid upon him. He thought it was someone seeking his life—maybe the stealthy outdoors man, Esau. He struggled for his life for several hours, seeming to be holding his own until his assailant touched his thigh and he was instantly crippled. But he continued to hold on.

Then it was that Jacob realized whom he had been wrestling with. "It was Christ, 'the Angel of the covenant,' who had revealed Himself to Jacob" *(ibid.,* p. 197). Can you imagine the greatness of our awesome God? He came personally to Jacob in his time of need!

As the light of dawn began to creep across the horizon the Angel made an effort to release Himself, telling Jacob, "Let Me go, for the day breaketh;" but Jacob answered, "I will not let You go unless You bless me!" (Genesis 32:26). Jacob was not being presumptuous in his statement but was rather showing his trust in the faithfulness of a covenant-keeping God.

In His parting blessing God told Jacob, "Your name shall no longer be called Jacob, but Israel, for you have struggled with God and with men and have prevailed" (v. 28). Jacob had received the blessing for which his soul had longed. His sin had been pardoned. The crisis of his life was over. He no longer feared to meet Esau because he knew that God would be with him. In fact we are told, "While Jacob was wrestling with the Angel, another heavenly messenger was sent to Esau. In a dream, Esau beheld his brother, for twenty years an exile from his father's house; he witnessed his grief at finding his mother dead; he saw him encompassed by the hosts of God. This dream was related by Esau to his soldiers, with the charge not to harm Jacob, for the God of his father was with him" *(Patriarchs and Prophets,* p. 198). So when they finally met, Esau ran to meet Jacob, embraced him, and fell on his neck and kissed him, and they wept.

"Jacob's experience during that night of wrestling and anguish represents the trial through which the people of God must pass just before the second coming. The prophet Jeremiah, in holy vision looking down to this time, said, 'We have heard a voice of trembling, of fear, and not of peace. . . . All faces are turned into paleness. Alas! For that day is great, so that none is like it: it is even the time of Jacob's trouble; but he shall be saved out of it' " Jeremiah 30:5-7 *(ibid.,* p. 201).

After the close of probation the people of God will face the death decree. And, "As Jacob was threatened with death by his angry brother, so the people of God will be in peril from the wicked who are seeking to destroy them. And as the patriarch wrestled all night for deliverance from the hand of Esau, so the righteous will cry to God day and night for deliverance from the enemies that surround them" *(ibid.).* We can't let go. We must hold on until the blessing comes! We will plead the promises of God made through Christ. As dangers surround us we must depend solely upon the merits of the atonement. "We can do nothing of ourselves. In all our helpless unworthiness we must trust in the merits of a crucified and risen Saviour. None will ever perish while they do this" *(ibid.,* p. 203).

After Jacob's family had met Esau, God again came to him and said, "Arise and go up to Bethel." He was almost home now! Bethel was Jacob's most honored place on earth. Many times over the years he had told his family about the dream of the ladder and God's promised blessings to him. And now he was taking them to Bethel. What do you do when you go to Bethel? You meet with God. You experience revival. You renew your covenant. So Jacob told his family, "Put away the foreign gods that are among you, purify yourselves, and change your garments. Then let us arise and go up to Bethel; and I will make an altar there to God, who answered me in the day of my distress and has been with me in the way which I have gone" (Genesis 35:2, 3). And God appeared to Jacob again and blessed him.

Have you had a Bethel experience with God? Is there some time or place that you made a mature Christian commitment to trust God with your life? We all must do so to be able to successfully withstand the trials ahead. Jacob's experience with God at Bethel has been an encouragement to thousands of believers since then.

The enslavement of Joseph vividly illustrates a saving faith. Joseph sold by his brothers to Ishmaelite traders, found himself bound hand and foot, riding the caravan south to Egypt. As he rode along he could see in the distance the hills where his father's tents were pitched. He wept bitterly and with a trembling heart he looked to the future. His situation had changed drastically, from a cherished son to a helpless slave. For a time he cried uncontrollably.

"But in the providence of God, even this experience was to be a blessing to him. He had learned in a few hours that which years might not otherwise have taught him . . . Then his thoughts turned to his father's God. In his childhood he had been taught to love and fear Him. Often in his father's tent he had listened to the story of the vision that Jacob saw as he fled from his home an exile and a fugitive. He had been told of the Lord's promises to Jacob, and how they had been fulfilled—how, in the hour of need, the angels of God had come to instruct, comfort, and protect him. And he had learned of the love of God in providing for men a Redeemer. Now all these precious lessons came vividly before him. <u>Joseph believed that the God of his fathers would be his God.</u> He then and there gave himself fully to the Lord, and he prayed that the Keeper of Israel would be with him in the land of his exile. . . . One day's experience had been the turning point in Joseph's life. Its terrible calamity had transformed him from a petted child to a man, thoughtful, courageous, and self-possessed" *(Patriarchs and Prophets,* pp. 213, 214).

Many years later Jacob moved down to Egypt and lived there till he died. But before he died he made Joseph and his other sons swear that they would not bury him in Egypt. He told them that he wanted to be buried in the cave of Machpelah because, "There they buried Abraham and Sarah his wife, there they buried Isaac and Rebekah his wife, and there I buried Leah" (Genesis 49:31). So after Jacob's death Joseph had him embalmed and they took his body and buried him with his fathers. Years later when Joseph was dying he also asked his brethren to swear that they would carry his body out of Egypt when they were delivered.

When God called Moses to deliver the Israelites from Egypt He first appeared to him in a burning bush. God introduced Himself to Moses from the bush by saying, "I am the God of your father—the God of Abraham, the God of Isaac, and the God of Jacob" (Exodus 3:6). It is fascinating to me that God has chosen to identify Himself by the names of His faithful children who had entered into the covenant with Him. In fact when Moses asked God who should he say had sent him to be the deliverer, God said, "Thus you shall say to the children of Israel: <u>'The Lord God of your fathers, the God of Abraham, the God of Isaac, and the God of Jacob, has sent me to you. This is My name forever, and this is My memorial to all generations'</u> " (Exodus 3:15). Jesus referred to this name of God in Matthew 22:32 as did Stephen in his speech before the council in Acts 7:32.

There is to be a very happy ending to Jacob's story. Somewhere, not far from Bethel, there is a cave in the midst of a field. Inside it are the remains of six individuals; one of the bodies was mummified in the manner of Egypt. Very soon now a very awesome event will impact that cave. Let me share it with you as it is described in Psalm 50:1-5.

"The Mighty One, God the Lord, has spoken and called the earth from the rising of the sun to its going down.

"Out of Zion, the perfection of beauty, God will shine forth.

"Our God shall come, and shall not keep silent; A fire shall devour before Him, and it shall be very tempestuous all around Him.

"He shall call to the heavens from above, and to the earth, that He may judge His people."

Can't you picture it? As that little black cloud about the size of a man's hand comes closer to the earth it becomes a glorious cloud of angels that can be seen by everyone on earth at the same time. Somewhere, high above the cave of Machpelah, the cloud stops. Atop the cloud is a powerfully glorified Jesus. He holds up His hands, and there is absolute silence. Then in a voice of rolling thunder He speaks the words, "Awake! Awake, ye that sleep in the dust of the earth!" There is movement in the cave. The six people begin to stir. Abraham, Isaac, and Jacob, after whom God has chosen His name forever, along with their wives, Sarah, Rebekah, and Leah, rush out of the cave as the words of Jesus echo around the earth! I believe that God will take particular joy in calling forth those six people. What a reunion! Can you picture the glory, the triumph, of that scene?

When Jacob fled for his life as a handsome young man, "Rebekah bitterly repented the wrong counsel she had given her son; it was the means of separating him from her, and she never saw his face again" (*Conflict and Courage*, p. 62). But now after 4,000 years they see each other again. She, that beautiful young woman chosen by the servant Eliezer for his master Abraham's son, Isaac. And he, that handsome young son who had been the pride of her life. He shouts, "Momma!" She shouts, "Jacob!" You'd better believe there will be a lot of hugging and shouting! And a lot of praising God as they behold His glory.

Then Jesus tells the angels: "Gather My saints together to Me, Those who have made a covenant with Me by sacrifice" (Psalm 50:5). Immediately the angels fold their wings and dive to the earth. They go straight to their assigned places on the earth. At least six of them come to the mouth of the cave. There they find Abraham and Sarah, Isaac and Rebekah, Jacob and Leah. (Remember that Rachel was buried in Bethlehem, where she died following the birth of Benjamin.) The angels excitedly say, "It's time to go home. The man at the top of the ladder is waiting for you. The God of Abraham, Isaac, and Jacob is calling." Wow! Is that awesome or not?

You know, as I have contemplated this event I want the God of Abraham, Isaac, and Jacob to be my God too, don't you? I want to be in covenant relation with Jesus. I don't want anything on earth to divert my eyes or attention from Him. I want to be in that group that sees Him come. "Happy is he who has the God of Jacob for his help, whose hope is in the Lord his God" (Psalm 146:5).

> "And I saw a new heavens and a new earth, for the first heaven and the first earth had passed away. Also there was no more sea.

> "Then I, John, saw the holy city, New Jerusalem, coming down out of heaven from God, prepared as a bride adorned for her husband.

> "And I heard a loud voice from heaven saying, 'Behold, the tabernacle of God is with men, and He will dwell with them, and they shall be His people, and God Himself will be with them and be their God.

> "And God will wipe away every tear from their eyes; there shall be no more death, nor sorrow, nor crying; and there shall be no more pain, for the former things have passed away" (Revelation 21:1-4).

> "And he showed me a pure river of water of life, clear as crystal, proceeding from the throne of God and of the Lamb.

> "In the middle of the street, and on either side of the river, was the tree of life, which bore twelve fruits, each tree yielding its fruit every month. And the leaves of the tree were for the healing of the nations.

> "And there shall be no more curse, but the throne of God and of the Lamb shall be in it and His servants shall serve Him.

> "They shall see His face, and His name shall be on their foreheads" (Revelation 22:1-4).[2]

If I could compress the message of this book into one statement, I could simply say that <u>God is right on schedule.</u> Things are working out just exactly as He said they would. The four world empires spoken of in Daniel's prophecies have all come and gone. The little horn power of Daniel 7 has come to power and received the deadly wound, which has now healed. The beast with horns like a lamb has grown into a super-power. The Protestants of America are reaching out to unity with the papacy. Spiritualism is rapidly bringing the world under its deception. The world is eager to welcome the new millennium of peace. God's people are getting ready to proclaim the third angel's message with power. The God of Abraham, Isaac, and Jacob is calling, "Come, for all things are now ready!" In the words of the old gospel song, We can almost see the lights of home.

"We are homeward bound. A little longer, and the strife will be over. May we who stand in the heat of the conflict, ever keep before us a vision of things unseen—of that time when the world will be bathed in the light of heaven, when the years will move on in gladness, when over the scene the morning stars will sing together and the sons of God will shout for joy, while God and Christ will unite in proclaiming, 'There shall be no more sin, neither shall there be any more death.' 'Forgetting those things which are behind, and reaching forth unto those things which are before' let us 'press toward the mark for the prize of the high calling of God in Christ Jesus.'"[3]

Maranatha! Our Lord is coming!

---

[1] See Genesis 32:1, 2 and *Patriarchs and Prophets,* p. 195.
[2] See Exodus 3:15 for God's name forever.
[3] This message was frequently written by Ellen White in gift copies of her books.

Appendixes

The following chapters are given as a prophetic background to the contemporary developments of this book:

I. Prophecy Is Simple (The Four World Empires)
II. The Rise and Fall of the Little Horn Power
III. The United States—World Superpower
IV. Unmasking the Antichrist
V. The Seal of God
VI. The Mark of the Beast

For extra reading on the subject I recommend:

The Bible—first and foremost—get to know Christ and His prophetic guidance in the books of Daniel, Matthew, and Revelation.

Books by Ellen White:
The Great Controversy
Maranatha
Last Day Events
Early Writings
Selected Messages, vol. 3, pp. 380-431

Other books:
God Cares, vols. 1 and 2, by C. Mervyn Maxwell
Jesus Is My Judge—Meditations on the Book of Daniel,
        by Leslie Hardinge
Even at the Door, by G. Edward Reid

Personal Bible Study Guides:
Discover, The Voice of Prophecy, P.O. Box 55,
        Los Angeles, CA 90053
Unlocking Revelation, Light Bearers Ministry, P.O. Box 1888,
        Malo, WA 99150

For top-quality inspirational tapes from Adventist speakers:
Contact American Cassette Ministries, P.O. Box 922,
        Harrisburg, PA 17108 (Free Catalog)

APPENDIX I

Prophecy Is Simple

(The Four World Empires)

O nly two Bible books are primarily apocalyptic. Two very unique books pull back the veil and display the ultimate destiny of mankind. They portray a revelation of God in history and predict the future with precise accuracy. These two books are Daniel and Revelation. Both Daniel and John were in their later years when they penned their works. Both had since their youth developed a deep and abiding relationship with the God of heaven.

Understanding Daniel is a prerequisite for understanding Revelation. And understanding the first part of Daniel is essential to understanding the last part. Apocalyptic prophecy is progressive and presupposes an understanding of previous prophecy and of each previous step in the revelation. As indicated in the appendix title above, God never intended that prophecy would be complex. In fact, just the opposite is true. He wants prophecy to be a "revelation" of Himself and His activities on behalf of mankind. However, we are told that "None of the wicked shall understand, but the wise will understand" (Daniel 12:10). In other words, spiritual things are spiritually discerned. The Bible is its own best interpreter and by spending time in the Word we will gain understanding.

The Babylonian captivity of Israel was a real low point in the history of God's people. Warned of—predicted—for many years by Jeremiah and other prophets, this experience was devastating for the morale of Israel. Their thoughts were characterized by the words of the psalmist:

> "By the rivers of Babylon,
> "There we sat down, yea, we wept
> "When we remembered Zion.

"We hung our harps
"Upon the willows in the midst of it.
"For there those who carried us away
        captive asked of us a song.
"And those who plundered us requested mirth,
"Saying, 'Sing us one of the songs of Zion!'
"[But] How shall we sing the Lord's song
        in a foreign land?" (Psalm 137:1-4).

And yet in spite of the captivity problems, which were the result of their own course of action, God was with them and prospered the faithful ones.

Since the first chapter of Daniel gives the setting for the book, it cannot be overlooked. It tells the story of four young men—only in their late teens—Jewish captives far from home. Offered the rich and unhealthful foods of the king the young men asked for simple food. They recognized their bodies as the temple of God. "Daniel purposed in his heart that he would not defile himself with the portion of the king's delicacies, nor with the wine which he drank . . . 'give us vegetables to eat and water to drink,'" he requested. (See Daniel 1:8, 12.) During their training period, "God gave them knowledge and skill in all literature and wisdom; and Daniel had understanding in all visions and dreams" (Daniel 1:17). At the end of their training period they were personally examined by the king. "And in all matters of wisdom and understanding about which the king examined them, he found them ten times better than all the magicians and astrologers who were in all his realm" (v. 20).

The second chapter of Daniel is fundamental to an understanding of the rest of that book and to the later book of Revelation. In the wisdom of God, chapter two is remarkably pleasant to read and easy to understand. And like the first chapter, its profound message is delivered to us as a story. It is simple enough to tell a child and yet in 45 short verses it lays out the entire course of history from Daniel's day to the second coming of Christ!

We read that the Babylonian king Nebuchadnezzar had a remarkable dream one night. It woke him up and he couldn't go back to sleep. The Bible says that "his spirit was so troubled that his sleep left him."

He then called in all his "wise men" or counselors. The Bible calls them "magicians, astrologers, sorcerers, and Chaldeans." He told them that his dream was very significant but that he couldn't remember it, and furthermore he wanted to know its meaning. The "wise men" were used to giving their "interpretations" of dreams, but they were powerless to come up with the dream as well. Nebuchadnezzar told them that if they could tell him what he had dreamed they would be given gifts, rewards, and great honor. If not, they would be cut in pieces and their houses would be made an ash heap. One can only imagine the fear that swept over the wise men.

The wise men made a final appeal. No king or ruler had ever asked his wise men such a thing as that before, they said, and no one could do what he was asking them to do "except the gods, whose dwelling is not with flesh." The king became furious and gave a command to his guards that all the wise men should be destroyed.

Apparently Daniel and his three faithful friends were not in the group before the king. Perhaps their junior status had kept them away. When the king's guard came to take Daniel and his companions to the execution, the Bible says Daniel, with tact and wisdom, asked Arioch, the captain of the king's guard, "Why is the decree from the king so harsh?" Obviously, Daniel was well-liked by those who knew him because Arioch then told him the whole story.

Upon hearing the story, Daniel ventured into the king's presence and begged time to petition his God to reveal the dream and its interpretation. The king granted the request. Immediately Daniel ran to his house and contacted his three friends, Hananiah, Mishael, and Azariah (their Hebrew names), asking them to join him in prayer "that they might seek mercies from the God of heaven concerning this secret, so that Daniel and his companions might not perish with the rest of the wise men of Babylon" (v. 18).

These young men had confidence in God. He had been with them before. They had turned to Him many times before for guidance and protection. Now, with contrition of heart they submitted themselves anew to the Judge of the earth, pleading that He would grant them deliverance in this their time of special need.

God revealed the secret dream of the king to Daniel in a night vision. No doubt when Daniel woke, he quickly wrote out some notes so he wouldn't forget his dream. He offered a prayer by saying,

> "I thank You and praise You, O God of my fathers;
> "You have given me wisdom and might,
> "And have now made known to me what
>   we asked of You,
> "For You have made known to us the king's
>   demand" (v. 23).

Going to Arioch, Daniel told him, "Don't kill the wise men, take me to the king and I will give him the interpretation." The Bible says that "Then Arioch quickly brought Daniel before the king, and thus said to him [apparently taking a little credit to himself], 'I have found a man of the captives of Judah, who will make known to the king the interpretation'" (v. 25).

There stood Daniel, the Jewish captive, courteous, calm, and self-possessed. The king, perhaps remembering him as the outstanding student he had examined some time before, asked, "Are you able to make known to me the dream which I have seen and its interpretation?" Daniel could have just said, "Yes." But he didn't. Instead he gave a little preface to his answer. He said, "The secret which the king has demanded, the wise men . . . cannot declare to the king. But there is a God in heaven who reveals secrets, and He has made known [not to me but] to King Nebuchadnezzar <u>what will be in the latter days</u>" (vs. 27, 28). Here is an indication that God wants us to know about future events and the last days!

Then Daniel began to tell the dream. You can be sure that everyone in the room, especially the king, was listening closely.

"You, O king, were watching; and behold, a great image! This great image, whose splendor was excellent, stood before you; and its form was awesome." The king moved to the edge of his throne and exclaimed, "That's it! You've got it! Go on!" Daniel continued,

> "This image's head was of fine gold, its chest and
>   arms of silver, its belly and thighs of bronze,
> "Its legs of iron, its feet partly of iron and partly
>   of clay.

"You watched while a stone was cut out without
      hands, which struck the image on its feet
      of iron and clay, and broke them in pieces.
"Then the iron, the clay, the bronze, the silver, and
      the gold were crushed together, and became
      like chaff from the summer threshing floors;
      the wind carried them away so that no trace
      of them was found. And the stone that struck
      the image became a great mountain and filled
      the whole earth" (vs. 32-35).

I can imagine the king, forgetting royal protocol, springing to his feet and hugging Daniel and saying, "You are exactly right, young man. Now, what does it mean?" Since he knew it was the very dream which had troubled him, he was receptive for its interpretation. Daniel responded, "Now <u>we</u> [apparently including his three friends as is later evident] will tell the interpretation of it before the king" (v. 36).

The interpretation, recorded in your Bible, is a model of clarity. The Bible interprets itself—it is indeed simple!

The Interpretation

The king sat back down and Daniel continued,

"You, O king, are a king of kings. For the God of heaven
has given you a kingdom, power, strength, and glory;

"And <u>wherever the children of men dwell</u> [the known
world], or the beasts of the field and the birds of the heaven,
<u>He has given them into your hand, and has made you ruler
over them all</u>—**you are this head of gold**" (vs. 37, 38).

As you can see from what I have underlined above, the king of Babylon ruled the entire known world. But is the head of gold referring to the king himself or to his kingdom? The next verse gives the answer.

"But after you shall arise <u>another kingdom</u> [not another "king"] inferior to yours; then another, a third **kingdom** of bronze, which shall rule over all the earth."

Please note that these successive kingdoms "rule over all the earth." They are world empires! But Daniel is not finished yet.

"And the fourth kingdom shall be as strong as iron, inasmuch as iron breaks in pieces and shatters everything; and like iron that crushes, that kingdom will break in pieces and crush all the others.

"Whereas you saw the feet and toes, partly of potter's clay and partly of iron, the kingdom shall be divided; yet the strength of the iron shall be in it, just as you saw the iron mixed with ceramic clay.

"And as the toes of the feet were partly of iron and partly of clay, so the kingdom shall be partly strong and partly fragile.

"As you saw iron mixed with ceramic clay, they will mingle with the seed of men; but they will not adhere to one another, just as iron does not mix with clay.

"And in the days of these kings [following the division of the fourth empire] the God of heaven will set up a kingdom which shall never be destroyed; and the kingdom shall not be left to other people; it shall break in pieces and consume all these kingdoms, and it shall stand forever" (vs. 39-44).

The bottom line is simple. There would be four world empires starting with Babylon—only four. The fourth one would not be conquered as the first three were by a succeeding world empire; but the fourth would be "divided" or broken up among various "kings." Oh yes, many leaders would try to make another world empire, but their attempts would fail.

Daniel concluded the interpretation for King Nebuchadnezzar by saying, "Inasmuch as you saw that the stone was cut out of the mountain without hands, and that it broke in pieces the iron, the bronze, . . . the silver, and the gold—the great God has made known to the king what **will** come to pass after this. **The dream is certain, and its interpretation is sure"** (v. 45). Daniel was confident of the dream and its interpretation because he was confident in God!

Picture the scene in the king's royal quarters. The king prostrated himself before Daniel (v. 46) and commanded that they should present an offering and incense to him. The king told Daniel that his God is the God of gods, and truly the Lord is a revealer of secrets—"since you could reveal this secret."

The king gave Daniel many great gifts and made him ruler over the whole province of Babylon and the chief administrator of the wise men. Daniel, in his greatness and humility, petitioned the king on behalf of his three friends, and they were given positions of leadership as well.

Sometimes in a study of history it appears that events were shaped because of the strength or prowess of man, but this prophecy reveals the hand and wisdom of God. Before these world empires came upon the stage of action, God looked down the ages and predicted their rise and fall. When we now look back, by studying history, we can see the literal fulfillment of divine prophecy.

Daniel lived long enough to see the beginning of the second world empire. The elder statesman was summoned to come to Belshazzar's feast for another interpretation—the handwriting on the wall! Daniel's last words to the king were, "Your kingdom has been divided, and given to the Medes and Persians" (Daniel 5:28).

The prophet Ezra confirms this in the words of the Persian king: "Thus says Cyrus king of Persia: All the kingdoms of the earth the Lord God of heaven has given me" (Ezra 1:2).

Then later through a "heavenly messenger" God revealed to Daniel the identity of the third empire as well! The messenger asked, "Do you know why I have come to you? And now I must return to fight with the prince of Persia; and when I have gone forth, indeed the prince of Greece will come" (Daniel 10:20). Three out of four is not bad. Do you think the Bible also reveals the identity of the fourth empire? Yes, it does—In the New Testament! In Luke 2:1 we learn that Caesar Augustus issued a decree that "all the world" should be registered for tax purposes. He must, then, have had jurisdiction over all the world.

Who was Caesar Augustus?—a Roman emperor. So Rome was the fourth kingdom. The legs of iron in Nebuchadnezzar's dream could represent no other kingdom, because Rome was the only universal kingdom that came to power after Grecia. So when Jesus appeared among men almost 2,000 years ago the course of history had already reached the legs of iron.

Dr. C. Mervyn Maxwell, in his excellent Daniel resource book summarizes the sequence this way: "After he [Nebuchadnezzar] died in 562 B.C. the Babylonian Empire ran rapidly downhill. Media and Persia, powers inferior to Babylon during Nebuchadnezzar's lifetime, were united together and linked to Lydia by Cyrus, king of Persia. They conquered Babylon in 539 B.C. The Medo-Persian Empire continued for a while to expand in wealth, power, and size (adding Egypt); but like Babylon it too went into decline. In 331 B.C. it was vanquished by Alexander the Great, founder of the Macedonian Greek Empire. At Alexander's death his dominion was divided into a number of Hellenistic Greek kingdoms. Meanwhile Rome was evolving in the west and, in due course, began to influence the Hellenistic kingdoms. By 168 B.C. Rome dominated the Mediterranean as the fourth empire of the statue prophecy.

"Babylonian, Medo-Persian, Greek, Roman—the list of empires is simple and can be memorized in a moment. Any good history book will confirm the sequence" (Maxwell, *God Cares,* vol. 1, pp. 34, 35).

How could this vision and history lesson ever be relevant to *Sunday's Coming!*? The answer: Daniel 2 is foundational. It is basic to understanding all prophecy that historically follows it. It provides the structure upon which one can add the additional details from other prophecies regarding these same and subsequent players in human history.

The Bible's own interpretation is sure. And a basic truth of Daniel 2 is that all of the major elements but the second coming of Christ are already written in the history books! We are indeed living in those "later times" spoken of by Daniel.

APPENDIX II

The Rise and Fall
of the Little Horn Power

The second chapter of Daniel gives us the basic structure of world history right down to the second coming of Christ. In fact, by the time of Christ's first advent, history had already reached the time of the fourth and final "world empire." So what about all the time between then and now? Do we have any indication from Bible prophecy what we should expect in those intervening years? Certainly: God wants us to know what is happening and what we may expect in the future. And in Daniel 7 we are informed in great detail of the activities of players in the drama of the ages. It is a wonderful validation of the truth that "Amidst the strife and tumult of nations, He that sitteth above the cherubim still guides the affairs of the earth.

"The history of nations that one after another have occupied their allotted time and place, unconsciously witnessing to the truth of which they themselves knew not the meaning, speaks to us. To every nation and to every individual of today God has assigned a place in His great plan. Today men and nations are being measured by the plummet in the hand of him who makes no mistake. All are by their own choice deciding their destiny, and God is overruling all for the accomplishment of His purposes.

"The history which the great I AM has marked out in His word, uniting link after link in the prophetic chain, from eternity in the past to eternity in the future, tells us where we are today in the procession of the ages, and what may be expected in the time to come. All that prophecy has foretold as coming to pass, until the present time, has been traced on the pages of history, and we may be assured that all which is yet to come will be fulfilled in its order.

"The final overthrow of all earthly dominions is plainly foretold in the word of truth. . . . That time is at hand. Today the signs of the times declare that we are standing on the threshold of great and solemn events. Everything in our world is in agitation. . . . The present is a time of overwhelming interest to all living. Rulers and statesmen, men who occupy positions of trust and authority, thinking men and women of all classes, have their attention fixed upon the events taking place about us. They are watching the strained, restless relations that exist among the nations. They observe the intensity that is taking possession of every earthly element, and they recognize that something great and decisive is about to take place—that the world is on the verge of a stupendous crisis.

"Angels are now restraining the winds of strife, that they may not blow until the world shall be warned of its coming doom; but a storm is gathering, ready to burst upon the earth; and when God shall bid His angels loose the winds, there will be such a scene of strife as no pen can picture.

"The Bible, and the Bible only, gives a correct view of these things" (Education, pp. 178-180). So let's get back to the Word for its exciting unveiling of more truth.

Daniel 7 begins by giving the date as "the first year of Belshazzar king of Babylon." This helps us to date the time of the vision. Historians tell us that Nebuchadnezzar was succeeded on the Babylonian throne by Nabonidus who "entrusted the kingship" to Belshazzar in 553 B.C.— the date of this vision. Nebuchadnezzar had been dead for nine years, and things weren't going very well for Babylon.

Daniel was no longer a young man. He was about 70, though apparently not fully retired. The fall of Babylon described in chapter 5 and his experience in the lions' den of chapter 6 were still in the future. The chapters of the book of Daniel—like that of Revelation—are not all arranged chronologically. Fifty years had passed since the vision of Daniel 2. No doubt that experience was still vivid in the mind of Daniel.

Then we read that "Daniel had a dream and visions of his head while on his bed" (v. 1). He wrote down the dream, making an outline of the main facts. What he saw was "the four winds of heaven were stirring up the Great Sea.

"And four great beasts came up from the sea, each different from the other.

"The first was like a lion, and had eagle's wings. I watched till its wings were plucked off; and it was lifted up from the earth and made to stand on two feet like a man, and a man's heart was given to it.

"And suddenly another beast, a second, like a bear. It was raised up on one side, and had three ribs in its mouth between its teeth. And they said to it: 'Arise, devour much flesh!'

"After this I looked, and there was another, like a leopard, which had on its back four wings of a bird. The beast also had four heads, and dominion was given to it.

"After this I saw in the night visions, and behold, a fourth beast, dreadful and terrible, exceedingly strong. It had huge iron teeth; it was devouring, breaking in pieces, and trampling the residue with its feet. It was different from all the beasts that were before it, and it had ten horns" (vs. 2-7).

Then Daniel observed a very unique feature in the dream—a little horn. It is really the focus of this chapter because it—the little horn—describes something not mentioned in the empire progression of Daniel 2. Daniel puts it this way:

"I was considering the horns, and there was another horn, a little one, coming up among them, before whom three of the first horns were plucked out by the roots. And there, in this horn, were eyes like the eyes of a man, and a mouth speaking pompous words" (v. 8).

Daniel continued to watch the heavenly portrayal until he was shown the awesome view of a heavenly judgment where "the Ancient of Days was seated . . . the court was seated, and the books were opened." Then he was apparently distracted by the sounds of the little horn.

"I watched then <u>because of the sound of the pompous words
which the horn was speaking;</u> I watched till the beast was
slain, and its body destroyed and given to the burning flame.

"As for the rest of the beasts, they had their dominion
taken away, yet their lives were prolonged for a season and
a time" (vs. 11, 12).

In his account Daniel says that he was next given a view of the second coming of the Son of Man and the setting up of His kingdom
"which shall not pass away." But the vision troubled him and he
wanted a better understanding of what it meant. He was particularly
concerned about the fourth beast with its ten horns and curious about
its "little horn." Daniel states that he came near to "one of those who
stood by." We may assume that it was an angel—a heavenly messenger. He asked the angel, "the truth of all this."

The Interpretation

God clearly wants us to understand prophecy. He does not want us
to be in darkness. Immediately, He provided an interpretation to Daniel
through an angel. So "he told me and made known to me the interpretation." The angel first gave Daniel a short summary:

"Those great beasts, which are four, are four kings which
arise out of the earth. But the saints of the Most High shall
receive the kingdom, and possess the kingdom forever, even ·
forever and ever" (vs. 17, 18).

Just two sentences. That's all he was given until he asked for more.
But surely the angel wanted Daniel to see the similarity with the vision
of chapter 2—the vision of the metal image. There would be four kingdoms and then God's everlasting kingdom. But Daniel wasn't satisfied
with that simple explanation. He wanted to know more about the
fourth beast and its horns and the strange "little horn." And so the
Bible record continues:

"Thus he [the angel] said:

"The <u>fourth beast</u> shall be a <u>fourth kingdom</u> on earth,

"Which shall be different from all other kingdoms, and shall devour the whole earth, trample it and break it in pieces" (v. 23).

Knowing that the fourth beast is the <u>fourth kingdom,</u> we recognize at once that we are seeing the same series of world powers that we discussed in the last chapter while reviewing Daniel 2: Babylonian, Medo-Persian, Greek, and Roman empires, followed in due time by the kingdom of God. But now more details are given.

The angel continued his interpretation:

"The ten horns are ten kings who shall arise from this kingdom.

"And another shall rise after them;

"He shall be different from the first ones,

"And shall subdue three kings.

"He shall speak pompous words against the Most High,

"Shall persecute the saints of the Most High,

"And shall intend to change times and law.

"Then the saints shall be given into his hand for a time and times and half a time" (vs. 24, 25).

The angel's interpretation of the mysterious little horn clearly helps to identify it as papal Rome—later to be known as the Roman Catholic Church. Let's review the clues given by the angel for a positive identification.

1. **Location.** It arose out of the fourth beast. It came up among

the ten horns (nations) of western Europe into which the civil or pagan Roman Empire was divided (vs. 8, 24).

Did papal Rome originate out of the old Roman Empire? Yes.

2. **Time of rise.** It appeared after the ten other horns, that is, after the breakup of the Roman Empire—during the sixth century A.D. Further, it would rise after three of the horns (kings) had been uprooted (vs. 8, 20, 24).

The "Christian church" founded by Christ and the apostles existed from the first century, but the papal domination did not begin until after the fall of the Roman Empire. Did papal Rome arise after the fifth century? Yes.

(Three of the barbarian kingdoms that arose out of the Roman Empire espoused the views of Arius, who denied the divinity of Christ. All the other barbarian kingdoms came to accept the Christian faith.)

From A.D. 476 on, the three Arian powers dominated portions of the territory of Rome, but each in turn met defeat as the rulers of the Eastern Roman Empire rallied to support the Roman Church in the West. In 533 Justinian, the emperor of the Eastern Empire, officially recognized the bishop (later to be called pope) of Rome as the head of all the Christian churches. But because of the Arian domination of Rome, the pope had no opportunity to actually exercise this officially recognized power. Five years later, in 538, Belisarius, one of Justinian's generals, routed the Ostrogoths, the last of the Arian powers, from the city of Rome. So by the military intervention of the Eastern Empire the pope was freed from the dominating influence of states that restrained his activities in the civil sphere. This date, A.D. 538, plays a significant part in another clue that helps to identify the little horn as the papacy.

3. **The nature of the little horn.** It was "different" or diverse from the other horns and though it was little at first it became "greater than his fellows" (vs. 7, 8, 20, 24). The little horn was different—it would speak against the Most High and persecute the saints. The "difference" was that it would be both political and religious in nature.

Was papal Rome different than the other "kingdoms" that emerged from the Roman Empire? Yes, indeed.

4. **Rise to power.** It would "put down three kings" or "pluck them up by the roots" (vs. 8, 24). As mentioned in two above, three of the ten kingdoms that emerged from the ashes of pagan Rome were "Arian" in religious thinking. These were the Heruls, the Vandals, and the Ostrogoths. They were, with the aid of the Eastern Empire, defeated by Rome to allow for its more dominant control. These three kingdoms have no modern counterparts.

Did papal Rome uproot three kingdoms as it "came to power"? Yes.

5. **Attitude toward God.** The little horn would speak great things against the Most High (vs. 8, 20, 25). What does it mean to "speak great words against the Most High"? It is generally understood among Bible scholars that speaking against the Most High is equivalent to taking on the prerogatives of God and/or blaspheming His name. Much could be written on this topic. The following should be sufficient to make the point of identification.

"The pope's power—and his religious and political claims—increased for centuries. In 1076 Pope Gregory VII informed the subjects of Henry IV, emperor of Germany, that if Henry would not repent of his sins, they would not need to obey him. Henry was the most powerful monarch in Europe at the time, but he nonetheless made a pilgrimage to Canossa in the Alps, where the pope was residing, and waited three painful days, barefoot in the snow, until Pope Gregory forgave him.

"Taking his cue from Gregory VII, Pope Pius V in 1570, in the bull (or decree) *Regnans in excelsis* ('He who reigns in the heavens') declared that the Protestant queen of England, Elizabeth I (1558-1603), was an accursed heretic who hereafter should have no right to rule and whose citizens were all, by papal authority, forbidden to obey her. 'Professor McKenzie [Jesuit professor John L. McKenzie of Notre Dame University] acknowledges in his gracious manner that 'the teaching authority of the Roman Catholic Church is vested at any given moment in men, who are not all of equal virtue and competence.' He continues: '[Pope] Pius V was and is respected as a holy and learned man, but his deposition of Elizabeth I of England is recognized as one of the greatest blunders in the history of the papacy.'

"The admission that the 'teaching authority of the Roman Church' is vested in men of unequal virtue and competence contrasts with the claim made as recently as the 1890's by Pope Leo XIII. In an encyclical letter, 'On the Chief Duties of Christians as Citizens,' dated January 10, 1890, Leo XIII asserted that 'the supreme teacher in the Church is the Roman Pontiff. Union of minds, therefore, requires . . . complete submission and obedience of will to the Church and to the Roman Pontiff, as to God Himself.' On June 20, 1894, in 'The Reunion of Christendom,' Leo claimed further that 'we [that is, we popes] hold upon this earth the place of God Almighty' " (Maxwell, *God Cares,* vol. 1, p. 125).

Does papal Rome claim the prerogatives of God? Yes.

6. **Attitude toward God's people.** The little horn was to persecute or "wear out the saints of the Most High" (vs. 21, 25). According to the angel's interpretation to Daniel this power would persecute God's people. Those whom papal Rome considered heretical faced civil punishment. History attests that millions were put to death under this religio-political system.[*] For a firsthand look, visit the archbishop's fortress in Salsburg, Austria, where during the "middle" or "dark ages" for a period of over 400 years Salsburg was a "city state" and the archbishop was also the king. Take the guided tour of the fortress and see the torture chamber where enemies of the archbishop and "heretics" were tortured until they "confessed" and then they were executed.

Did papal Rome persecute the saints? Yes.

7. **Attitude toward God's law.** The little horn would attempt to or "think to" change times and law (v. 25). It would view God's law as needing changes and would attempt to make changes in that law by its own authority. Several examples will illustrate this. Many could be given. Significantly, the Roman Catholic Church does not adhere to the basic Protestant notion that the Bible and the Bible only should be the standard of faith and practice. There are three major "sources of truth" for the Roman Catholic: the Bible, the "magisterium" or the teaching authority of the church, and, of course, the ex-cathedra words of the pope.

Now here are some claims of the Roman Church regarding changes in God's law:

"Around the year 1400 Petrus de Ancharano made the claim that 'the pope can modify divine law, since his power is not of man, but of God, and he acts in the place of God on earth, with the fullest power of binding and loosening his sheep.'

"This astonishing assertion came to practical fruitage during the Reformation. Luther claimed that his conscience was captive only to Holy Scripture. *Sola Scriptura* was his slogan. 'The Bible and the Bible only.' No churchly tradition would be allowed to guide his life.

"But one day it occurred to Johann Eck and to other Catholic churchmen to taunt Luther on his observance of Sunday in place of the Bible Sabbath. Said Eck, 'Scripture teaches: "Remember to hallow the Sabbath; six days shall you labor and do all your work, but the seventh day is the Sabbath day of the Lord your God," etc. Yet,' insisted Eck, 'the *church* has changed the Sabbath into Sunday on its own authority, on which *you* [Luther] have no Scripture.'

"At the great Council of Trent (1545-1563), convened by the pope to staunch the onrush of Protestantism, Gaspare de Posso, the archbishop of Reggio, in an address of January 18, 1562, brought the issue up again. 'The authority of the church,' he said, 'is illustrated most clearly by the scriptures; for while on the one hand she [the church] recommends them, declares them to be divine, [and] offers them to us to be read, . . . on the other hand, the legal precepts in the Scriptures taught by the Lord have ceased by virtue of the same authority [the church]. The Sabbath, the most glorious day in the law, has been changed into the Lord's day . . . These and other similar matters have not ceased by virtue of Christ's teaching (for He says He has come to fulfill the law, not to destroy it), but they have been changed by the authority of the church'" (Maxwell, *God Cares,* vol. 1, p. 128).

Hundreds of years later the Roman Church still asserts she can change God's law. Recently I purchased two books from a Catholic organization, Our Lady's Book Service, operated by the "Servant and Jesus and Mary" in Constable, New York. Both books are proported to have the "Imprimatur" or blessing of the church. One book, by the renowned James Cardinal Gibbons, archbishop of Baltimore, states: "The scriptures alone do not contain all the truths which a Christian is obliged to practice. Not to mention other examples, is not every Christian obligated to sanctify Sunday and to abstain on that day from unnecessary servile work? Is not the observance of this law among the most prominent of our sacred duties? But you may read the Bible from Genesis to Revelation, and you will not find a single line authorizing the sanctification of Sunday. The Scriptures enforce the religious observance of Saturday, a day which we never sanctify" (Gibbons, *The Faith of Our Fathers,* pp. 72, 73, 1876, reprinted by TAN Books and Publishers, 1980).

The other book is Peter Geiermann's Catechism. His comments, in question-and-answer format, on the Sabbath commandment are as follows:

"Q. *What is the Third Commandment?* [note: Catholics place the Sabbath Command third]

"A. The Third Commandment is: Remember that thou keep holy the Sabbath day.

"Q. *Which is the Sabbath day?*

"A. Saturday is the Sabbath day.

"Q. *Why do we observe Sunday instead of Saturday?*

"A. We observe Sunday instead of Saturday because the Catholic Church transferred the solemnity from Saturday to Sunday" (Rev. Peter Geiermann, C.SS.R., *The Convert's Catechism of Catholic Doctrine,* p. 50).

In addition, in Catholic listings of the Ten Commandments the second commandment is dropped altogether. Many of the others have been abbreviated, robbing them of their full meaning. And the tenth is divided in order to make a total of ten. In the comments on the fourth commandment in the New Catechism (called the third by the RCC) paragraph number 2190 it states: "The sabbath, which represented the completion of the first creation, has been replaced by Sunday which recalls the new creation inaugurated by the Resurrection of Christ" *(The Catechism of the Catholic Church,* 1994 edition, p. 529).

Did papal Rome try to change God's law? Yes.

8. **Length of time permitted to rule.** It—the little horn—was to rule for "a time, and times and half a time" (v. 25). Again, this is not

complicated. A time = one year or 360 days in prophecy. Times = two years or 720 days, and half a time = half a year or 180 days. Add them up and you get 1260 days. This harmonizes with Revelation 13:5 where this period is spoken of as 42 months (42 months x 30 days per month = 1260 days) and in Revelation 12:6 where the time is actually recorded as 1260 days.

Maxwell gives a good explanation of this. "We are dealing here with symbols. The Bible says that the four beasts are symbols of four kings or kingdoms, that the horns likewise symbolize kingdoms, and that the waters are symbolic of multitudes of people [Rev. 17:15]. The Bible also indicates that in symbolic prophecy days represent years.

"You may recall that when Daniel lived in Babylon, the prophet Ezekiel lived at Nippur, not very far away. In the symbolic prophecy of Ezekiel, chapters 4 to 6, God said expressly to Ezekiel, 'I assign you, a day for each year.' Ezekiel 4:6" (Maxwell, *God Cares,* vol. 1, p. 124).

Remember, as we noted in number 2 (Time of rise), the papal Roman Catholic Church came to power in 538 A.D. If we add to that the 1260 years of the time it was given to rule, that brings us to 1798. And so it happened in 1798, 1260 years after 538, that the French general Berthier, under the direction of the military government of France, arrested Pope Pius VI in the Sistine chapel and took him captive, where he ultimately died in exile.

Did papal Rome dominate Europe during the 1260-year period from 538 to 1798? Yes.

These eight identifying characteristics of the "little horn" clearly point to the papal Roman Church. What other power, different than other powers, arose after the fall of the Roman Empire from among the divided kingdoms, destroyed three of the kingdoms, spoke blasphemy against God, persecuted God's saints, tried to change God's law, and dominated Europe for 1260 years? None but the Roman Catholic Church. No other power or entity even comes close to meeting the conditions. The little horn power is quite obviously the Roman Catholic Church.

But this takes us only to 1798. Does God leave us there to wonder what will happen next? Not at all. Remember how prophecy is progressive and builds on what happens or is given before? In order to fill in the prophetic picture right up to the 1990s we go to the apocalyptic book of Revelation. God gave the apostle John the same view of the future that He gave Daniel. However, by the time of John the first three world empires were already history, and he was living during the fourth and final world empire. Summarizing what had been given before, God quickly brought John up to speed in an impressive vision.

"Then I stood on the sand of the sea. And I saw a beast rising up out of the sea, having seven heads and ten horns, and on his horns ten crowns, and on his heads a blasphemous name. Now the beast which I saw was like a leopard, and his feet were like the feet of a bear, and his mouth like the mouth of a lion. And the dragon gave him his power, his throne, and great authority" (Revelation 13:1, 2).

This beast rose up out of the sea, which represents a populated area (Rev. 17:15). Then John saw a unique symbol—a beast with the body of a leopard, the feet of a bear, and the mouth of a lion. These are the same symbolic animals of Daniel 7. In his vision Daniel saw a lion (symbolizing Babylon), a bear (Medo-Persia), a leopard (Greece), and finally a "dreadful and terrible" beast (Rome). According to his vision, the fourth empire, Rome, would come to be dominated in its final stage by a "little horn," a terrible power that would persecute God's people for "a time, times, and half a time."

John's vision and prophecy are so similar to the description of the little horn in Daniel 7, and it unquestionably points to the time when the apostate papal church system of the Middle Ages began to dominate the state. The apostle Paul referred to this power as the "man of sin," and the "mystery of iniquity" (see 2 Thessalonians 2:3, 4).

One aspect of Revelation 13 is most significant. After ruling for 1260 years during the Middle Ages until 1798, the papacy appeared to receive a deadly wound. But this chapter in Revelation reveals an additional fact. The deadly wound heals, and all the world wonders after the beast (Revelation 13:3). Evidently, the papacy will play a major role in end-time events.

In identifying the role of the papacy and Roman Catholicism, I want to emphasize that I have no bone to pick with Catholic people. Without question there are many wonderful, God-fearing individuals in the Roman Catholic Church. The Bible is quite clear on that

(Revelation 14:7 and 18:4). God does not condemn these dear people. Rather, it is the system to which God objects—the mingling of church and state, or as Revelation 17:1 shows, the prostitution of the church to the state.

The bottom line here is very simple and straightforward. In the outline of prophecy as given through the books of Daniel and the Revelation, papal Rome as a system is a major player. One can draw no other logical conclusion.

---

* For considerable documented evidence see my book *Even at the Door,* chapter four and the appendix to chapter four.

APPENDIX III

The United States— World Superpower

Many nations have played important bit parts in history. However, only a relatively small number actually play a major role in Bible prophecy and salvation history. They are Babylon, Medo-Persia, Greece, Rome, the papacy, and the United States of America. There are many explicit characteristics of the sixth power that help to identify it as the last great earthly power to play a role in salvation history.

Daniel was promised by an angel that his book, though it would be sealed for a period of time, would be opened and understood at the time of the end (see Daniel 12:4, 9, 10). Revelation, on the other hand, was to be just that—a revelation of Jesus Christ which would show His servants things which must shortly take place (see Revelation 1:1; 22:6, 7). It is when we use our own human speculation regarding prophetic interpretation instead of using the Bible itself to be its own interpreter that we come up with all kinds of weird interpretations. Remember, God wants us to know.

It has been the traditional interpretation of Seventh-day Adventists that the second beast, mentioned in Revelation 13 (v. 11), the land beast, the beast with horns like a lamb, is the United States of America. The reason it is important to identify this beast is that whatever nation it is eventually cooperates with the revived or "healed" papacy at the end of time. These two will be the final players in the great drama of the ages.

In the last chapter when discussing the little horn, we noted that apparently when God gave John his vision in Revelation 13, He took it for granted that His servant John would be familiar with the book of

Daniel and its beasts in chapter 7. So basically, Revelation 13 does not go all the way back to Babylon and move systematically forward as Daniel 2 and 7 do. Instead, the vision of Revelation 13 makes a quick two-verse summary to bring John up to speed and then proceeds to give more details that help to make a positive ID of the little horn power.

But now another beast rises out of the earth. "He had two horns like a lamb and spoke as a dragon" (Revelation 13:11). Again the biblical clues give unmistakable evidence as to its identity. Here are some of the biblical identifying characteristics of this beast with horns like a lamb.

1. It arises about the time when the first beast, the papacy, is wounded (vs. 3, 11).
2. It, unlike the first beast of Revelation 13 and the beasts of Daniel 7, comes up out of the earth (v. 11).
3. It has two horns like a lamb (v. 11).
4. It speaks like a dragon (v. 11).
5. It has a worldwide influence (vs. 12, 14).
6. It has authority like the first beast (v. 12).
7. It supports the first beast (vs. 14, 15).
8. It encourages worship of the first beast (v. 15).
9. It performs great signs (vs. 13, 14).
10. It becomes a persecuting power (vs. 15, 17).
11. It causes many to receive the mark of the beast (v. 16).

"Beasts" in apocalyptic language represent kings or kingdoms. Accordingly, we can begin by looking for a kingdom or nation that fits the clues given in Revelation 13. It is an almost inescapable conclusion that the clues point to the United States of America. The clues reveal:

1. **The time of its rise to power.** We should look for a country that is rising to power around 1798, the time when the papacy received its "deadly wound." The pilgrims landed in the "New World" in the early 1600s. The various settlements known as colonies slowly began to bond together during the "colonial period." In 1776 the colonies unified to the point that the Declaration of Independence was drawn up. In 1787 the Constitution was ratified, and in 1789 the Bill of Rights was formulated. In 1791 the Bill of Rights was adopted. As we noted in the last appendix it was a French general (Berthier) who took the pope captive in 1798, and it is no doubt significant that it was that very same year that the French government recognized the United States as a nation.

Ellen White makes this observation: "What nation of the New World was in 1798 rising into power, giving promise of strength and greatness, and attracting the attention of the world? The application of the symbol admits of no question. One nation, and only one, meets the specifications of this prophecy; it points unmistakably to the United States of America" *(The Great Controversy,* p. 440).

2. **The location of the new power.** The other beasts or kingdoms in the prophetic lineup all rose from the sea, which as we have seen from Revelation 17:15 represents "peoples, multitudes, nations, and tongues." All of the other nations came to power amidst the peoples of the earth by conquering them. Babylon conquered its surrounding nations including Israel; Medo-Persia conquered Babylon, etc., but this beast came up "out of the earth." So the nation we are looking for is one that "developed" or "grew up" by exploration, colonization, and development. Only one place on earth was "undeveloped" as far as the rest of the world was concerned—the North American continent. And it certainly was colonized by people moving here from other nations. Literally millions came to America from Ireland, Italy, Germany, and other countries of Europe initially and then from all parts of the world. Who hasn't heard of Ellis Island and the Statue of Liberty? In fact, fitted right into the pedestal or base of the Statue of Liberty is this famous poem:

The New Colossus
"Not like the brazen giant of Greek fame,
With conquering limbs astride from land to land;
Here at our sea-washed, sunset gates shall stand
A mighty woman with a torch, whose flame
Is the imprisoned lightning, and her name
Mother of Exiles. From her beacon-hand
Glows world-wide welcome; her mild eyes command
The air-bridged harbor that twin cities frame.

"'Keep ancient lands, your storied pomp!' cries she with silent lips.
'Give me your tired, your poor,
Your huddled masses yearning to breath free,
The wretched refuse of your teaming shore.

<u>Send these, the homeless, tempest-tost to me,</u>
<u>I lift my lamp beside the golden door!' "</u>
—Emma Lazarus

And so they came—by the millions! And still today they want to come! The new nation idea called by many the "American experiment," has been a part of the core of American history. But it was not without a struggle. There was a great civil war: Americans fighting Americans over differences in ideology.

Just a little over an hour's drive from my home is the little community of Gettysburg, Pennsylvania. The battle fought there on July 1 to 3 of 1863 marked a turning point in the war. The circumstances leading to this particular battle are very intriguing. General George G. Meade led a Northern army of about 90,000 men to victory against General Robert E. Lee's Southern army of about 75,000. The two forces met accidently in the little town of Gettysburg, Pennsylvania. The shooting began when a Confederate brigade ran into Union cavalrymen in Gettysburg on July 1.

The two armies spent the first day maneuvering for position. Northern troops settled south of town in a strong defensive position. Lee tried to crack the left side of the Union's defenses on the second day. The attack crushed a Northern corps, but failed to occupy the position. On July 3, Lee decided to aim directly at the Union center. In a famous charge, General George E. Pickett's troops advanced across an open field and up the slopes of Cemetery Ridge into murderous Northern fire. They reached the crest of the ridge, but could not hold the position. Lee withdrew his battered forces to Virginia. But the casualty list was long. More than 38,000 men lay dead on the battlefield.

Later that same year it was decided that a memorial should be established at Gettysburg. Part of that battlefield would be dedicated to be a cemetery for those who died there. On November 19, 1863, President Abraham Lincoln came up on the train "to say a few words" on the occasion of setting aside this special cemetery. He was not the featured speaker. The famous orator Edward Everett spoke for two hours before Lincoln gave his two-minute talk. Few have any knowledge of what Everett said in those two hours, but Lincoln's "few words" are known by all Americans as the Gettysburg Address. In those days everyone knew that America was unique, but wondered if the American experiment could work.

> "Four score and seven years ago <u>our fathers brought forth on this continent, a new nation,</u> conceived in Liberty, and dedicated to the proposition that all men are created equal.
>
> "<u>Now we are engaged in a great civil war, testing whether that nation, or any nation so conceived and so dedicated, can long endure.</u> We are met on a great battlefield of that war. We have come to dedicate a portion of that field, as a final resting place for those who here gave their lives that that nation might live. It is altogether fitting and proper that we should do this.
>
> "But, in a larger sense, we can not dedicate—we can not consecrate—we can not hallow—this ground. The brave men, living and dead, who struggled here, have consecrated it, far above our power to add or detract. The world will little note, nor long remember what we say here, but it can never forget what they did here. It is for us the living, rather, to be dedicated here to the unfinished work which they who fought here have thus far so nobly advanced. It is rather for us to be here dedicated to the great task remaining before us—that from these honored dead we take increased devotion to that cause for which they gave the last full measure of devotion—<u>that we here highly resolve that these dead shall not have died in vain—that this nation, under God, shall have a new birth of freedom—and that government of the people, by the people, for the people, shall not perish from the earth.</u>"
>
> —Abraham Lincoln, Gettysburg, Pennsylvania, Nov. 19, 1863

The Emma Lazarus poem on the Statue of Liberty and Lincoln's Gettysburg Address show clearly that from a simply historical perspective the United States is truly a "new nation." There can be no question that the United States fits the second clue.

3. **It has two horns like a lamb.** Some interpreters have called this beast a lamblike beast. The Bible doesn't call the beast lamblike. It says that its horns are lamblike. Lamblike describes the horns not the beast. Ellen White makes 17 references to this in her writings and she <u>always</u> says the horns are lamblike—not the beast. There is a great dif-

ference in meaning. The beast grows to be big and powerful but it has "lamblike" horn. Maybe a buffalo—which some have pictured—would be more like the beast which John saw.

Why make such a big deal out of the lamblike description? It is quite simple. A misinterpretation can lead to a wrong conclusion! A former Adventist minister with nearly a million copies of his book in print, believes that the second beast of Revelation 13 is the antichrist. His reasoning is simple. He says if this beast is lamblike but <u>not</u> "the" lamb or Christ, then it must be the antichrist. This error could not have come up if one would just read the scripture carefully. The "horns" are "lamblike," not the beast. What do the two horns represent, then? I believe they could quite logically represent the "gentle" characteristics of Republicanism and Protestantism—a nation without a despotic king and a church without an authoritarian pope. The bottom line here is that the new nation would have civil and religious liberty.

"At the time when the Papacy, robbed of its strength, was forced to desist from persecution, John beheld a new power coming up to echo the dragon's voice, and carry forward the same cruel and blasphemous work. This power, <u>the **last** that is to wage war against the church and the law of God, is represented by a beast with lamblike horns.</u> The beasts preceding it had risen from the sea; but this came up out of the earth, representing the peaceful rise of the nation which it symbolized—the United States.

"<u>The 'two horns like a lamb' well represent the character of our own government, as expressed in its two fundamental principles,— Republicanism and Protestantism.</u> These principles are the secret of our power and prosperity as a nation. Those who first found an asylum on the shores of America, rejoiced that they had reached <u>a country free from the arrogant claims of popery and the tyranny of kingly rule. They determined to establish a government upon the broad foundation of civil and religious liberty</u>" (Ellen White, *The Signs of the Times,* Feb. 8, 1910).

4. **It becomes very powerful.** Revelation says, "speaks like a dragon." The United States is the only remaining world "superpower" today. No country on earth has the political or military muscle of the United States today. Yet this clue is fulfilled only partially at present. We may expect to see it further fulfilled in the near future.

"The dragon," of course, is Satan. But Satan also works through the other dragon-like beasts of prophecy. So apparently the United States will become more "Satan-like" near the end. Some might wonder how the United States could ever "speak as a dragon" and become a persecuting power. But the Bible says it will happen.

"The founders of the nation wisely sought to guard against the employment of secular power on the part of the church, with its inevitable result—intolerance and persecution. The Constitution provides that 'Congress shall make no law respecting an establishment of religion, or prohibiting the free exercise thereof' and that 'no religious test shall ever be required as a qualification to any office of public trust under the United States.' Only in flagrant violation of these safeguards to the nation's liberty, can any religious observance be enforced by civil authority. But the inconsistency of such action is no greater than is represented in the symbol. It is the beast with lamblike horns—in profession pure, gentle, and harmless—that speaks as a dragon" *(The Great Controversy,* p. 442).

5. **It has worldwide influence.** With the demise of the former Soviet Union the United States "leads" the world. For example, there would have been no "liberation" of Kuwait without the United States. The success of the "Desert Storm" war was possible only with the power and technology of the United States.

This worldwide influence was recognized by Malachi Martin in *The Keys of This Blood,* published in 1990. On the cover and in the introduction to his book Martin says that there was a three-way struggle going on for world dominion between the pope (Roman Catholicism), Gorbachev (the Soviet Union), and the Capitalist West (the United States and its allies). Martin expects the pope to be the victor in the struggle and that "those of us under seventy will at least see the basic structures of the new world government installed" (pp. 15, 16). He goes on to say, "It is not too much to say, in fact, that the chosen purpose of John Paul's pontificate—the engine that drives his papal grand policy and that determines his day-to-day, year-by-year strategies—is to be the victor in that competition, now well under way" (p. 17).

There can be no question that the United States does have worldwide influence today. But in the future, "As America, the land of religious liberty, shall unite with the papacy in forcing the conscience and compelling men to honor the false sabbath, the people of every country on the globe will be led to follow her example." Ellen White concludes, "Our people are not half awake to do all in their power, with the facilities within their reach, to extend the message of warning" *(Testimonies for the Church,* vol. 6, p. 18).

6. **It exercises all the authority of the first beast (the papacy).** This will be fulfilled "When the Protestant churches shall unite with the secular power to sustain a false religion, for opposing which their ancestors endured the fiercest persecution; when the state shall use its power to enforce the decrees and sustain the institutions of the church— then will Protestant America have formed an image to the papacy [the beast], and there will be a national apostasy which will end only in national ruin" (Ellen G. White, *Signs of the Times,* March 22, 1910).

7. **It—the United States—supports the first beast—the papacy.** Many state Sunday laws were established around the turn of the century. But one essential ingredient was missing for them to constitute "the" national Sunday law. The missing ingredient was a cooperation between the United States and the papacy. In fact, as history bears out, there was a very strong anti-Catholic bias in the United States. How things have changed today! During Ronald Reagan's presidency we established "full diplomatic relations with the central government of the Roman Catholic Church," and additionally, in what has been called the "Holy Alliance," we cooperated with the papacy in bringing about the downfall of Communism.

8. **It encourages worship of the first beast.** One of the major factors in the identification of the first beast (of Revelation 13 and the little horn of Daniel 7) is that it is "different." This "worship" clue does include that the allegiance involves not only a civil but also a religious entity. In plain language the United States will eventually encourage support of the Roman Catholic Church. In fact, that is happening right now! Churchmen like Chuck Colson, Pat Robertson, Billy Graham, and others are encouraging support of Rome. And civil leaders like President Clinton, Vice President Gore, and most of the Republican establishment are giving political support for the aims of Rome.

9. **It would perform great signs.** The "signs" mentioned in Revelation 13 are things like "fire coming down from heaven." Significantly this type of sign is now being predicted by "The Blessed

Virgin Mother, Mary" in apparitions around the world.

10. **It becomes a persecuting power.** This characteristic of the beast with lamblike horns has yet to be revealed. "Our land is in jeopardy. The time is drawing on when its legislators shall so abjure the principles of Protestantism as to give countenance to Romish apostasy. The people for whom God has so marvelously wrought, strengthening them to throw off the galling yoke of popery, will, by a national act, give vigor to the corrupt faith of Rome, and thus arouse the tyranny which only waits for a touch to start again into cruelty and despotism. With rapid steps are we already approaching this period" (Ellen White, *Signs of the Times,* July 4, 1899).

11. **It causes many to receive the mark of the beast.** The United States, founded on the principles of civil and religious liberty, and so blessed of God, will be instrumental in bringing about the mark of the beast.

Taken together these clues are very clear. They point unmistakably to the United States as the second beast of Revelation 13—the beast with lamblike horns.

Unmasking the Antichrist

The antichrist is described as the great opponent and counterfeit of Christ, by whom he is finally to be conquered. The term antichrist may mean one who is opposed to Christ, or one who assumes the place of Christ, or one who combines both of these roles by assuming the prerogatives of Christ. The term antichrist occurs only in the New Testament and only in the writings of John (1 John 2:18, 22; 4:3; and 2 John 7).

It seems that John takes it for granted that his readers understand that the full manifestation of antichrist is in the last days. He speaks, however, of many antichrists in his day (1 John 2:18). He also uses the singular term "antichrist." Under the figure of the leopard beast of Revelation 13 he depicts a great power that would oppose Christ and His people.

Satan is "the ultimate" antichrist. He has opposed Christ through various human agencies. He has introduced many heresies through the centuries, all suited to deceive. In John's day Docetism and Gnosticism were doubtless considered anti-Christian. Through the centuries many Bible scholars, even some Roman Catholics, have identified the papacy as antichrist. I concur with this view and will share the evidence for this conclusion in this appendix.

At the very end of human history Satan will play a direct, personal role in world affairs (2 Thessalonians 2:9). In fact, Satan's personation of Christ will be followed quickly by the real second coming of Christ.

If the antichrist was already working in John's day and will be working intensely at the end of time, it could not be a specific man. It is rather the devil working through a "system" of evil.

In *Jesus Is My Judge—Meditations on the Book of Daniel*, Dr. Leslie Hardinge gives over 100 Bible clues for the identity of the antichrist. He makes the point, as do many other scholars, that the antichrist John speaks of is also the little horn of Daniel 7 and 8.

Chuck Colson, writing in *Evangelicals and Catholics Together*, observes, "About the only moral value postmodernists [our generation] seem to be able to advance is total, undiscriminating tolerance, but being able to tolerate anything is a formula for accepting the status quo. Those who accept people as they are have no interest in helping them change, even when their condition and behavior is ruining their lives . . . Mere tolerance is a weak and passive virtue compared to the active energy of Christian love" (p. 22).

The attitude that says I'm OK—you're OK, or just do your own thing, or if it makes you feel good—do it, is not appropriate for a Christian who is committed to fulfilling the gospel commission. Failure to warn of error and danger is unconscionable. Failure to state what the danger is in a clear and concise way is also just as bad.

While maintaining a spirit of love toward those deceived, Ellen White called Romanism a "mammoth system of deception" and wrote that "The people need to be aroused to resist the advances of this most dangerous foe to civil and religious liberty." She went on to say, "Papists place crosses upon their churches, upon their altars, and upon their garments. Everywhere is seen the insignia of the cross. Everywhere it is outwardly honored and exalted. But the teachings of Christ are buried beneath a mass of senseless traditions, false interpretations, and rigorous exactions. . . . Conscientious souls are kept in constant terror fearing the wrath of an offended God, while many of the dignitaries of the church are living in luxury and sensual pleasure" *(The Great Controversy,* pp. 570, 566, 568).

"The apostle Paul warned the church not to look for the coming of Christ in his day. 'That day shall not come,' he says, 'except there come a falling away first, and that man of sin be revealed.' 2 Thessalonians 2:3. Not until after the great apostasy, and the long period of the reign of the 'man of sin,' can we look for the advent of our Lord. The 'man of sin,' which is also styled 'the mystery of iniquity,' 'the son of perdition,' and 'that wicked,' **represents the papacy,** which, as foretold in prophecy, was to maintain its supremacy for 1260 years. This period ended in 1798. The coming of Christ could not come before that time" *(ibid.,* p. 356).

But how could the "Christian" church become so enmeshed with error as to be an antichrist power? The answer seems to be the "Christianizing" of paganism. It is quite clear to students of church history that Constantine's "conversion" to Christianity and his acceptance into the church was a matter of mutual convenience. Over the years much of paganism came into the belief and practice of the church. John Henry Newman, Rome's most famous English convert, gave the following list of church practices that came directly from paganism:

"The use of temples, and those dedicated to the particular saints, and ornamented on occasion with branches of trees, incense, lamps and candles; votive offerings on recovery from illness, holy water, asylums, holy days and seasons, use of calendars, processions, blessings on fields, sacerdotal vestments, the tonsure, the ring in marriage, turning to the East, images at a later date, perhaps the ecclesiastical chant, and Kyrie Eleison are all of pagan origin, and sanctified by adoption into the Church" (Cardinal J. H. Newman: *An Essay on the Development of Christian Doctrine,* p. 373).

There are many other pagan practices in Romanism today such as: "The sacrificing Priesthood, penances, absolution and the Confessional, Papal Infallibility, the titles 'Holy Father' and 'supreme pontiff,' the worship or veneration of Saints and relics (such as the Turin Shroud) and of idols, images, statues and symbols; stone altars; the rosary, the monstrance and wafer, prayers for the dead, extreme unction, purgatory and limbo, plenary indulgences, ritualism, monasticism and mysticism; add to these pilgrimages, crosses and crucifixes, celibacy, the Mother and Child worship; Mary's continuing virginity, the scapular, canonization of Saints, Cardinals, nuns, the mitre, fish on Friday, the (mystic) keys, Lent; the sign of the cross, the 'Sacred Heart,' Easter (from Astarte the goddess of spring, associated with the sun rising in the east), baptismal regeneration and justification by works; Peter 'the rock,' rather than Peter's faith in Christ; all these things and many besides, are at the heart of modern Roman Catholicism. Not all are widely practiced in Western Protestant countries, but they are nevertheless deeply embedded in Church tradition. All are unsupported by Scripture and many are expressly forbidden in the Bible" (Michael de Semlyen, *All Roads Lead to Rome,* pp. 61, 62).

The discerning student will quickly note that the two major doctrinal errors in the end-time scenario, Sunday sacredness and the immortality of the soul, both come directly from paganism—from the devil—and not the Holy Scriptures.

The Authority of Scripture

Some say that it is unfair to judge the modern church by the church of the past. The church has changed, they say. Yes, many public practices have changed such as using English in the services here in America, the priest facing the congregation, etc. But what doctrine or pagan practice has changed? Can you name even one? I can't. Sadly, the Roman Catholic Church holds that the Bible alone is not a sufficient guide for faith and practice. I will quote three Catholic authors for evidence of that "antichrist" position.

"The Scriptures alone do not contain all the truths which a Christian is bound to believe, nor do they explicitly enjoin all the duties which he is obliged to practice. Not to mention other examples, is not every Christian obliged to sanctify Sunday and to abstain on that day from unnecessary servile work: Is not the observance of this law among the most prominent of our sacred duties? But you may read the Bible from Genesis to Revelation, and you will not find a single line authorizing the sanctification of Sunday. The Scriptures enforce the religious observance of Saturday, a day which we never sanctify.

"The Catholic Church correctly teaches that our Lord and His Apostles inculcated certain important duties of religion which are not recorded by the inspired writers. For instance, most Christians pray to the Holy Ghost, a practice which is nowhere found in the Bible.

"We must therefore, conclude that the Scriptures alone cannot be a sufficient guide and rule of faith because they cannot, at any time, be within the reach of every inquirer; because they are not of themselves clear and intelligible even in matters of the highest importance, and **because they do not contain all the truths necessary for salvation"** (James Cardinal Gibbons, *The Faith of Our Fathers,* pp. 72, 73).

In 1994 the Roman Catholic Church produced the new *Catechism of the Catholic Church.* The full edition of the Catechism had not been revised since the sixteenth century (1566). It was also the first full edition of the Catechism to be printed in English. It sold over 10,000,000 copies in the first six month of circulation. Significantly, it has the Imprimatur of the Vatican in the form of the signature of Cardinal Joseph Ratzinger, the director of the Congregation for the Doctrine of the Faith which is "the Roman Inquisition's latest incarnation" *(Time,* December 6, 1993, p. 58). *Time* goes on to report that "The Cardinal [Ratzinger] likes to explain his faith through the story of one of his theology professors, a man who questioned the thinking behind the church's 1950 declaration that the Assumption of the Virgin Mary into Heaven was an infallible tenet. He said, 'No this is not possible—we don't have a foundation in Scripture. It is not possible to give this as dogma.' This led the professor's Protestant friends to hope they had a potential convert. But the professor immediately reaffirmed his abiding Catholicism. 'No, at this moment I will be convinced that the church is wiser than I.' Ratzinger asserts, 'It was always my idea to be a Catholic, to follow the Catholic faith and not my own opinions.' Theologians may wrangle all they want, he says, but faith in the end is something ineffable, springing from the heart. And once it is felt there, he says, 'then the mind will accept it too'" *(Time,* Dec. 6, 1993, p. 60). This great enforcer of the Catholic faith states in essence that it doesn't matter if your belief is biblical or not—if the church teaches it, you will accept it.

Ellen White gave this very perceptive insight into this topic. "The Roman Church reserves to the clergy the right to interpret the Scriptures. On the ground that ecclesiastics alone are competent to explain God's word, it is withheld from the common people. Though the Reformation gave the Scriptures to all, yet the selfsame principle which was maintained by Rome prevents multitudes in Protestant churches from searching the Bible for themselves. They are taught to accept its teachings *as interpreted by the church;* and there are thousands who dare receive nothing, however plainly revealed in Scripture, that is contrary to their creed or the established teaching of their church" *(The Great Controversy,* p. 596).

But here again hasn't the church changed? Now the Catholic Church encourages the study of the Bible. There are even Bible study groups. Yes, one can study all he wants to, but to remain a Catholic you must accept the interpretation of the church above the plain meaning of Scripture.

Perhaps the best example of this is the stated belief of Roman Catholic attorney and author, Keith Fournier. He is a college graduate, a law school graduate, a college administrator, and now works full-time for the Christian Coalition as the director of the American Center for Law and Justice. He states that he is a born-again Christian, a tongues-speaking, Holy Spirit-filled, Evangelical Catholic. He is a "professional Christian," who has been involved in the Charismatic movement and the ecumenical movement and has written several books on religious topics—and yet in spite of all this he will not make a biblical decision apart from the teaching of the church. He says, "I am thoroughly convinced that the church of Christ must be both hierarchial and charismatic, institutional and dynamic, and that she is indeed the universal sign (sacrament) of salvation still revealing Christ's presence in the world. Therefore I have submitted myself to the teaching office of the Catholic Church and its leadership. I do this willingly and by conscious choice."

Fournier goes on to say, "I have often heard friends refer to themselves as 'Bible-toting believers.' Well, I am too, but as a Catholic, I believe that there is a magisterium, a teaching office, that provides ongoing guidance in the application of that Book to my life. **Hence I am a magisterium-toting Catholic.** I appreciate the moral clarity the magisterium provides" (Keith Fournier, *A House United,* p. 32).

Anti-Catholic Bigotry?

Many "politically correct" Christians say that to point out the errors of the Catholic Church is prejudiced and bigoted. We need to keep in mind that "It is true that there are real Christians in the Roman Catholic communion. Thousands in that church are serving God according to the best light they have . . . But Romanism as a system is no more in harmony with the gospel of Christ now than in any former period of her history. The Protestant churches are in great darkness, or they would discern the signs of the times. The Roman Church is far-reaching in her plans and modes of operation. She is employing every device to extend her influence and increase her power in preparation for a fierce and determined conflict to regain control of the world, to re-establish persecution, and to undo all that Protestantism has done. Catholicism is gaining ground on every side . . . Protestants have tampered with and patronized popery; they have made compromises and concessions which papists themselves are surprised to see and fail to understand" *(The Great Controversy,* pp. 565, 566).

Is it prejudice to expose error? Is it bigotry to stand for the truth of God's Word and encourage others to join you? If you think it is, then what kind of message will you give during the latter rain and the loud cry? The message of Revelation 18 is twofold: "Babylon is fallen" and "Come out of her My people." Think about it! The bottom line is that the truth must be spoken in love—but it must be spoken.

"As the time comes for it [the third angel's message] to be given with greatest power, the Lord will work through humble instruments . . . The sins of Babylon will be laid open. The fearful results of enforcing the observances of the church by civil authority, the inroads of spiritualism, the stealthy but rapid progress of the papal power—all will be unmasked. Thousands upon thousands will listen who have never heard words like these. In amazement they hear the testimony that Babylon is the Church, fallen because of her errors and sins, because of her rejection of the truth sent to her from heaven" *(ibid.,* pp. 606, 607).

Catholics Discuss the Papacy

Over the years many Catholic leaders have deplored the gross immorality in the Catholic Church. In fact, Martin Luther, "as an Augustinian monk in the University of Wittenberg, came reluctantly to believe 'the papacy is in truth . . . very Antichrist.'" And "Through the centuries, various Roman Catholic spokesmen have felt that the pope—either the current one or a future one, or the papacy as a whole (the entire line of popes)—was the Antichrist. For example, during a time of deep spiritual laxness in Rome, Arnoff, the bishop of Orleans, deplored the Roman popes as 'monsters of guilt' and declared in the council called by the king of France in 991 that the pontiff, clad in purple and gold, was 'Antichrist, sitting in the temple of God, and showing himself as God.'

"When the Western church was divided for about 40 years between two rival popes, one in Rome and the other in Avignon, France, each pope called the other pope antichrist—and John Wycliffe is reputed to have regarded them both as being right: 'two halves of

Antichrist, making up the perfect Man of Sin between them'" (Maxwell, *God Cares,* vol. 1, p. 117).

In the thirteenth century a terrible feud developed between Frederick II, ruler of the Holy Roman Empire, and Pope Gregory IX. During this controversy Eberhard II, archbishop of Salzburg, who was a supporter of Frederick, reported in public the results of his biblical studies—that the pope was the antichrist and the little horn of Daniel 7. "His boldest statement was made at a synod of Bavarian bishops held in Regensburg, or Ratisbon, in 1240 or 1241; where he gave utterance at the same time to a new interpretation of some lines of prophecy. Here, during this council, Eberhard, in a brilliant oration preserved by Aventinus, or Turmair, in his noted Bavarian Annals, clearly sets forth this identification of the prophecy of the Little Horn. In this striking presentation Eberhard not only openly calls the pope a wolf in shepherd's garb, the Son of Perdition, and Antichrist, but also gives his revolutionary exposition of the pope as the Little Horn of Daniel 7" (Leroy Edwin Froom, *The Prophetic Faith of Our Fathers,* vol. 1, pp. 797, 798).

Eberhard's declaration came at the height of the papal power, which was the midnight of Bible truth and religious freedom. Ellen White describes those days in this manner: "The Holy Scriptures were almost unknown, not only to the people, but to the priests. Like the Pharisees of old, the papal leaders hated the light which would reveal their sins. God's law, the standard of righteousness, having been removed, they exercised their power without limit, and practiced vice without restraint. Fraud, avarice, and profligacy prevailed. Men shrank from no crime by which they could gain wealth or position. The palaces of popes and prelates were scenes of vilest debauchery. Some of the reigning pontiffs were guilty of crimes so revolting that secular rulers endeavored to depose these dignitaries of the church as monsters too vile to be tolerated. For centuries Europe had made no progress in learning, arts, or civilization. A moral and intellectual paralysis had fallen upon Christendom" *(The Great Controversy,* p. 60).

Sadly, the papacy, Roman Catholicism, does indeed fit the prophetic definitions of the system through which the great antichrist, Satan, is working. "The papacy is just what the prophecy declared that she would be, the apostasy of the latter times" *(ibid.,* p. 571).

APPENDIX V

The Seal of God

In the Bible the seal of God is good and its counterpart, the mark of the beast, is bad. No one gets both. Everyone who lives to see Jesus come will get one or the other. It is important to clearly identify the seal of God. We need to prepare for it. Actually, the sealing process is a trigger point in the book of Revelation. John says, "After these things I saw four angels standing at the four corners of the earth, holding the four winds of the earth, that the wind should not blow on the earth, on the sea, or on any tree.

"Then I saw another angel ascending from the east, having the seal of the living God. And he cried with a loud voice to the four angels to whom it was granted to harm the earth and the sea.

"Saying, 'Do not harm the earth, the sea, or the trees till we have sealed the servants of our God on their foreheads.'

"And I heard the number of those who were sealed. One hundred and forty-four thousand of all the tribes of the children of Israel were sealed" (Revelation 7:1-4).

Evidently, God's wrath is not poured out until His seal is placed on His servants. The seal, placed on their foreheads, identifies them and provides protection.

The King James Bible has 25 references to the word "seal." The general usage denotes something official: something with a permanent mark. The book of Esther records the word of the Persian king to Esther following the hanging of Haman. Wanting to protect Esther and all of the Jews in his realm, he told them, "You yourselves write a decree for the Jews, as you please, in the king's name, and seal it with the king's signet ring; for a letter which is written in the king's name and sealed with the king's signet ring <u>no one can revoke</u>" (Esther 8:8).

God loves each one of us dearly. A study of His seal reveals some amazing concepts. We are His by virtue of creation and redemption. He paid for us. And He is coming back soon to get us! Note the following exciting passage: "Now He who establishes us with you in Christ and has anointed us is God, who also has sealed us and given us the Spirit in our hearts as a deposit" (2 Corinthians 1:21, 22, NKJV). Here God seals us with His Spirit as a deposit. The KJV says, "He has given the earnest [as in earnest money] of the Spirit in our hearts." The NIV says, "He has put his Spirit in our hearts as a deposit, guaranteeing what is to come." And who is given the Holy Spirit? Acts 5:32 states, "And we are His witnesses to these things, and so also is the Holy Spirit whom <u>God has given to those who obey Him.</u>" This is one of the clues we are looking for. Obedience involves God's law. God's seal is given to those who obey His law.

Isaiah 8:16 commands, "Bind up the testimony, seal the <u>law</u> among my disciples." Here again the seal involves God's law. When we go to God's great moral law, the Ten Commandments as recorded in Exodus 20, it is easy for one to observe that the fourth commandment in particular identifies its author and on what basis He should be worshiped. A seal typically gives the name, title, and territory of a ruler. The fourth commandment contains these elements in regard to God. The name—"The Lord Thy God"; title—"Creator"; territory—"Heaven and Earth." With the fourth commandment, the Creator plainly indicates that it is the Sabbath which is to stand as His eternal seal. God plainly said this to Moses. "Speak also to the children of Israel, saying: '<u>Surely My Sabbaths you shall keep, for it is a sign between Me and you throughout your generations,</u> that you may know that I am the Lord who sanctifies you'" (Exodus 31:13). There is more evidence from Scripture: God says, "Moreover <u>I also gave them My Sabbaths, to be a sign between them and Me, that they might know that I am the Lord who sanctifies them.</u> 'I am the Lord your God: Walk in My statutes, keep My judgments, and do them; <u>hallow My Sabbaths, and they will be a sign between Me and you, that you may know that I am the Lord your God'</u>" (Ezekiel 20:12, 19, 20).

"<u>The Sabbath</u> is not introduced [at Mt. Sinai] as a new institution but as having been founded at creation [see Genesis 2:1-3]. It is to be remembered and observed as the memorial of the Creator's work. Pointing to God as the Maker of the heavens and the earth, it <u>distinguishes the true God from all false gods.</u> All who keep the seventh day signify by this act that they are worshipers of Jehovah. Thus the Sabbath is the sign of man's allegiance to God as long as there are any upon the earth to serve Him. The fourth commandment is the only one of all the ten in which are found both the name and the title of the Lawgiver. It is the only one that shows by whose authority the law is given. Thus it contains the seal of God, affixed to His law as evidence of its authenticity and binding force" *(Patriarchs and Prophets,* p. 307).

In changing the Sabbath the papal power violated the seal of God on the law. God's followers are called upon to restore the Sabbath of the fourth commandment to its rightful position as the Creator's memorial, the sign of His authority and His covenant with His people.

The Significance of the Seal

"Not all who profess to keep the Sabbath will be sealed" *(Testimonies for the Church,* vol. 5, p. 213). A survey of the chapter from which this statement is taken indicates that knowledge of the Sabbath and a merely legalistic observance of it falls far short of evidencing a saving relationship with God. Then what, in addition to Sabbathkeeping, is necessary to receive the seal of God? "The seal of God will never be placed upon the forehead of an impure man or woman. It will never be placed upon the head of an ambitious, world-loving man or woman. It will never be placed upon the forehead of men or women of false tongues or deceitful hearts. All who receive the seal must be without spot before God—candidates for heaven" *(ibid.,* p. 216). In other words, those who receive the seal of God will not only be Sabbathkeepers, they will also be converted, committed, loving, and honest Christians.

Ellen White explains that those who are sealed have settled "into the truth, both intellectually and spiritually, so that they cannot be moved" *(Manuscript Releases,* vol. 10, p. 252). They believe the truth and they practice the truth. They believe in the perpetuity of God's law and they trust Him to sanctify them. "No other institution which was committed to the Jews tended so fully to distinguish them from surrounding nations as did the Sabbath. God designed that its observance should designate them as His worshipers. It was to be a token of their separation from idolatry, and their connection with the true God. But in order to keep the Sabbath holy, men must themselves be holy. Through faith they must become partakers of the righteousness of Christ" *(The Desire of Ages,* p. 283).

Earlier we noted that 2 Corinthians 1:22 states we are sealed by God's Spirit as an earnest pledge, deposit, or guarantee. Let's now consider what that truly means. "The sealing is a pledge from God of perfect security to His chosen ones (Ex. 31:13-17). Sealing indicates you are God's chosen. He has appropriated you to Himself. As the sealed of God we are Christ's purchased possession, and no one shall pluck us out of His hands. The seal given in the forehead is God, New Jerusalem. 'I will write upon him the name of My God, and the name of the city of My God' (Rev. 3:12)" *(Manuscript Releases,* vol. 15, p. 225).

Neither the seal of God nor the mark of the beast are visible marks to the human eye. It is also important to note that though the mark of the beast can be received either in the hand or on the forehead, the seal of God can be received only on the forehead. Most Bible students believe that with regard to the Sunday law and the mark of the beast one can choose to believe and support it—mark on the forehead, or choose to not make any waves and just go along with it—mark in the hand. Obviously, no one will "just go along" with the seal of God. It is something one must be willing to die for.

So, then, what is this seal that is placed on the foreheads of the saved? "It is a mark which angels, not human eyes, can read; for the destroying angel must see the mark of redemption. The intelligent mind has seen the sign of the cross of Calvary in the Lord's adopted sons and daughters. The sin of the transgression of the law of God is taken away. They have on the wedding garment, and are obedient and faithful to all God's commands" *(The Gospel Herald,* June 11, 1902). The living righteous will receive the seal of God prior to the close of probation and it will be their passport through the gates of the Holy City. (See *Maranatha,* p. 211 and *The SDA Bible Commentary,* vol. 7, p. 970.)

Certainly the Sabbath is central to obeying God and receiving His seal. It is central to recognizing the great end-time apostasy. It is not an obscure interpretation by one or two Bible scholars. It is woven into the very fabric of God's Word to us. Early Adventists held the Sabbath aloft and treasured it. The following "facts" on the Sabbath come from an old tract published by the Review and Herald Publishing Association about the year 1885. Read through these significant—and still very true—facts to understand the continuing significance of the Sabbath.

One Hundred Bible Facts Upon the Sabbath Question

Why keep the Sabbath day? What is the object of the Sabbath? Who made it? When was it made, and for whom? Which day is the true Sabbath? Many keep the first day of the week, or Sunday. What Bible authority have they for this? Some keep the seventh day, or Saturday. What scripture have they for that? Here are the facts about both days, as plainly stated in the Word of God:

Sixty Bible Facts Concerning the Seventh Day

1. After working the first six days of the week in creating this earth, the great God rested on the seventh day. Genesis 2:1-3.

2. This stamped that day as God's rest day, or Sabbath day, as Sabbath day means rest day. To illustrate: When a person is born on a certain day, that day thus becomes his *birthday*. So when God rested upon the seventh day, that day became His rest, or Sabbath day.

3. Therefore the seventh day must always be God's Sabbath day. Can you change your birthday from the day on which you were born? No. Neither can you change God's rest day to a day on which He did not rest. Hence the seventh day is still God's Sabbath day.

4. The Creator blessed the seventh day. Genesis 2:3.

5. He sanctified the seventh day. Exodus 20:11.

6. He made it the Sabbath day in the garden of Eden. Genesis 2:1-3.

7. It was made before the fall; hence it is not a type; for types were not introduced till after the fall.

8. Jesus said it was made for *man* (Mark 2:27); that is, for the race, as the word man here is unlimited; hence, for the Gentile as well as for the Jews.

9. It is a memorial of creation. Exodus 20:11; 31:17. Every time we rest upon the seventh day, as God did at creation, we commemorate that great event.

10. It was given to Adam, the head of the human race. Mark 2:27; Genesis 2:1-3.

11. Hence through him, as our representative, to all nations. Acts 17:26.

12. It is not a Jewish institution; for it was made 2,300 years before there ever was a Jew.

13. The Bible never calls it the Jewish Sabbath; but always, "the Sabbath of the Lord thy God." Men should be cautious how they stigmatize God's holy rest day.

14. Evident reference is made to the Sabbath all through the patriarchal age. Genesis 2:1-3; 8:10, 12; 29:27, 28, etc.

15. It was a part of God's law before Sinai. Exodus 16:4, 27-29.

16. Then God placed it in the heart of His moral law. Exodus 20:1-17. Why did He place it there if it was not like the other nine precepts, which all admit to be immutable?

17. The seventh-day Sabbath was commanded by the voice of the living God. Deuteronomy 4:12, 13.

18. Then He wrote the commandment with His own finger. Exodus 31:18.

19. He engraved it in the enduring stone, indicating its imperishable nature. Deuteronomy 5:22.

20. It was sacredly preserved in the ark in the holy of holies. Deuteronomy 10:1-5.

21. God forbade work upon the Sabbath, even in the most hurrying times. Exodus 34:21.

22. God destroyed the Israelites in the wilderness because they profaned the Sabbath. Ezekiel 20:12, 13.

23. It is the sign of the true God, by which we are to know Him from false gods. Ezekiel 20:20.

24. God promised that Jerusalem should stand forever if the Jews would keep the Sabbath. Jeremiah 17:24, 25.

25. He sent them into the Babylonian captivity for breaking it. Nehemiah 13:18.

26. He destroyed Jerusalem for its violation. Jeremiah 17:27.

27. God has pronounced a special blessing on all the Gentiles who will keep it. Isaiah 56:6, 7.

28. This is in the prophecy which refers wholly to the Christian dispensation. See Isaiah 56.

29. God has promised to bless any man who will keep the Sabbath. Isaiah 56:2.

30. The Lord requires us to call it *"honorable."* Isaiah 58:13. Beware, ye who take delight in calling it the "old Jewish Sabbath," "a yoke of bondage," etc.

31. After the holy Sabbath has been trodden down "many generations," it is to be restored in the last days. Isaiah 58:12, 13.

32. All the holy prophets kept the seventh day.

33. When the Son of God came, He kept the seventh day all His life. Luke 4:16; John 15:10. Thus He followed His Father's example at creation. Shall we not be safe in following the example of both the Father and the Son?

34. The seventh day is the Lord's day. See Revelation 1:10; Mark 2:28; Isaiah 58:13; Exodus 20:10.

35. Jesus was the Lord of the Sabbath (Mark 2:28); that is, to love and protect it, as the husband is the lord of the wife, to love and cherish her. 1 Peter 3:6.

36. He vindicated the Sabbath as a merciful institution designed for man's good. Mark 2:23-28.

37. Instead of abolishing the Sabbath, He carefully taught how it should be observed. Matthew 12:1-13.

38. He taught His disciples that they should do nothing upon the Sabbath day but what was *"lawful."* Matthew 12:12.

39. He instructed His apostles that the Sabbath should be prayerfully regarded 40 years after His resurrection. Matthew 24:20.

40. The pious women who had been with Jesus carefully kept the Sabbath after His death. Luke 23:56.

41. Thirty years after Christ's resurrection, the Holy Spirit expressly calls it *"the Sabbath day."* Acts 13:14.

42. Paul, the apostle to the Gentiles, called it "the Sabbath day" in A.D. 45. Acts 13:27. Did not Paul know? Or shall we believe modern teachers, who affirm that it ceased to be the Sabbath at the resurrection of Christ?

43. Luke, the inspired Christian historian, writing as late as A.D. 62, calls it "the Sabbath day." Acts 13:44.

44. The Gentile converts called it the Sabbath. Acts 13:42.

45. In the great Christian council, A.D. 52, in the presence of the apostles and thousands of disciples, James calls it "the Sabbath day." Acts 15:21.

46. It was customary to hold prayer meeting upon that day. Acts 16:13.

47. Paul read the Scriptures in public meetings on that day. Acts 17:2, 3.

48. It was his custom to preach upon that day. Acts 17:2.

49. The book of Acts alone gives record of his holding 84 meetings upon that day. See Acts 13:14, 44; 16:13; 17:2; 18:4, 11.

50. There was never any dispute between the Christians and the Jews about the Sabbath day. This is proof that the Christians still observed the same day that the Jews did.

51. In all their accusations against Paul, they never charged him with disregarding the Sabbath day. Why did they not, if he did not keep it?

52. But Paul himself expressly declared that he had kept the law. "Neither against the law of the Jews, neither against Caesar, have I offended any thing at all." Acts 25:8. How could this be true if he had not kept the Sabbath?

53. The Sabbath is mentioned in the New Testament 59 times, and always with respect, bearing the same title it had in the Old Testament, *"the Sabbath day."*

54. Not a word is said anywhere in the New Testament about the Sabbath being abolished, done away with, changed, or anything of the kind.

55. God has never given permission to any man to work upon it. Reader, by what authority do you use the seventh day for common labor?

56. No Christian of the New Testament, either before or after the resurrection, ever did ordinary work upon the seventh day. Find one case, and we

will yield the question. Why should modern Christians do differently from Bible Christians?

57. There is no record that God has ever removed His blessing or sanctification from the seventh day.

58. As the Sabbath was kept in Eden before the fall, so it will be observed eternally in the new earth after the restitution. Isaiah 66:22, 23.

59. The seventh-day Sabbath was an important part of the law of God, as it came from His own mouth, and was written by His own finger upon stone at Mount Sinai. See Exodus 20. When Jesus began His work, He expressly declared that He had not come to destroy the law. "Think not that I am come to destroy the law, or the prophets." Matthew 5:17.

60. Jesus severely condemned the Pharisees as hypocrites for pretending to love God, while at the same time they made void one of the Ten Commandments by their tradition. The keeping of Sunday is only a tradition of men.

We have now presented 60 plain Bible facts concerning the seventh day. What will you do with them?

Forty Bible Facts Concerning the First Day of the Week

1. The very first thing recorded in the Bible is work done on Sunday, the first day of the week. Genesis 1:1-5. This was done by the Creator Himself. If God made the earth on Sunday, can it be wicked for us to work on Sunday?

2. God commands men to work upon the first day of the week. Exodus 20:8-11. Is it wrong to obey God?

3. None of the patriarchs ever kept it.

4. None of the holy prophets ever kept it.

5. By the express command of God, His holy people used the first day of the week as a common working day for 4,000 years, at least.

6. God Himself calls it a *"working"* day. Ezekiel 46:1.

7. God did not rest upon it.

8. He never blessed it.

9. Christ did not rest upon it.

10. Jesus was a carpenter (Mark 6:3), and worked at His trade until He was 30 years old. He kept the Sabbath and worked six days in the week, as all admit. Hence He did many a hard day's work on Sunday.

11. The apostles worked upon it during the same time.

12. The apostles never rested upon it.

13. Christ never blessed it.

14. It has never been blessed by any divine authority.

15. It has never been sanctified.

16. No law was ever given to enforce the keeping of it, hence it is no transgression to work upon it. "For where no law is, there is no transgression." Romans 4:15; (1 John 3:4).

17. The New Testament nowhere forbids work to be done on it.

18. No penalty is provided for its violation.

19. No blessing is promised for its observance.

20. No regulation is given as to how it ought to be observed. Would this be so if the Lord wished us to keep it?

21. It is never called the Christian Sabbath.

22. It is never called the Sabbath at all.

23. It is never called the Lord's day.

24. It is never even called a rest day.

25. No sacred title whatever is applied to it. Then why should we call it holy?

26. It is simply called "the first day of the week."

27. Jesus never mentioned it in any way, never took its name upon His lips, so far as the record shows.

28. The word Sunday never appears in the Bible at all.

29. Neither God, Christ, nor inspired men, ever said one word in favor of Sunday as a holy day.

30. The first day of the week is mentioned only eight times in all the New Testament. Matthew 28:1; Mark 16:2, 9; Luke 24:1; John 20:1, 19; Acts 20:7; 1 Corinthians 16:2.

31. Six of these texts refer to the same first day of the week.

32. Paul directed the saints to look over secular affairs on that day. 1 Corinthians 16:2.

33. In all the New Testament we have a record of only one religious meeting held upon that day, and it was even a night meeting. Acts 20:5-12.

34. There is not an intimation that they ever held a meeting upon it before or after that.

35. It was not their custom to meet on that day.

36. There was no requirement to break bread on that day.

37. We have an account of only one instance in which it was done. Acts 20:7.

38. That was done in the night—after midnight. Verses 7-11. Jesus celebrated it on Thursday evening, (Luke 22), and the disciples sometimes did it every day. Acts 2:42-46.

39. The Bible nowhere says that the first day of the week commemorates the resurrection of Christ. This is a tradition of men, which makes void the law of God. Matthew 15:1-9. Baptism commemorates the burial and resurrection of Jesus. Romans 6:3-5.

40. Finally, the New Testament is totally silent with regard to any change of the Sabbath day or any sacredness for the first day.

Here are 100 plain Bible facts upon this question, showing conclusively that the seventh day is the Sabbath of the Lord in both the Old and New Testaments.

Reprinted from a tract published by the Review and Herald Publishing Association about the year 1885.

APPENDIX VI

The Mark of the Beast

In Christian circles having the "mark of the beast" is synonymous with being "lost." And well it should. In every case those who receive the mark of the beast are contrasted with God's people and in most references they are consigned to hellfire.

The term "mark of the beast" is found only in the book of Revelation. "And that no one may buy or sell except one who has the mark or the name of the beast, or the number of his name" (Revelation 13:17). At first blush it would seem that receiving the mark of the beast is desirable because without it you can't buy or sell. Upon reading the context, however, one soon discovers that those who follow the leopard-like beast and the two-horned beast do not have their names written in the Book of Life (Revelation 13:8). And also the beast giving this mark receives his power, throne, and authority from the dragon— who is Satan!

The next two references to the mark of the beast are found in Revelation 14:9-12, right in the heart of the third angel's message. "And a third angel followed them, saying with a loud voice, 'If anyone worships the beast and his image, and receives his mark on his forehead or on his hand, he himself shall also drink of the wrath of God, which is poured out full strength into the cup of His indignation. And he shall be tormented with fire and brimstone in the presence of the holy angels and in the presence of the Lamb.

"And the smoke of their torment ascends forever and ever; and they have no rest day or night, who worship the beast and his image, and whoever receives the mark of his name.

"Here is the patience of the saints; here are those who keep the commandments of God and the faith of Jesus."

Those with the mark suffer the wrath of God [the seven last plagues] unmixed with mercy [His "strange"act] and are burned up. Those without the mark are those who keep the commandments of God and have faith in Jesus. The description of the saints in contrast with those who receive the mark of the beast is a significant point. The saints uphold God's commandments and have faith in Him. Could it be that those who receive the mark do not keep the commandments and have faith in Jesus? One thing we know for sure from this passage is that those who receive God's wrath are those who follow the beast and receive his mark.

The next mention of the mark of the beast is in Revelation 15:2, 3. John, seeing a vision of the future, says, "And I saw something like a sea of glass mingled with fire, and those who have the victory over the beast, over his image and over his mark and over the number of his name, standing on the sea of glass, having harps of God. They sing the song of Moses, the servant of God, and the song of the Lamb."

What an awesome, glad scene. It's one I plan to participate in one day soon. Those who refuse the mark of the beast—that is, gain the victory over the beast—eventually stand on the sea of glass in heaven and with one of God's harps sing the victory song—the song of Moses and the Lamb!

Again we read of the mark of the beast in Revelation 16:2. This entire chapter is taken up with the seven angels with the seven last plagues—the wrath of God. "So the first [angel] went and poured out his bowl [plague] upon the earth, and a foul and loathsome sore came upon the men who had the mark of the beast and those who worshiped his image."

Students of prophecy understand that the seven last plagues are poured out without mercy on those with the mark of the beast. This happens after the close of probation—when there is no longer mercy available for sinners. The wrath of God falls on those who have rejected Him and persecuted His faithful people. Thank God, His people are protected against these plagues by the seal of God!

The sixth mention of the mark of the beast is where we read of the fate of those who are deceived by the beast and the false prophet. "Then the beast was captured, and with him the false prophet who worked signs in his presence, by which he deceived those who received the mark of the beast and those who worshiped his image. These two were cast alive into the lake of fire burning with brimstone" (Revelation 19:20).

What a sad picture. <u>Those who receive the mark of the beast are deceived!</u> But because they rejected opportunities to hear the truth they receive the wrath of God and miss out on eternal life with God.

The seventh and final mention of the mark of the beast is in connection with the great judgment in heaven. Those who would not worship the beast or receive his mark live and reign with Christ 1,000 years! "And I saw thrones, and they sat on them, and judgment was committed to them. And I saw the souls of those who had been beheaded for their witness to Jesus and for the word of God, and who had not worshiped <u>the beast</u> or his image, <u>and</u> had not received <u>his mark</u> on their foreheads or on their hands. And they lived and reigned with Christ for a thousand years" (Revelation 20:4).

The conclusion, from a review of these passages, is basic and sobering: Those who receive the mark of the beast are lost—those who don't are saved.

Earth's Final Warning

I believe the Seventh-day Adventist Church is the "remnant" church of Bible prophecy. I believe God has called us to proclaim the worldwide message of the three angels of Revelation 14:6-12.

Prophecy indicates another angel/message will come just before the second coming of Christ. This is a final warning to the world to escape from the wrath of God. This message, which lightens the whole world with its glory, has two parts: "Babylon is fallen"—a repeat of the second angel's message, and "Come out of her My people"— which is a repeat of the third angel's message (Revelation 18:1-4).

To give this message one must know who Babylon is, what the beast is, what its mark is, and be convicted of the need to warn others of their danger. <u>This is a very sensitive subject, but we overlook it at the peril of our lives, our eternal lives, and those of many others.</u>

Who Is the Beast With the Mark?

The context of Revelation 13 indicates that "the beast" is the leopard beast—the first beast introduced in this chapter. A study of prophecy shows clearly that the little horn power of Daniel 7 and the leopard beast of Revelation 13 are one and the same.

Both derive their power and authority from the dragon—Satan.

They both rise out of pagan Rome.

They both blaspheme God.

They both rule for 1260 years.

They both make war on the saints.

They both have worldwide influence.

And in Revelation 13 this power receives a wound that appears deadly, but it heals, and all the world wonders after it.

Revelation 13 tells of the blasphemous beast power cooperating with a new beast with two lamb-like horns. This new beast can be identified as the United States of America. These are the two last great powers involved in the great controversy against God. The evidence is almost overwhelming—the leopard beast and the little horn power describe papal Rome, the Roman Catholic Church.

But Who Is Babylon?

In the book of Revelation, John presupposes or assumes that his readers have a knowledge of the book of Daniel and the other Old Testament writers. The book contains literally hundreds of quotes from the Old Testament. As one reads through Revelation, witnessing the working of God in history, there is suddenly the announcement "Babylon is fallen, is fallen, that great city" (Revelation 14:8). There is no definition given as to the identity of Babylon—just, Babylon is fallen.

Remember, in the previous chapter John has been shown a "composite" beast made up of the beasts of Daniel 7. He certainly knows what Babylon represents and he believes his readers will too.

Ancient Babylon—the first world empire—came to its end, rejecting God. God's "handwriting on the wall," announced that "You have been weighed in the balances, and found wanting" (Daniel 5:27). That very night king Belshazzar was killed as the Medes and Persians attacked the city of Babylon and overthrew its kingdom.

In John's day the actual city of Babylon lay in ruins. But because of Babylon's oppression of His people in the days of Daniel, God used it as a symbol of how near the close of history Satan would try to destroy His people through a corrupt church. As ancient Babylon rejected God, so much of the professed Christian world is rejecting Him today, if not in actual words, certainly by their actions. Those who reject the judgment hour message of the first angel of Revelation 14 can only fall farther and farther away from God. According to the second angel, when the churches of Christendom unite themselves fully with the principles of the world, then the fall of Babylon will be complete.

God's people will then repeat the second angel's message with such power that in Revelation 18:1-4 it is described as illuminating the whole earth! Those who reject this message clearly fail to recognize Babylon's fall and will see in the union of church and state something good. Only those who keep the commandments and have the faith of Jesus will realize the nature of sin in the light of the cross, and will speak with power against the corruption of Babylon.

In particular they will expose Babylon's erroneous teachings, the "wine" that she induces all nations to drink. Among other things, this wine includes the teaching that Sunday is sacred and that man has an immortal soul by nature. The first error forms a bond between Roman Catholicism and Protestantism, and the second connects both with spiritualism.

In Revelation, Babylon is described as the one who receives the plagues. And to Babylon goes the call to "Come out of her." Since "the mark of the beast power" is the composite, leopard-looking beast, it is apparent that it and Babylon are one and the same. And we can see that the antichrist power is a system through which Satan works to war against the cause of God. Accordingly, all who act this part are part of the "system."

The Beast Describes His Mark

The beast, as we have noted several times before, represents papal Rome or the Roman Catholic system. One could surmise that the mark of the beast has to do with Sunday worship since the seal of God is found in the Sabbath and since the saints are described as those who keep the commandments. But beyond these clear biblical proofs we can make a positive identification of the mark by listening to Roman Catholic spokesmen.

In the thirteenth century Thomas Aquinas, whose authority as a

Catholic theologian is unequaled, declared specifically, "In the New law the keeping of the Sunday supplants that of the Sabbath, not in virtue of the precept of the law, but through determination by the church and the custom of the Christian people" (Thomas Aquinas, *Summa theologiae,* 2a2ae, 122.4 ad 4, cited in *Daniel & Revelation Committee Series,* vol. 7, p. 95). Aquinas, the single most respected teacher of Roman Catholicism, taught that the change from Sabbath to Sunday was indeed brought about by the Roman Catholic Church.

This was also acknowledged at the great Council of Trent in an address by Gaspare [Ricciulli] de Fosso (Archbishop of Reggio), in an address in the 17th session of the Council, Jan. 18, 1562. He stated, "The Sabbath, the most glorious day in the law, has been changed into the Lord's day . . . These and other similar matters have not ceased by virtue of Christ's teaching (for He says He has come to fulfill the law, not to destroy it), but they have been changed by the authority of the church." (Original source cited in the SDA *Bible Student's Source Book,* p. 887.)

Many Catholic Catechisms make the claim that the "Church" changed the day of worship from the Sabbath to Sunday because of her power and authority. Here is one of many such examples:

"Q. *Have you any other way of proving that the Church has power to institute festivals of precept?*

"A. Had she not such power, she could not have done that in which all modern religionists agree with her; she could not have substituted the observance of Sunday the first day of the week for the observance of Saturday the seventh day, a change for which there is no Scriptural authority" (Stephen Keenan, *A Doctrinal Catechism,* p. 174).

Cardinal Gibbons of Baltimore stated, "The Divine institution of a day of rest from ordinary occupations and of religious worship, transferred by the authority of the Church from the Sabbath, the last day, to Sunday, the first day of the week, has always been revered in this country, has entered into our legislation and customs, and is one of the most patent signs that we are a Christian people.

"The neglect and abandonment of this observance would be sure evidence of a departure from the Christian spirit in which our past national life has been moulded. In our times, as in all times past, the enemies of religion are the opponents, secret or avowed, of the Christian Sabbath. A close observer cannot fail to note the dangerous inroads that have been made on the Lord's Day in this country within the last quarter of a century. He renders a service to his country who tries to check this dangerous tendency to desecration.

"It would not be difficult to show that the observance of Sunday is fraught with the greatest social blessing; as proof, look at the social ills that have befallen those Christian nations that have lost respect for it. Solicitous to avert from the United States those disastrous consequences, the Catholic Church has been a strenuous upholder of the sacred character of the Lord's Day" (James Cardinal Gibbons, *The Claims of the Catholic Church in the Making of the Republic,* in John Gilmary Shea and others, *The Cross and the Flag, Our Church and Country,* pp. 24, 25; cited in full in *SDA Bible Students' Source Book,* p. 987).

Reading those three short paragraphs from Cardinal Gibbons lets one know of the significance of Sunday and the desire of the Catholic Church to see it observed in the United States as a "sign" that we are Christian people.

What Is the Mark of the Beast?

Synthesizing what we have covered in the last four chapters, it can be seen that, **"The mark of the beast is willful, knowledge-able, end-time approval of coercive Sunday observance in *opposition* to the clear light on the Sabbath question and in *harmony* with classic Roman Catholicism. As such, the mark of the beast is evidence of personal *character* matured in opposition to God"** (Daniel & Revelation Committee Series, vol. 7, *Symposium on Revelation—Book II,* p. 118; bold and italics in original). Remember in the last chapter we discovered that the seal of God was evidence of an intellectual and spiritual settling into the truth? The mark of the beast is evidence of a character "matured" in opposition to God.

"When the test comes, it will be clearly shown what the mark of the beast is. It is the keeping of Sunday. Those who, after having heard the truth, continue to regard this day as holy bear the signature of the man of sin, who thought to change times and laws" (Ellen G. White, Letter 12, 1900, quoted in *The SDA Bible Commentary,* vol. 7, p. 980).

When Will the Mark of the Beast Be Given?

From our study to this point, we understand that the seal of God and the mark of the beast are given just before the close of probation and just before the seven last plagues begin to fall. Just before the end the gospel will go to all the world with great power. The Bible says, "Therefore, to him who knows to do good and does it not, to him it is sin" (James 4:17). Thousands have died keeping Sunday, thinking it was the Bible Sabbath. But men will not be judged for light they never had. "Many have gone to their graves in full faith that Sunday was the Sabbath. . . . If we are rational beings, and the light has come to us, we shall be accountable for it. But those who have not had the light which is now shining upon the people of God concerning the Sabbath question, will not be accountable for the light; for it has never been brought before them, and they have died without condemnation" (Ellen G. White, *Review and Herald,* April 25, 1893).

The real "when" of the mark of the beast is answered in this statement: "When Sunday observance shall be enforced by law, and the world shall be enlightened concerning the obligation of the true Sabbath, then whoever shall transgress the command of God, to obey a precept which has no higher authority than that of Rome, will thereby honor popery above God. He is paying homage to Rome, to the power which enforces the institution ordained by Rome. As men then reject the institution which God has declared to be the sign of His authority, and honor in its stead that which Rome has chosen as the token of her supremacy, they will thereby accept the sign of allegiance to Rome,— 'the mark of the beast.' And it is not until the issue is thus plainly set before the people, and they are brought to choose between the commandments of God and the commandments of men, that those who continue in transgression will receive 'the mark of the beast'" *(The Great Controversy,* [1888 edition], p. 449).

Only Two Sides at the End of Time

C. Mervyn Maxwell expresses graphically the situation in our world at the moment of crisis.

"Scripture indicates clearly that at the end of time personal choices will cause everyone to be on one side or the other. No one will be left in the middle.

"One side will worship the Creator (Rev. 14:7). The other side will worship the beast and his image (13:12; 14:9; 16:2; 19:20).

"One side will be trustworthy and true, without any lies in their mouths (14:5). The other side will have accepted the lies of the false prophet (19:20).

"One side will be pure and spotless (14:4, 5). The other side will be cowardly, faithless, polluted, murderers, fornicators, sorcerers, idolaters, liars (21:8).

"One side will have their names in the book of life (Dan. 12:1). The other will have had their names blotted out of the book of life (Rev. 17:8).

"One side will be unable to buy or sell but will escape the plagues (13:17; 18:4). The other side will be able to buy and sell (for a time) but will then suffer the plagues (13:17; 14:9-11; 16:2).

"One side is composed of guests invited to the Lamb's joyous wedding supper (19:9). The other side is fed to birds of prey at the terrible supper of God (19:17-21).

"One side praises God and sings joyfully in the presence of the Lamb (15:2-4; 14:3). The other side curses God and suffers torment in the presence of the Lamb (16:9-11, 21; 14:9-11).

"One side enters the eternal kingdom (Dan. 7:27; Rev. 22:14). The other suffers permanent punishment (Rev. 14:9-11).

"One side has the seal of God (7:1-3). The other side has the mark of the beast (13:16; 14:11).

"The easiest thing to do when the image of the beast is set up will be to go with the crowd. People who have believed the serpent's lies, that God's laws either should not, ought not, or cannot be obeyed, will find compliance easy. They will be influenced by Satan's signs and wonders (2 Thess. 2:9-12). They will "bow" to the image—and receive the mark of the beast, indicating their submission and obedience to human authority.

"But those who cherish Jesus and the 'faith of Jesus' and have learned to 'conquer' as Christ conquered (Rev. 3:21), will choose at the risk of their lives to honor God and worship Him in the way He has directed. They will consider loyalty to their Creator and Redeemer the most important consideration possible. These courageous ones will soon find themselves singing on the sea of glass (15:1-5)" (C. Mervyn

Maxwell, *"Roman Catholicism and the United States, Daniel & Revelation Committee Series, vol. 7,* Symposium on Revelation—Book II, pp. 119, 120).

Bible prophecy has indeed indicated the entire course of human history. All the world powers have taken their places and passed from the scene of action—just as God predicted. And, then, as predicted, the little horn power arose from among the kingdoms of the divided Roman empire. That power, we have identified as papal Rome, the Roman Catholic Church. It virtually ruled the world for 1260 years before receiving a deadly wound in 1798. Many thought that the papacy was "done for," but as the Bible predicted, the wound has been healed. Now—all the world is wondering after the beast. The United States has indeed arisen as a "new nation," maturing into the most powerful nation on the earth—the world's only superpower.

These two powers, the papacy and the United States, are to be the leading characters in the last act in the drama of the ages.

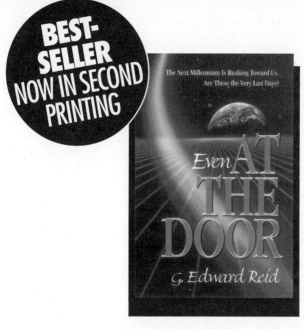

The Next Millennium Is Rushing Toward Us.
Are These the Very Last Days?

Even AT THE DOOR

G. Edward Reid

Even at the Door

G. Edward Reid presents overwhelming evidence that we are the generation that will see the literal second coming of Christ. You will be startled at the plainness of scriptural predictions, roused by the testimony of Ellen White and other Adventist pioneers, and amazed to see how completely world conditions indicate that these are the final days. And above all, you will find encouragement in preparing for the most spectacular event in history.

Distributed by Review and Herald.
Paper, 250 pages
US$14.99, Cdn$21.49.

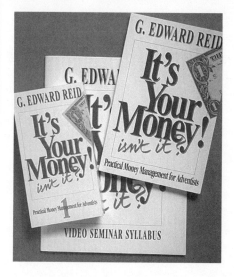

- pouring of the 7 last plagues Rev. 16
- the second coming of Christ   John 14: 1-3
- resurrection of righteous   } 1 Thess. 4: 13-1
- binding of Satan Rev. 20: 2, 3
- translation to Heaven John 14: 1-3
- descent of New Jerusalem c̄
      Christ + the saints Rev. 21: 1-4
- resurrection of the wicked Rev. 20: 5
- loosening of Satan Rev. 20: 7
- destruction of the wicked Rev. 20: 14, 15

Malachi 3: 7